COLLINS POCKET
GUIDE TO THE SEA SHORE

COLLINS POCKET GUIDES

COLLINS POCKET GUIDE TO BRITISH BIRDS
by R. S. R. Fitter
Illustrated by R. A. Richardson

COLLINS POCKET GUIDE TO NESTS AND EGGS
by R. S. R. Fitter
Illustrated by R. A. Richardson

COLLINS GUIDE TO BIRD-WATCHING
by R. S. R. Fitter

COLLINS POCKET GUIDE TO WILD FLOWERS
by David McClintock and R. S. R. Fitter

COLLINS GUIDE TO MUSHROOMS AND TOADSTOOLS
by Morten Lange and F. B. Hora

COLLINS FIELD GUIDE TO ARCHAEOLOGY
by Eric S. Wood

A FIELD GUIDE TO THE BIRDS OF BRITAIN AND EUROPE
by Roger Tory Peterson, Guy Mountfort
and P. A. D. Hollom

A FIELD GUIDE TO THE MAMMALS OF BRITAIN AND EUROPE
by F. H. van den Brink

A FIELD GUIDE TO THE BIRDS OF EAST AND CENTRAL AFRICA
by J. G. Williams

A FIELD GUIDE TO THE BIRDS OF NEW ZEALAND
by R. A. Falla, R. B. Sibson
and E. G. Turbott

THE BIRDS OF THE WEST INDIES
by James Bond

THE BIRDS OF TRINIDAD AND TOBAGO
by G. A. C. Herklots

A FIELD GUIDE TO THE STARS AND PLANETS
by Donald Menzel

COLLINS GUIDE TO FRESHWATER FISHES OF BRITAIN AND EUROPE
by Bent Muus and Preben Dahlstrøm

COLLINS
POCKET GUIDE TO THE
SEA SHORE

JOHN H. BARRETT
C. M. YONGE

ILLUSTRATED BY
Elspeth Yonge, Shirley Townend,
Dorothy Fitchew, Richard Pike,
John Norris Wood, David Pratt,
Dido Berry

COLLINS
8 GRAFTON STREET, LONDON W1

Editorial Adviser

R. S. R. FITTER

FIRST PUBLISHED	1958
REPRINTED	1960
REPRINTED	1962
REPRINTED	1965
REPRINTED	1967
REPRINTED	1970
REPRINTED	1972
REPRINTED	1973
REPRINTED	1976
REPRINTED	1977
REPRINTED	1980
REPRINTED	1983
REPRINTED	1984
REPRINTED	1985

ISBN 0 0 219321 3

HOW TO USE THIS BOOK

IF you want to look up a seaweed or a fish or any other animal whose name you know, there is an index beginning on page 260.

To name a seaweed or a fish or other animal that you do not know, turn first to TYPES OF SHORE LIFE on p. 25. Here marine life is divided into six main groups, viz.:

> Plant-like, p. 26.
>
> Encrusting, p. 28.
>
> Worm-like, p. 30.
>
> Crustaceans and related animals, p. 33.
>
> Other shelled animals, p. 35.
>
> Swimming animals, p. 37.

From each of these main groups you will be guided to the right part of the text and plates.

THE TEXT, pages 41-255, is itself cast in the form of a key. Under each main group of animals and seaweeds you are led from one set of characters to another, till finally you arrive at the solution. Sea creatures are not like birds, which fly away. By having them under close observation in your hand or in a jar, you should be able to see all the characters needed for identification.

The text is written in as simple language as possible. Those technical terms which are unavoidable are explained in the general introduction to each group of animals, so if you come across an unfamiliar term, turn back to the beginning of the section.

THE ILLUSTRATIONS consist of 40 colour plates between pages 64-65, 40 black and white plates between pages 128-129, and over 300 line drawings scattered through the text. If you can place the animal or plant you want to identify in a broad grouping, such as sea-anemones or brown seaweeds, you can also check through the plates, which are listed on pp. 9-10.

ACKNOWLEDGMENTS

The introductory sections of this guide, many of the introductory accounts of groups of animals and the section on the Molluscs have been written by C. M. Yonge, the remainder by J. H. Barrett. Each author has freely emended and, it is their united opinion, improved the work of the other, but they do also feel that the complete work represents very much of a joint effort by writers and artists. They wish to acknowledge the skill and patience of those who have succeeded in producing what is surely the best series of illustrations of seashore plants and animals available to the general public at the present time.

Besides his work on many plates, Dr. R. B. Pike provided much advice and guided artists who were not themselves also naturalists. We owe him special thanks. Various specialists have helped us and we wish to acknowledge our gratitude. Mr. A. E. Wade of the National Museum of Wales helped over lichens; Dr. Mary Parke and Dr. Harry Powell over seaweeds; Professor T. A. Stephenson gave advice about sea-anemones and agreed to the copying of certain of his coloured figures of these animals and also of the tube worm, *Myxicola*; Professor E. W. Knight-Jones gave advice about *Spirorbis*; Mr. E. Ford about fish; Dr. R. H. Millar about sea-squirts; Dr. H. O. Bull, Dr. Sumner Jones and Dr. D. P. Wilson about nudibranch sea-slugs as did Dr. Burdon Jones who also helped with information about enteropneusts; Professor F. W. Rogers Brambell and Dr. H. A. Cole permitted the copying of their coloured drawing of *Saccoglossus*. Most of the text figures have been copied from the literature. The sources are acknowledged in the list on p. 259. Mr. R. S. R. Fitter has made useful suggestions and has helped in many ways with the preparation of the guide. Mr. Raleigh Trevelyan and other members of the staff of Messrs. Collins have borne patiently with difficulties presented by the authors themselves and by the wide range of animals they have attempted to describe and have illustrated. The authors are most conscious that much of what may be of value in this book comes from others.

J. H. BARRETT
C. M. YONGE

CONTENTS

CONTENTS

COLOUR PLATES

between pages 64-65

9

BLACK AND WHITE PLATES

between pages 128-9

Plates 1-3, 5-9, 14-16, 24-31 are by Elspeth Yonge; Plates 4, 10-13, 18-21, 33-40, xxvi-xl by Shirley Townend; Plates 17, 22-23, xiv-xxi by Dorothy Fitchew; Plates i-iii, vi-xiii by Richard Pike; Plates 32, xxii, xxiii, xxiv by John Norris Wood; Plates iv, v, xxv by David Pratt. The line drawings in the text are by Dido Berry, Richard Pike, Shirley Townend and C. M. Yonge

INTRODUCTION

THIS BOOK has modest aims. It is intended as no more than an introduction for the amateur naturalist, assuming no prior knowledge, to the common and more easily identified animals and plants of the shore. For the student with some technical knowledge of zoology and botany excellent books exist. By the shore we mean the full extent of that fringe between land and sea which is uncovered at the lowest tides and covered at the highest. While this represents no great area when compared with the land on the one side and the still greater extent of the sea on the other, yet it is inhabited by a remarkable variety of living things. Many of these, moreover, are of types never encountered elsewhere. So, in a very real sense, when we go on to the shore we enter a new world and, like travellers visiting strange countries, we need a guide-book to help us. That is the function of this book, to be supplemented later should the traveller remain for long and need fuller information.

Just as such a guide stresses the more obvious and important features of a country, so must this one confine itself to the more obvious animals and plants. Anything like a comprehensive account of the inhabitants of the sea shore is out of the question, nor perhaps does it seem so important these days. Our Victorian ancestors loved to have a name for everything and to make collections of all they found to fill their shell cabinets or books of dried seaweeds. To-day we are just as much concerned with the general picture of intertidal life as we are with minute details about different species. But there are in any case too many; almost every group of animals is represented, to say nothing of the seaweeds of which there are some hundreds. Some plants and animals are large but the majority are small; something more than the naked eye is very often necessary for their identification. It is assumed that all readers will have the aid of a ×10 lens; it should then be possible to see all details mentioned in this guide.

But still smaller animals and plants are omitted, together with many small species which are difficult even for the expert to identify. Certain larger but very rare animals or plants are also passed over. The variety of life on the shore is so great and the animals so unusual that it is much better to draw the attention of the novice to those he is certain to encounter and can be expected to identify. Furthermore certain objects which are common on the shore, such as empty shells, skeletons, egg cases and the like, come from animals that live offshore. Such jetsam needs to be noted when it is large or common. Where, as we hope it will be, interest that runs beyond the contents of this book is roused,

11

the reader is referred to the list of books (p. 255) where he can gratify a most rewarding curiosity.

Shores vary enormously in character; some are of rock draped with seaweeds and interspersed with pools, others are of sand with little evidence of life when the tide is out, and again there are mud flats and steep shingle beaches. And there are regions where one type of shore merges into another. Each kind of shore has its typical population, so that as well as describing shore species something must be said about where each is likely to be found. Moreover as well as finding out the name of the animal or plant, an indispensable label but not an end in itself, we should also try to find out how each species manages to live where it does, perhaps by clinging to rocks or by sheltering beneath them, or how it resists being dried up when the tide is out, or how it burrows into sand or mud or even, in some cases, into wood or stone.

Shore life varies from one part of Great Britain to another and also from one zone to another on the same stretch of shore. The population near high water mark is always very different from that around low water mark. The first variation is due chiefly to climate and more the climate of the sea than of the land. Our southern and western shores are bathed with warmer waters coming from the south-west, so that the life upon them has species in common with the population on the Atlantic coasts of France, Spain and Portugal. But on the east coast colder water comes from the north and shore life has more in common with that of Norway. The precise distribution of many, even very common, shore animals and plants is still far from fully known. Moreover it is changing all the time with southern species spreading north and new species invading British shores. If by arousing popular interest in such matters this book helps to increase knowledge both of present and future distribution of intertidal species it will have performed a most useful function.

The manner in which animals and plants occupy a series of zones at various levels on the shore, some even living above high tide level in the so-called splash zone, is one of the most interesting aspects of life on the shore. This zonation can be strikingly obvious on a rocky shore where there are bands of obviously different kinds of seaweeds but many animals of both rocks and sands are similarly restricted. Although some animals, such as shore crabs, seem to scuttle about almost everywhere, for many others the limits of the zone they inhabit represent the confines of a prison but one that the prisoner strives most strenuously to re-enter should chance release him from it.

Clearly a guide to the seashore must be something very different from a guide to birds or to wild flowers. Everyone knows what a bird is and realises the broad difference between a flowering plant and a fern or a moss. But very few are knowledgeable about the inhabitants, both plant and animal, of the shore; the very names of many of the major groups of animals may be unknown. So inevitably these must first be described in popular terms so that the beginner may come to distinguish between a hydroid and a polyzoan and between the many—and in fundamental structure very different—groups of worms, and begin to learn the names and distinguish between the various groups of the spiny-skinned animals or echinoderms which comprise the starfishes, the brittle stars, the sea urchins, the sea cucumbers and the feather stars. Long series of impressive volumes have been written about the inhabitants of the shore and some of this information must be compressed within the covers of this small book. But the species here described represent only a portion of the vast wealth of life that exists between tide marks around the British Isles.

TIDES AND TIDAL EFFECTS

When considering sea shores and shore life tides are all-important. Although the effects of winds and waves produce some small width of shore in virtually tideless seas such as the Mediterranean, or even in large lakes, the wide exposure of rocks, sand or mud around the coasts of Great Britain is due to the rise and fall of the tides. These are produced by the gravitational pull of all the heavenly bodies upon the waters of the globe, but particularly by the sun, which is so large, and the moon which is so close.

If a bath is partly filled with water, it is quite easy to establish an oscillation of the water about the middle line of the bath; at one moment the water is going back up the taps and at the next it has sloshed out on to the floor. All the time the depth of the water at the middle line, the node, will not have changed. A mathematician would describe the water's movement as a uninodal seiche. In the same bath it is possible to establish a binodal seiche with a high and low water level (tide) at both ends of the bath and also across the middle, the two nodes being at the quarter and three-quarter marks. But any attempt to produce any other type of oscillation always ends in chaos. The periods of the waves so produced, their rate of oscillation, are a function of the length of the bath and of the depth of the water. They have nothing to do with the width of the bath.

The oceans of the world are divided into natural baths or basins. Some of these have a natural period of oscillation of about twelve hours and that is approximately the daily rhythm of the gravitational pulls exerted by the sun and the moon. It is these forces, according to the recent stationary wave theory of tides, that keep the bodies of water oscillating. The basins within which they oscillate have no hard and fast boundaries at the surface of the oceans. There is a great deal of over-spilling and masking of effect between neighbouring basins. As the water level sinks at one end of one basin, it may be replaced by water flowing over from the high tide in the next basin. Further and great complications come from the shallowing edge of the oceans and the irregular shape of the continents jutting out into them. These shallow water effects do little to mask the underlying simplicity of the idea of water oscillating in basins under gravitational pulls of the sun and moon.

At both full and new moon the sun and moon are pulling more or less in a straight line and the vertical range of the tide is at a maximum; then we have spring tides, the word " spring " having nothing to do with the season of the year. For seven days after the full or new moon the angle between the pulls of the sun and the moon increases so that their combined effect decreases and we come to a neap tide. Then for seven days the angle closes again, the combined effect increases and we are back at a spring tide. And so on.

Overlying this monthly rhythm of tides is an annual rhythm. The spring tides become progressively larger as the equinoxes (about March 21 and September 21) are approached, for only then are the pulls of the sun and moon exactly in a straight line. In mid-December and mid-June the spring tides, though of course still the biggest tide of their fourteen-day period, are much smaller than in September or March because the sun's pull is not in line with the moon's.

All tides oscillate about mean sea level; indeed that is the definition of mean sea level (p. 16). So at spring tides not only does the water come high up the beach, it also goes a long way down. These are the tides which are best for seeing the plants and animals of the seashore. At equinoctial springs we have both the highest and lowest tides of the year; the tidal range is the greatest. This contrasts with the neap tides when high tide by no means reaches the top of the shore nor does it go very far down. In Pembrokeshire the average spring tide range is about 20 feet and the average neap range is only about 7 feet.

Essentially tide is a vertical movement of water, although most people's experience of it may only be shuffling back their deck chairs to avoid the horizontal component. It is this horizontal component that causes the tidal coastal currents which are particularly well known round, say, Portland Bill or St. Ann's Head or in the Pentland Firth. The coasts are being constantly sandpapered by the passing water and this horizontal tidal current has some effect on the distribution of plants and animals along the shore.

At any one place spring low water always occurs at about the same time of day. Most seaside towns publish tide tables that give the time of the tide and also the predicted height of high water. The local datum point may be a board on the pier or the sill of the lock gates. The figures in the tide tables may amount to nonsense until this local datum is known.

From the collector's point of view there are advantages and disadvantages in having spring low tides at about midday and midnight. He has one convenient time for working, whereas a 6 a.m. tide drags him out of bed in the chilly hours of an April morning and brings him back to the shore again in the dusk. But with low tide at midday the heat of the sun will beat down on the lowest exposed zone of the shore, where the animals and plants are least adapted for withstanding the effects of heat and consequent drying up. However, such plants and animals will be found elsewhere exposed on shores where the time of low tide is earlier, and so before the heat of the sun has developed, or later when it has to some extent diminished.

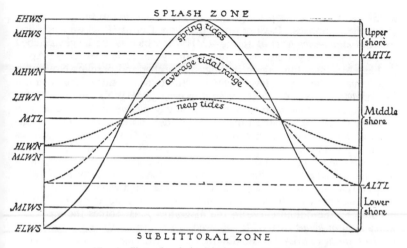

Fig. 1. Shore levels in relation to tidal changes

As a rough guide for periods of several days together it is safe to say that both high and low water are fifty minutes later each day. In the short run this will lead to trouble because in the three or four days around springs each day's tide will be only about twenty minutes later. At neaps the next day's tide will be as much as eighty minutes later. The average of these two is fifty minutes and that is the origin of the approximation.

Zonation—Apart from their influence on the configuration of the coastline, the effects of tidal movements are profound and they are, of course, complicated by the increase and decrease in tidal range as neaps change to springs and back again to neaps. Thus the region between the extremes of tidal movement, namely the shore, may be divided into a series of horizontal zones according to the extent to which each is covered and uncovered during the full cycle of tidal movements. Each of these zones represents a distinct environment for plants and animals, most obviously so on rocky shores where even a superficial glance may often reveal the presence of successive belts of different kinds of seaweeds between low and high water levels. Subsequent examination will reveal a similar zonation of the animal life so that it is important from the start to understand the *major subdivisions of the shore*. These subdivisions, as they will be considered and referred to in this guide, are shown in Fig. 1. The highest level there shown is that attained by the *extreme high water level of springs* (EHWS), the lowest level being that to which these same tides recede, namely *the extreme low water level of springs* (ELWS). But the tide goes as high and low as this perhaps only two to four times in the year, round about the equinoxes. Passing down the shore from EHWS we come first to *mean high water level of springs* (MHWS) which is the height reached by half the spring tides in a year, namely those in February, April, perhaps May and July, again in August, October and perhaps November and January. Below this level (referring still to the left side of the diagram) we come to the *mean high water level of neaps* (MHWN) followed by the lowest level to which high tides attain, namely the *lowest high water level of neaps* (LHWN). At the time of these tides more of the shore is uncovered during an entire day than at any other time; subsequent tides lap higher and higher until they merge into springs. Below this level comes the *mean tide level* (MTL) or mean sea level, which is a line running along the middle of the shore. Below again comes the *highest low water level of neaps* (HLWN) which corresponds to the lowest high water level of neaps, i.e. the extremes of the smallest tidal range in the lunar cycle. This is denoted by the dotted curve in the diagram. Then comes the *mean low water level of neaps* (MLWN) followed in its turn by the *mean low water level of springs* (MLWS) and finally by the *extreme low water level of springs* (ELWS) representing the lowest level of the shore.

The unbroken curved line in the diagram represents the extent, over the full width of the shore, of the greatest, i.e. the equinoctial, spring tides. Between the extremes of the springs and neaps the *average tidal range* is indicated by a curve which extends from the *average low tide level* (ALTL) to the *average high tide level* (AHTL), the curve and the levels being indicated by broken lines, and the lettering being on the right. On the basis of these levels the most convenient subdivision of the shore can be made into:

A. **THE UPPER SHORE.** This is the area above the average high tide level and, as shown in the diagram, it is the region which is continuously uncovered *except* when the tides exceed average range, i.e. when they have passed from neaps into springs. It is therefore the most difficult zone for occupation by marine plants and animals and is, in fact, the most sparsely populated in variety of species, though not necessarily in numbers of individuals.

B. THE MIDDLE SHORE. This is an extensive region bounded above by the average high tide level and below by the average low tide level. In the main, therefore, it experiences twice daily first submergence under the sea and then exposure to the air. These represent typical shore conditions and the animals and plants which occur here in great abundance both of species and individuals are the most typical inhabitants of the shore.

C. THE LOWER SHORE. This is the narrower region extending from the average low tide level down to the limit of the shore at the extreme low water level of springs. The opposite in character to the upper shore, this region is only *uncovered* when the tides exceed average range. It is therefore the easiest for marine animals to colonise and on to it extend animals and plants from the area below tidal levels.

In addition to these three major subdivisions of the shore (or intertidal or littoral zone as it is often termed), there are two marginal zones:

The Sublittoral Fringe. This lies below the extreme low water level of springs and represents the margin of what is truly marine. The plants and animals that inhabit this zone are never uncovered although they live in shallow water which has a greater range of temperature than the open sea. The tall brown oar weeds (*Laminaria*) which typically grow in profusion in this region off rocky shores project above the surface of the water at low water of springs although the hold-fasts that secure them to the rocks are never exposed.

The Splash Zone. Above the technical limits of the shore, i.e. extreme high water level of spring tides, there is a zone which may be drenched with spray. The width of this depends on the degree of exposure and around the British Isles is greatest on western coasts fully exposed to the Atlantic surf. On to this zone extend a number of true shore-dwelling animals and plants, notably small periwinkles and the channelled wrack. But the effect of exposure is also to raise the levels—at any rate as indicated by the presence of typical animal and plant populations—of the middle and upper shores. We must therefore add the effect of wind and waves to those of the tides when considering the zonation of life on the shore.

TYPES OF SHORE

The shore is formed by interaction of sea and land; in some regions the sea, aided by the action of weather, cuts into the land, in others pebbles, sand or mud are deposited. Outcrops of hard rock may project seaward, sometimes forming high cliffs, and fringed by rocky shores. Material broken away by weather or sea together with that washed down by rivers is carried alongshore in tidal currents to be deposited in descending order of size of particles as water movement diminishes. First pebbles drop to the bottom, then—usually in wide bays—the medium-sized particles which constitute sand drop out of suspension and collect to form what are often wide and deep beaches. Finally in areas where water movements are least—in deep inlets which are often estuaries—the finest particles accumulate. They consist of the finest fragments of rock but also of still finer, often flocculent, pieces of organic matter derived from the dead bodies of plants and animals. This material, much of which is edible, may be of great importance to the animals which live in or upon mud.

These different types of shore, of rock, shingle, sand or mud, must be considered separately although, of course, they intergrade into one another, rock being often surrounded by sand which may itself in places merge into mud. There is inevitably a stage at which any scheme of classification must break down, but the characteristic physical features of the major types of shore may briefly be considered.

A. ROCKY SHORES. These are much the most variable in character depending on the type of rock, hard or soft, igneous or sedimentary, and if the last-named on the nature and slope of the strata. Where rocks are mixed, the harder ones stand up better to erosion by air and sea, for instance igneous dykes among softer sandstones. The wearing away of the softer strata in sedimentary rocks undercuts the harder strata, which may break away and form boulders. The slope of the strata is most important: if horizontal, a flat rocky platform may be formed and constitute the shore; if inclined, high pools or sheltered crevices may be found, both harbouring highly characteristic assemblages of animals and plants. Undoubtedly the most attractive of all shores are those where pools abound. The surface of the rock is a most important factor; if it weathers smooth, it offers little opportunity for attachment of either plant or animal. This is indeed the case with igneous rocks in general, but limestone and especially shales and slates offer all manner of fissures and crevices where animals and plants may attach themselves.

The slope of rocky shores varies very greatly, ranging from almost horizontal (usually below the base of a cliff) to steeply piled rocks that represent the narrowest of shores. Because rocky shores are the most exposed of all, their effective extent is increased by the action of spray well above extreme high water mark to form the *splash zone* (see p. 17). Finally, owing to the rigour of the conditions to which they are exposed, rocky shores are the most permanent of shores. Only the hardest and most securely based rocks can maintain themselves, and the thick carpet of seaweeds which covers most rocky shores helps to protect them both from the force of the sea and from the effects of exposure to the air.

B. SHINGLE BEACHES. These are composed of pebbles, i.e. of smooth rounded pieces of rock ranging from about ¼-inch to 6 inches across. A beach so composed has a very steep slope (about 12° for pebbles 2½ inches across), the waves rolling the pebbles over one another as they rush up and then fall back over the beach, the slope of which varies from time to time with changes in the force of the sea. There may be a constant lateral movement (especially noticeable where groynes run out), which is due to the oblique approach of the waves to the shore. Shingle beaches are the most unstable of shores. Because the pebbles are so big, water cannot be retained (unlike sand and still less like mud) when the tide falls, while everything on the surface is crushed by the constantly rolling pebbles. Hence nothing, plant or animal, can live either upon or within a shingle beach, which nevertheless remains the hunting ground of those who delight in the beauties to be found in beach pebbles, a rewarding pastime as described by Clarence Ellis (*The Pebbles on the Shore*, London, 1954).

C. SANDY SHORES. These are made up of fine fragments of very hard rock, usually of quartz grains because everything less hard soon gets reduced to the still smaller grain size of mud. The slope of a sandy beach is much less than that of shingle, about 2° for medium sand although this also is influenced by the effect of heavy seas. Owing to the small size of the particles (less than 1/5-inch in diameter), water is retained by capillary action within the minute spaces between the individual grains of sand. This has the dual effect of preventing the sand grains from rubbing against each other and of permitting animals to live, still effectively in water, within the sand after the level of the sea has fallen below it. Two effects may be observed on the surface of wet sand when pressure, as of a foot, is applied. If the water content is below a certain figure, the sand will be seen to turn pale or white. This is because pressure has disturbed the close packing of the sand grains and there is not enough water to fill the enlarged spaces between them. This condition is known as *dilatancy* and causes increased resistance to movement through the sand. But if the water content is somewhat higher, pressure and agitation by your foot makes the sand go soft and wet. This is *thixotrophy*, resistance being lowered. It is probably of the greatest importance to animals working their way through sand, because by agitating the sand they reduce its resistance to their passage.

A further advantageous property of sands from the standpoint of animals is that within the sand salinity and temperature, both factors of prime importance, are little affected by changes on the surface such as are caused by a hot sun or pouring rain falling on to an exposed rocky shore. In the sense that animals cannot construct permanent burrows in sand (unless this is mixed with a fair amount of mud) and

19

that the surface layers may be churned up by heavy seas, sand is not a fully stable medium; but it is far more so than shingle and also, except high up on the shore, retains water within it. There is abundant, although necessarily rather specialised, life in sandy shores.

D. MUDDY SHORES. Here accumulate the finest particles of all, of organic as well as of inorganic origin. There is almost no slope, so that exposed muddy shores are suitably termed *mud flats*. Because of the relative lack of water movement (or mud would not accumulate in the first place) and the coherence of the particles which compose it, mud forms a highly stable medium in which animals can and do make permanent burrows. Moreover the absence of slope on the surface and the very fine grade of the mud particles—particularly if these are of clay—often prevents the mud from drying out even at the surface when the tide retreats. The presence of organic matter in mud is both an advantage and a disadvantage. It represents food for many animals that burrow into it, such as the lugworm, which although it also occurs in sand does so only when this contains some mud. But at the same time this organic matter removes oxygen (normally present in the water contained in sand), so that life becomes difficult at any depth below the surface, water having continually to be drawn into the burrow. The fine particles of mud also represent a problem because they tend to clog delicate mechanisms concerned with feeding or with respiration. Hence the fauna within (although not necessarily upon) mud is more restricted than that in sand just as that is less varied in species (although not necessarily in total numbers) than the population of rocky shores.

WHERE AND HOW TO FIND SHORE ANIMALS AND PLANTS

While an exposed rocky shore richly covered with seaweeds will often give an immediate impression of great diversity of life, there is usually little or no indication of life of any kind on an exposed sandy beach. Mud flats, because they tend to retain water on their surface, may have a good number of sometimes not very conspicuous animals upon them. But in all cases what is immediately visible is but a minute proportion of the actual population, so much of which lives under rocks or seaweeds, burrows in sand or mud, or even bores into solid rock. There are a number of distinct faunal, and in some cases also floral, areas or environments, which are best considered in relation to the major types of shore, with some indication of the general characteristics of the animals and plants that inhabit them.

WHERE TO FIND ANIMALS AND PLANTS

A. ROCKY SHORES

i. **Bare Rock Surface.** Rocks fully exposed to the Atlantic surf may be bare, but even in regions of great water movement, where there are no seaweeds, the rock surface may be well covered with animals although these will consist of a few species all highly adapted for life under such exposed conditions. They are either permanently attached (e.g. acorn barnacles), or capable of gripping firmly (e.g. limpets) or being rolled about without damage (e.g. dog whelks).

ii. **Weed-covered Rocks.** These occur in somewhat more sheltered conditions and represent a major floral as well as a major faunal area. The species of seaweeds vary not only on the different levels on the shore but also in relation to exposure and to the presence of fresh water. The zonation of the brown fucoid seaweeds is very obvious; those highest on the shore have the greatest resistance to the effects of drying up but have little tensile strength, while those lowest on the shore, where they are fully and continuously exposed to wave action, have great tensile strength but cannot withstand for long the effects of being dried. Passing from sheltered to more exposed rocky shores, one species of weed replaces another while the presence of a stream or even of a permanent trickle of fresh water over the rocks may be shown by a downward extension of the green weeds which normally live in brackish water high on the shore.

A great population of animals occurs on and under the weed, which provides shelter from wave action and from the drying effect of sun and air; only a few of them eat the weed. Many of these animals are permanently attached (sponges, hydroids, sea mats, tube worms, sea squirts, etc.); the others either hold on firmly by one means or another (sea anemones, periwinkles and other snails, crustaceans, etc.) or crawl about as do the numerous bristle and other worms. Many of these animals are small.

iii. **Rock Pools.** These represent local areas which never dry out and they are the most beautiful as well as often the most rewarding environments to examine on the shore. The seaweeds and the animals which occur in them include many of those already encountered on bare and weed-covered rocks, but also species which cannot withstand even very temporary drying up, being often inhabitants of shallow offshore waters. While the immediate effect of disturbance may be to drive the very actively swimming prawns and fishes into corners or cracks and to cause the anemones and tube worms to contract, all will re-emerge into view if the pool is left undisturbed although it may be necessary to put aside the often dense growth of seaweeds. Sea urchins, starfish and crabs may all be found in numbers, as well as several kinds of sea anemones.

iv. Overhangs of Rock. The sides and roof of caves or well-protected overhanging surfaces of massive rocks have a particularly rich fauna, because the surface remains damp as well as sheltered from sun and wind when the tide is out. The surface is often completely covered with encrusting, usually plant-like animals, though plants themselves are few because light is reduced. They include many kinds of sponges, hydroids, sea anemones, sea mats, tube worms and sea squirts, as well as the sea slugs, snails and worms which prey upon them. Colours are particularly rich and varied and few areas on the sea shore are more beautiful.

v. In Crevices. These may be very special faunal areas occupied by a diverse and very interesting assemblage of often very small animals. The crevices are usually damp and shady, so resembling the over-hangs, but the space within them is restricted and conditions vary considerably according to whether they are high or low on the shore and whether they face seaward or landward; the type of rock also influences the shape and depth of crevices. The amount of food in the form of organic debris which is carried in by water movements is also important. Broadly speaking the population can be divided into those that live around the entrance to the crevice, those that penetrate into the outer regions and those that dwell in the inner recesses. Plants are naturally largely confined to the outer regions while the animals that enter consist largely of small crustaceans (including the larger sea slater), together with essentially terrestrial mites and insects, with many interesting small snails and bivalve molluscs and some ribbon worms and bristle worms. In some places sea cucumbers may be found insinuated within very narrow cracks.

vi. Within Rocks. Some of the animals, notably bivalve molluscs but also perhaps some worms, which once nestled in crevices came eventually to extend these by actively boring into the rock. Other bivalves, such as the common piddock and its relatives, would seem to have reached the same habit following an apprenticeship spent burrowing into stiffer and stiffer clay where they do often still occur. Other rock borers include bristle worms and a yellow sponge. All need to be sought by breaking into the rock with a hammer and cold chisel, but nothing will be found in really hard rocks like granite.

vii. Beneath Boulders. Detached rocks that are small enough to be moved should be turned over to expose the animals below. Particular care should be taken always to *replace the boulders as they were*. Failure to do so may ruin a shore both by killing the animals exposed and by smothering the animals and plants that were on the overturned surface of the rock. This is often a rich source of specimens, with animals both attached to the under surface of the rock and living in the gravel, sand or mud beneath. It is a good place to find crabs, hermit crabs, starfish and small sea urchins, together with certain kinds of bivalve molluscs and many kinds of worms, both crawling on the rock and living within the often gravelly mud below. Where there is a depression, a shore fish such as a butter fish, rockling or blenny may be found lurking, while sucker fish may be attached to the rock.

viii. On Pier Piles. Here man has provided an extensive settling surface, often over the entire tidal range and beyond it for the large group of animals and plants that normally inhabit rocky shores. The most typical inhabitants are probably barnacles high up and mussels low down, but piles are usually admirable collecting grounds for both solitary and compound sea squirts and for sea anemones (notably the plumose anemone which assumes many colours), sponges and hydroids. Many worms also live among these encrusting animals or insinuate themselves among the attaching threads of the mussels. Seaweeds often drape the piles, especially on the exposed and illuminated faces; small fishes and jellyfish are often common in the still water. With the aid of a small boat the exploration of pier piles, or the face of a jetty, especially in sheltered unpolluted harbours, may be most rewarding.

ix. Within Wooden Piles. While iron piles are often corroded, wooden ones, unless suitably protected, tend to become eaten away by animals. These are of two types, the molluscan shipworms (actually much more like worms than bivalve molluscs in general appearance), species of *Teredo* which excavate deep borings but give hardly any outward indication of their presence, and the small crustacean borers. Among the latter, an isopod, known as the gribble, makes superficial galleries which are immediately obvious, and with it is usually a larger amphipod crustacean. The surface of these piles will, of course, often be encrusted with the usual assemblage of animals and plants. Old wooden ships and floating timber are similarly affected by these wood borers.

B. SHINGLE BEACHES. Here, as already noted, life of any kind is conspicuously absent.

C. SANDY SHORES

i. Within Sand. Plants are absent and only by digging will the wealth of animal life be revealed; there is a zonation here as well as on the rocks. All animals living in sand are capable of moving into and through it: a fact which may be demonstrated by placing them in a sandy pool, when they will immediately proceed to burrow. Probably the most numerous are bivalve molluscs, from the rounded and very superficially burrowing cockle (*Cardium*) to the extremely flattened tellinids (*Tellina*) and the elongated, almost straight razor shells (*Ensis* or *Solen*) which burrow vertically with great speed and are correspondingly difficult to secure. Certain carnivorous snails also burrow in sand, together with great numbers of small crustaceans, chiefly of the amphipod or " hopper " type, and, low on the shore, the larger shrimp, *Crangon*, and the still larger masked crab, *Corystes*, which may be dug at extreme low water level of spring tides. Worms are numerous, some in tubes or burrows, others freely moving through the sand and of carnivorous habit. Also low on the shore live the burrowing sea urchin, *Echinocardium*, the burrowing starfish, *Astropecten*, the sand eel, *Ammodytes*, and other sand-burrowing fishes. The population of exposed beaches is less than that of sheltered beaches; the former are pounded by surf and their sand far from stable. The very smooth-shelled bivalve, *Donax*, is a characteristic inhabitant of such beaches. Sheltered sands are more stable and contain more organic debris, beginning to change in character towards mud flats. They are typified by the presence of the burrowing lugworm, *Arenicola*, which makes characteristic castings and feeds on the organic matter in the surface sand.

ii. **Strand Line.** This is a region occupied by masses of dead seaweed and other jetsam thrown up by the sea. Its position (here and also along the upper levels of rocky shores) oscillates with the position of high tide level as springs change to neaps and then to springs again. It is *par excellence* the habitat of the scavenging sand hoppers, *Talitrus*, marine animals which have become almost terrestrial. Here also are many land-living insects, notably beetles and flies, which feed on organic debris.

D. MUDDY SHORES

i. **Surface of Mud.** On this there may be boulders or moderate-sized stones with standing water around them and weed and encrusting animals on them. Shore crabs, periwinkles and various bristle worms are common on the surface, which, if it is gravelly, may in places be bound together by mussels. In very quiet but fully saline inlets the projecting tubes of peacock worms and other tube worms may rise above the surface. Though the population changes progressively up estuaries as the lowered salinity cuts out more and more marine animals, there may still be large numbers of small snails together with shrimps, various small crustaceans and bristle worms.

ii. Burrowing in Mud. Many bivalve molluscs occur, including cockles and the deep-burrowing clams, *Mya arenaria* (where there is admixture with sand) and *Mya truncata* (where the bottom is of stiff clay). Unlike razor shells, these animals cannot escape the spade and it is often hard, although rewarding, work digging them out. Characteristic of very compact mud is the large very flat-shelled bivalve *Scrobicularia* which actively draws in surface debris through its long and very mobile siphonal tube. These animals occupy what amounts to a permanent burrow, and so do the burrowing shrimps (really relatives of hermit crabs) which may be encountered along southern shores.

E. COMMENSALS AND PARASITES. Some animals live on or within the bodies of other animals (occasionally plants) and must be sought with their partners or, if they are parasites, their " hosts." Commensals feed with, rather than on, their partners and there are many examples of such relationships on the shore, such as the small bivalves which live attached near the anus of certain sea urchins and the anemones which live only upon the shells occupied by hermit crabs (the shells often also harbouring a bristle worm). Parasites are often too small to be noticed, but prawns which have a swelling on one side of the shell—looking as though they had a swollen face—are harbouring a sizeable crustacean (isopod) parasite. Shore crabs may often be found with a growth under the tail region which, surprisingly enough, is the reproductive organs of a parasite allied to the barnacles. The small pea crabs found in mussels and other bivalves are far less degenerate in form but probably no less parasitic. Swellings on the surface of some brown seaweeds are due to numbers of small parasitic round worms.

TYPES OF SHORE LIFE

A major attraction of the shore is undoubtedly the great array of plants and animals to be found upon it, but this presents an initial difficulty to the beginner, who has to learn how to distinguish the many new kinds of animals he will now encounter. Indeed he may often find it difficult to decide whether he is dealing with a plant or an animal. In any scientific account of the animal or plant kingdoms the various groups are separated from one another according to the manner in which they are organised, each having, as it were, a characteristic ground plan. This is the only sound method of classification, but it is one we can seldom employ on the sea shore where we cannot usually study or compare internal structure. So we must do as best we can with outward appearance, and in the account which follows plants and animals are arranged in an arbitrary series of groups according to what they look like. This, it is hoped, will make it possible for the beginner to decide what kind of animal or plant he has encountered and then, by the use of the faunistic and floristic surveys, to determine its name and learn something about it.

A. PLANT-LIKE. Here are included most of the plants (the remainder forming encrusting growths to be considered next) but also many animals which are attached and which grow like plants.

   i. Plants. These can be initially divided into three groups according to their nature, namely lichens, algae (seaweeds) and flowering plants.

     (*a*) *Lichens* (p. 254, Plate 40). These are compound plants composed of intertwining fungal threads with scattered green algal cells. The majority of shore lichens form grey or yellow encrusting growths, but a tufted species, *Lichina pygmaea*, so dark green as to appear black, and about 1 inch high occurs on the upper half of the shore.

     (*b*) *Algae* (p. 218; Plates 33-39, xxvi-xl). These are the seaweeds, green, brown and red, occurring roughly in that order down the shore. They reproduce by spores, not by seeds. Attached to rocks or stones by holdfasts, they do not have roots, but obtain all their food from the surrounding sea water. They vary in texture from delicate green weeds to tough, almost leathery, brown ones. All can easily be cut, revealing little apparent internal structure; there is never anything resembling a mouth and there are no tentacles. Some small red weeds common in rock pools may mislead the observer. They form little tufted growths and contain so much lime that the branches are brittle and break when roughly handled. These are corallines.

     (*c*) *Flowering Plants* (p. 254; Plate 40). Just above high water level there are a number of characteristic coastal plants that flourish in the salty soil and atmosphere (see *Flowers of the Coast*, by I. Hepburn; New Naturalist, No. 24). Here we are virtually confined to flowering plants so low on the shore that they are only exposed at low water of spring tides, mostly species of eel grass (*Zostera*) which has long, strap-like, dark green leaves with the characteristic ribbing of flowering plants (absent in seaweeds). The flowers are inconspicuous.

   ii. Plant-like Animals. While plants will seldom be mistaken for animals, a number of animals may well be taken for plants. They live attached to rocks and form plant-like growths, often branched like little bushes. They may be distinguished as follows:

     (*a*) *Sponges* (p. 41; Plate 1). While most shore sponges form encrustations, the simplest consist of very pale grey tubular or flattened objects up to 2 in. long, which hang down from the underside of overhanging rocks where it is always damp. They have a single terminal opening known as an osculum (*not* a mouth). As in all sponges (except the group which includes the bath sponge) there is a skeleton of fine spicules which can be felt by the fingers and seen under low magnifications. Sponges constitute the *Porifera*.

(*b*) *Hydroids* (p. 45 *et seq.*; Plate 2,i). Owing to their mode of growth these were once termed zoophytes, because they were considered part plant and part animal. They are common on the shore while larger species are often washed up. They form tufted or branching colonies seldom much over 3 in. high (those from offshore may be much larger). They have an outer supporting skeleton of horny material through openings in which project the feeding heads or polyps, each with a ring of tentacles surrounding a mouth. These usually withdraw when exposed or touched. All the polyps are united by canals which run through the colony. A lens is needed to determine structure or identify species. The hydroids are members of the *Coelenterata*.

(*c*) *Polyzoa* or *Bryozoa* (Many-animals or Moss-animals) (p. 171; Plate iii). These animals were formerly included in the zoophytes with the hydroids, which superficially they resemble closely. They form similar colonies and have the same horny skeleton. Most of those found on the shore are encrusting and will be considered later, but a few produce branching colonies while others of this type, and much larger, are frequently washed up after storms, notably the common sea-mat or horn wrack. Unlike the hydroids, the numerous individuals which go to form a colony inhabit separate chambers or " zooecia," the openings of which often bear spines which can be seen under a lens. Viewed in life under water the surface of the colony may be covered with a whitish fur of projecting tentacles which, like those of hydroids, can be extended or else withdrawn within the shelter of the skeleton. But the individuals are more complex, each complete in itself with its own mouth and anus, not united by common canals. A second type of these animals may occasionally be found on seaweeds or amongst hydroids where, as in the tufted hydroids, separate stems end each in a small pear-shaped individual.

(*d*) *Sea-Anemones* (*Actinians*) (p. 56 *et seq.*; Plates 5-7). These are allied to the hydroids, but are much larger, grow as separate individuals without a surrounding skeleton and when fully expanded are the most flower-like of animals. They are common on the shore, though some of them need to be carefully sought because they live in clefts or under stones and weed and, in some cases, buried in sand. When exposed or touched, the tentacles are drawn in and the whole animal contracts down to a rounded mass which may be difficult to see or to recognise as an animal. Under water, especially when given food (all are carnivorous), the body or column extends, and the tentacles expand around the terminal disc in the centre of which lies the mouth. Sea-anemones or *Actiniaria* belong to the *Coelenterata*.

(*e*) *Corals* (p. 60; Plate 7). On rocky shores in the south-west, what appear to be sea-anemones may be found which have a firmly attached limy skeleton above which they can expand so as completely to obscure it, but into the shelter of which they can withdraw. These are stony corals of which we have only a few solitary species. The reef-building corals of the tropics are colonial and form the great skeletons which constitute coral rock. The animals, or polyps, of all such corals are just like individual anemones. Occasionally a white or orange-coloured " soft coral " is encountered at low tide. This is colonial with many small polyps embedded in a firm mass. Both stony corals (*Madreporaria*) and soft corals (*Alcyonacea*) are included in the *Coelenterata*.

(*f*) *Sea Squirts* (p. 185; Plate 29). While these creatures are not exactly plant-like they are certainly not like animals. They are bag-like with two small openings out of which water is squirted in fine jets when pressed—hence the common name. Some sea squirts are solitary and up to as much as 6 in. long, others are colonial with many small individuals, in the case of the commonest about the size and colour of a red gooseberry, growing together. A third type is discussed in the next section. All take in water through one opening and expel it, after removing oxygen and food, through the other. Sea squirts or tunicates, despite their simple structure, are distantly related to the vertebrates by possession of a " tadpole " stage in development. They are included in the *Chordata*.

B. ENCRUSTING. Rocks, on both exposed and sheltered surfaces, and also many of the larger seaweeds, are often encrusted with many forms of life some of which are very difficult initially to assign to any particular group of plants or animals. These include representatives of the groups already mentioned with a variety of others.

i. Plants

(*a*) *Lichens* (p. 254; Plate 40). Very thin coverings, little more than patches of colour, orange, grey or black, often at or above high tide level, are lichens.

(*b*) *Algae* (p. 249; Plate 35). The bottom and sides of rock pools are very often coated with a pink encrustation with gently rounded margins. This, like the tufted corallines, is a red seaweed, a nullipore, which incorporates lime in its tissues.

ii. Animals

(a) *Sponges* (p. 42; Plate 1). Most intertidal sponges grow in this way. There is little apparent structure but the tissues crumble when rubbed and the spicules may be felt. The surface is covered with many fine, and less numerous large, openings (oscula) new ones being formed as the colony grows. Many are brightly coloured, red, green, yellow or brown being common.

(b) *Hydroids* (p. 48; Plates 2, i). Encrustations common on snail shells occupied by hermit crabs are due to a hydroid named *Hydractinia*.

(c) *Polyzoa* (p. 172; Plate iii), here well-called moss-animals, usually grow as encrustations on the shore, both on rocks and on the larger seaweeds where they form delicate lace-like growths in which the separate compartments (zooecia) occupied by individual little animals can easily be seen with a lens. Polyzoa growing on rocks are often limy and red or orange in colour; others form gelatinous masses often on seaweeds, and in these colonies the separate compartments are not easily distinguished.

(d) *Sea Squirts* (p. 192; Plate 29). Compound sea squirts are common growing as thin sheets over the surface of rocks and seaweeds. Within a jelly-like matrix many minute individuals are arranged in double rows or in star-like patterns. While each individual has its own opening where water enters, the outflow from many leaves by a common opening. The commonest are brightly and most variably coloured; others, commonest on seaweeds, are greyish but in all the characteristic pattern of the individuals, to be seen with the naked eye or with the aid of a lens, determines their nature.

(e) *Acorn Barnacles* (p. 90; Plate vi). These are the commonest objects on a rocky shore, covering the intertidal rocks in numbers up to 30,000 per square yard. Often they seem part and parcel of the rock, showing no evidence of life when exposed. Each is encased in a limy shell, broad-based and roughly conical, consisting of a series of plates the uppermost of which may open or close. If observed under water, or occasionally in air if the tide has just retreated and all is still very damp, these plates open and ten plume-like processes are alternately extended and withdrawn. These are " feet " and the animal is feeding. Barnacles spend their early life swimming in the sea, and then settle head downwards on rock, form a stout shell and use their feet to collect food. Barnacles are crustaceans belonging to the group known as the *Cirripedia*.

(f) *Limy Tube Worms* (p. 76; Plate iv). The intertidal brown weeds and the rocks are often thickly covered with very small, spirally coiled although flat, limy shells. They give a first impression of small snail shells but are firmly cemented and are formed by worms which can protrude a delicate crown of tentacles or withdraw them and close the opening of the shell with a neat plug or operculum. Larger worms, of irregular but never spiral arrangement, with a sharp longitudinal ridge ending in a point over the opening, are also encountered on rocks. This worm is worth observing in life because of its brilliantly coloured tentacles. These encrusting tube-dwellers are bristle worms, of which we shall encounter many representatives, some inhabiting different kinds of tubes, others free and active. These with limy tubes are *Serpulidae*.

(g) *Saddle Oysters* (p. 154; Plate xvii). A number of bivalve molluscs, such as mussels, live attached to rocks, but these are too well known and too obviously bivalves to raise difficulties. There are, however, certain bivalves which adhere very closely to the surface of rocks, their shells conforming to every irregularity. They look like small oysters and appear, like them, to be cemented by the under shell-valve. But if the animal is very carefully removed with a knife so that no damage is done to the under valve, this is then seen to have a hole in the centre through which the animal attaches itself, as does a mussel, to the rock. The shell itself is *not* attached. These saddle oysters are certainly encrusting animals; they belong, like all other such bivalves, to that sub-group of the Mollusca known as the *Lamellibranchia*.

C. WORMS AND WORM-LIKE ANIMALS.

We have now considered all the animals which might be confused with plants; all the remainder are obviously animal, although their precise nature may often baffle the novice (and sometimes the experienced zoologist as well). To begin with there are worms, elongate animals which crawl about on the surface or, more usually, under stones and weed and within sand, gravel or mud. Although all are " worms," and superficially alike, yet they belong to a number of widely different groups of animals. It is essential that we should learn to place each worm in its correct group, only then can we hope to discover its name. In all cases there are external characters which help us.

i. **Flatworms** (p. 62; Plate ii). These are all small, half an inch or less in length, but once seen are easily recognised because they are so flat; almost film-like they appear to flow rather than to crawl over the surface of rocks or weed. They are brown or whitish in colour. Allied to the parasitic flukes and tapeworms, these small free-living flatworms are *Turbellaria*.

ii. **Round Worms** (p. 87). While these animals, apart from the insects, are probably the most numerous group in the animal kingdom, occurring in the sea, in fresh water, and on land, and being among the commonest of parasites, they are always inconspicuous and never more so than on the shore. Species living there are all small and may be found in mud on the underside of stones or in washings from pools. One species is parasitic within brown seaweeds. It is difficult, and here unnecessary, to identify particular species but it is easy enough to tell a round worm from other worms. The body is circular in section, encased in a firm smooth covering and is pointed at each end. These worms constitute the *Nematoda*.

iii. **Ribbon Worms** (p. 63; Plate 8). These are almost entirely confined to the sea and are not uncommon, though sometimes difficult to find, on the shore. They vary in length from less than an inch to several feet. They are slimy, contract readily and are easily damaged. They are most often pink, red or black. The head is characteristic; unlike that of other worms of this general appearance, it has no protruding tentacles but is laterally grooved. The body has neither the firm covering of the round worms nor the subdivisions and lateral spines of the bristle worms next for consideration. If observed feeding—they are carnivorous—the ribbon worms are seen to possess a long proboscis which issues from an opening above the mouth and wraps around the prey. These worms are commonest under stones and round the holdfasts of seaweeds. They constitute the *Nemertini*.

iv. **Bristle Worms** (p. 66; Plates 9-13, iv, v). The majority of the common shore worms belong to this group which also includes the earthworms. While a typical bristle worm is easy enough to distinguish from other worms, there is great variation in appearance and in habit of life within this highly successful group. They possess bristles along each side of the body arranged in series corresponding to the body compartments or " segments " into which the worm is divided. (This segmentation is obvious in earthworms although the bristles are inconspicuous.) In the more active, crawling or swimming species these bristles are carried on conspicuous lateral lobes on each segment. The head is obvious, usually with conspicuous tentacles (unlike earthworms) and often eye spots. The rag worms in particular have powerful jaws and the largest, a foot or more long, can inflict a painful bite. Such worms are common under rocks and weed and among mud and gravel. But there are many kinds of active bristle worms, some long and thin, others short and squat and covered with scales on the back. All are obviously segmented, have tentacles on the head and laterally projecting spines. The burrowing worms, such as the common lugworms used extensively for bait, have no head tentacles and the spines and lateral projections of the body are reduced so that they come to resemble

31

earthworms. From burrowing worms we come to tube worms. Those constructing limy tubes have already been mentioned under encrusting animals, but there are many others in tubes of sand (separate or massed together to form impressive " reefs ") or of parchment-like or jelly-like consistency. All have conspicuous and beautifully coloured crowns of tentacles which are cautiously protruded and then withdrawn in a flash when even a shadow falls upon them. Although not uncommon, these worms are often difficult to find because the tubes are seldom conspicuous, but even when obtained it remains difficult to see them fully expanded. All show clear evidence of segmentation and have bristles. The bristle worms are *Chaetopoda*, including the marine worms with many bristles and the earthworms with few (there are some small worms of this type on the shore), and belong to the large group of the segmented worms or *Annelida*.

v. Sea Cucumbers (p. 183; Plate 28). Small members of this group—which has many large and brightly coloured members in deep and in warm seas—occur on the shore. They are about the size of a gherkin, from $1\frac{1}{2}$ to 6 in. long with a tough skin and five rows of what appear to be short tentacles running along the length of the animal. These " tube-feet " are organs—primarily of locomotion—which they possess in common with the related sea urchins and starfish. The mouth is at the one end and around it extend ten much branched tentacles, but these are withdrawn when the animal is exposed. Sea cucumbers are largely confined to the south-west and live usually in rock crevices. Other animals of the same type are occasionally found in sand; these have no rows of tube-feet, but the delicate skin adheres to a touching finger owing to the presence in it of minute anchor-shaped bodies with which the animal grips the sand when moving (i.e. they serve the same function as the bristles in the lugworm). Sea cucumbers or cucumarians are members of the *Holothuroidea* belonging to the very characteristic group of the *Echinodermata*.

vi. Other Worm-like Animals. Other animals having a worm-like appearance include some sea anemones (p. 59) that burrow in sand and have a long cylindrical column with a rounded (instead of the usual sucker-like) base. When laid in water and allowed to expand the number and nature of the tentacles and lack of any opening but that of the mouth indicates their true nature. Within old timbers in the sea long borings are made by the elongated " ship-worm " (p. 166; Plates xx and xxv). But this has two small shell valves at the inner end. Although used exclusively for boring, these are fundamentally the same as the shell of a mussel or a cockle. The ship-worm is a modified bivalve mollusc. Then there are worms for which no common name exists (p. 193), orange or yellow in colour, six or eight inches long, very fragile and making tubes in mud. Although not segmented, the body is clearly divided into three regions—proboscis, collar and trunk (shown in Plate 28). Finally some fishes (p. 202) are worm-like, especially the shore-living pipe-fishes (Plate xxii). But examination should soon reveal the small head with terminal mouth, eyes and gill openings, and the tail and the small fins—all indicating the nature of the animal.

D. CRUSTACEANS AND RELATED ANIMALS. Here we encounter a host of animals varying widely in size and form. Like the bristle worms they are segmented, but their bodies are hard, with jointed limbs, and they form with the insects and spiders, the *Arthropoda* (jointed-limbed), the largest group in the Animal Kingdom. Sometimes the entire body is obviously segmented, or only the hinder region as in lobsters or prawns, but always there are many pairs of jointed limbs (even in the otherwise very atypical barnacles already mentioned). Except for a few insects which have moved down from the land and the little sea-spiders (*no* connection with the land spiders), all shore animals of this kind are crustaceans and it will be helpful if at this stage the more obvious characteristics of each major subdivision of this most important group are summarised.

i. Insects (p. 121; Plate xiii). There are few truly marine insects but a number, small and not easy to identify, occur on the shore, most commonly in piles of rotting seaweed. They can be distinguished from crustaceans because they have only three pairs of legs and one (instead of two) pair of feelers (antennae).

ii. Sea-Spiders (p. 122; Plate xiii). These are all small (much bigger ones occur in the deep seas) resembling land spiders in possessing four pairs of legs, but the region behind the legs, technically known as the abdomen, which is large and rounded in land spiders is here very small. Once noted, there is no difficulty in recognising a sea-spider; they are usually found with sea-anemones or with hydroids on which they feed.

iii. Crustaceans (p. 89). To begin with the atypical, in addition to the acorn barnacles already mentioned, there are stalked barnacles (p. 92; Plate vi), somewhat flattened laterally but with similar encasing plates. They live attached to the undersides of ships or buoys and will be usually encountered attached to timber washed ashore. Other barnacles have become parasitic on crabs, forming a rounded mass beneath the undertucked tail region; these are not uncommon, but others which are parasitic on dogfishes and whales are unlikely to be encountered. The typical crustacean is not attached and is " shrimp-like," i.e. with a segmented body carrying many appendages the first two pairs of which are feelers (antennae), followed by feeding " mouth-parts," and then by others concerned with movement, i.e. walking, hopping and swimming. Certain of these may also have to do with reproduction. Finally there is a tail, often with an associated pair of appendages, by sudden flicks of which the animals can make darting backward " escape movements " when danger threatens. Numerous small crustaceans will be seen in almost any sample of water taken in spring and summer; some will be young stages of large species and need much experience to identify, others will be adult copepods which are amongst the commonest of all animals and possess long feelers with the series of feathered " oar-like " appendages which give the group its name. The larger crustaceans, which can be recognised as such by the naked eye (so excluding a few small groups), may conveniently be divided into: (a) those that are flattened from above to below, (b) others also flattened but from side to side, (c) " shrimp-like " and " lobster-like " animals, i.e. not flattened and with the body obviously divided into a region behind the head covered with a shield or carapace and a hinder tail region (technically abdomen), (d) the crabs with flattened carapace and the tail region tucked under this, (e) the hermit crabs. All demand a little further description.

(a) *Isopoda* (p. 96; Plates vii, viii) These are easily recognised because of their resemblance to the woodlice or slaters which are typical terrestrial members of this group. Marine, fresh-water and terrestrial isopods are very similar; there is no carapace and the young are carried in a " brood-pouch " under the hinder part of the body.

(b) *Amphipoda* (p. 102; Plates viii-x) They have more slender bodies while the lateral flattening is usually obvious. Many are agile jumpers, forming the sand or beach " hoppers " common on the shore. Again there is no carapace and the young develop in a brood-pouch.

(c) Two types of " shrimp-like " animals occur on the shore. The small almost transparent ones found in rock pools are probably opossum shrimps or *mysids* (p. 94). They have not the pincers or chelae of the true prawns; the eggs are retained in a brood-pouch, *not* attached to the under side of the tail region as in prawns and crabs. True shrimps and prawns (p. 111; Plate xi) together with lobsters and crabs, have five pairs of " walking legs " the first of which usually carries a pair of stout pincers while some of the others of these legs may carry small ones. Females " in berry " have masses of eggs attached to the swimming appendages under the tail region. Broadly speaking, prawns live in rock pools and shrimps within sand, but certain special types of prawns live in burrows in mud; they have a very wide tail region. Lobsters

(p. 115; Plate 14) are unmistakable, but there are smaller " squat lobsters (p. 116, Plate 14) in which the tail is usually carried under the broad short body but can be extended and used in vigorous backward movement.

(*d*) This habit of tucking the hinder portion of the body under the carapace has been carried to extremes in the crabs (p. 117; Plates 14-16, xii); here the tail region cannot be extended. But the female continues to carry her eggs there. This manner of organising the crustacean body has been a marked success and there are now many kinds of crabs.

(*e*) The hermit crabs (p. 116; Plate 15) have a naked tail region, which is protected within the cavity of the snail or whelk shell which they occupy, the hindermost appendages being used to grip the central column of the shell. The mouth of the shell is effectively blocked by the right pincer when the animal withdraws. Hermit crabs are very common. The crab may be induced to leave the shell by breaking this or heating it (very gently) with a match.

Prawns, lobsters, crabs and hermit crabs all belong to the *Decapod Crustacea*.

E. OTHER SHELLED ANIMALS.

The common expression shell-fish covers the crustaceans just considered but also the *Mollusca* which also usually live within a shell although one of a very different type that grows with the occupant and does not have to be cast from time to time. But here we might also consider other animals with a stout limy skeleton namely the sea urchins with their relatives the starfishes and brittle stars which, like the sea cucumbers already mentioned, are included in the *Echinodermata*.

i. Mollusca. Of this large and important group of animals there are five groups, all initially possessing shells, though in some the shell is lost, notably in the sea slugs which have special mention below, or is reduced and has become internal as in cuttlefish and squids. They may be recognised by the following characteristics:

(*a*) *Univalves* (marine snails and slugs) (p. 126; Plates 17-21, xiv-xvi). The shell (absent only in the sea slugs) is in one piece and usually spirally coiled like the garden snail, although the shape of the spiral and the number of coils vary widely. Coiling is absent in the numerous limpets, the conical shell representing the last, greatly enlarged coil, the earlier ones being lost. There is a tendency in one marine group for the shell to be reduced and finally lost, giving rise to the brightly coloured *sea slugs* which may usually be recognised by their elongated " slug-like " appearance, by the broad " foot " on which they crawl and the head armed with tentacles. Many of them have brightly coloured

35

processes, sometimes almost like a fur, along the back. The univalves constitute the *Gastropoda*.

(b) *Multivalves* (Chitons or Coat-of-mail Shells) (p. 125; Plate xiv). British species are all small and very flat, like a kind of molluscan woodlouse. They live on rocks, with the same habit of life as limpets, and may be distinguished from all other molluscs (from all other animals indeed) by the presence of eight shell-plates arranged one behind the other along the back. Far from conspicuous, when once spotted they cannot be mistaken. Scientifically they constitute the *Placophora* or *Loricata*.

(c) *Bivalves* (p. 147; Plates 22, 23, xvii-xx). Here the shell is composed of two plates, or valves, and a connecting elastic ligament. All bivalves are flattened from side to side (in that respect resembling the crustacean amphipods as the chitons do the isopods). Most bivalves, e.g. mussels, scallops, oysters, cockles and also the long and aptly named razor shells, are easily distinguished. Two of the exceptions to this, the encrusting saddle oysters and the elongated ship-worms, have already been mentioned. Many other bivalves bore into rock but they retain a large shell and cannot be confused with anything else. The bivalves are the *Lamellibranchia* or *Pelecypoda*.

(d) *Elephant Tusk Shells* (p. 147; Fig. 90). Mentioned only because the shells, although never the living animals, may be found washed up on the shore. They are a very small group of molluscs with a tubular, tusk-like shell somewhat wider at one end than the other and slightly curved, usually about 1 in. long. These are the *Scaphopoda*.

(e) *Octopods, Cuttlefish and Squids* (p. 169; Plate xxi). Although true molluscs, these animals are far more powerful and active than any of the others, while the reduced shell (e.g. cuttlefish " bone ") is enclosed within the body. They are more suitably considered with other swimming animals later. They represent the *Cephalopoda*.

ii. **Echinodermata.** These are all radially constructed animals and so essentially different from anything that occurs on land (hydroids, sea-anemones and jellyfish are also radially symmetrical). For this reason and because they are often large and brightly coloured, both sea urchins and starfishes are usually known and immediately recognised, but the following points might be stressed:

(a) *Sea Urchins* (p. 181; Plate 27). There are two kinds of these, one of which lives on the surface, usually of rocks, and is circular when viewed from above or below. The spherical shell is stoutly built. The other type burrows in sand or gravel and has a more delicate shell which is oval. Both are unmistakable; in life they are covered with spines which tend to drop off after death. These are the *Echinoidea*.

(b) *Starfishes and Brittle Stars* (p. 177; Plates 24-26). Usually with five arms, though some kinds have more (if less than five this is due to damage and new arms may be seen growing), these are common on the shore. The body is firm owing to internal limy plates like those that form the skeleton (or test) of sea urchins but here not fused together. Like urchins also, the mouth is on the underside of the central " disc," grooves along the underside of the arms converging on it. Brittle stars are distinguished from starfish because the disc and arms are distinct from one another whereas in the starfish the one merges into the other. The starfishes are the *Asteroidea* and the brittle stars the *Ophiuroidea*.

(c) *Feather Stars* (p. 177; Plate 26). These are mentioned because, with the sea cucumbers already mentioned (under Worm-like Animals), they complete the description of the echinoderms. There is but one species in British waters which may be seen on certain shores only. Its radial structure and ten feathery arms render it unmistakable. It is a member of the *Crinoidea*.

F. SWIMMING ANIMALS. Finally, associated in habit and not in appearance, come three groups of animals which, in varying manner swim, namely the *Jellyfish*, the *Octopods* and *Cuttlefish*, and the *Fish*.

i. **Jellyfish** (p. 54; Plates 2-4). These consist of transparent or translucent creatures which largely drift about in shallow waters, being often common in docks or estuaries although they may be left in rock pools or stranded on the beach when the tide retreats. Using the term jellyfish widely, there are three kinds:

(a) What may be called the jellyfish proper (p. 54), namely rounded hemispherical or saucer-shaped animals often of considerable size and some of them brightly coloured. They have long trailing tentacles and move by a leisurely pulsation of the bell which drives out water in that direction so that they swim with the dome of the bell foremost, the mouth being then hindmost. These are *Scyphozoa*, one of the major groups of the *Coelenterata*.

(b) For want of any popular name we must use the scientific name of siphonophores (p. 54; Plate 3) to cover the large Portuguese-man-o'-war and the smaller By-the-Wind-Sailor which may be encountered in the summer off our far western coasts. They float on the surface with a gas-filled bladder in the one and a gas-filled sail in the other. On the underside are trailing tentacles, a mouth or mouths, and reproductive organs. These *Siphonophora* are also included in the *Coelenterata*.

(c) Rounded or pear-shaped animals, very transparent and with at most two tentacles, sometimes appear in numbers in the summer. Examination in life shows lines of iridescence extending from one pole to the other like meridians of longitude. These are ctenophores (p. 61; Plate 2) for which we have no common name except for one known as the sea gooseberry, but to the Americans they are known as comb jellies (*Ctenophora*). The name *ctene*, meaning a comb, refers to the iridescent swimming plates which are composed of series of fine combs beating one after the other. Their motion causes the animals to swim with mouth foremost.

ii. **Octopods and Cuttlefish** (p. 169; Plate xxi). The former may be encountered in rock pools, the latter in shallow water over sand. The former have eight arms, the latter ten, armed with suckers and surrounding the mouth. Octopods may crawl with the arms, but both swim by sudden expulsion of water drawn into the respiratory chamber; so they proceed by jet propulsion. As already noted they are *Cephalopoda* and belong to the *Mollusca*.

iii. Many of the shore fishes (p. 194; Plates 30-32, xxii-xxiv) are poor swimmers and assume unusual shapes such as the rounded lumpsucker which holds on to rocks and the thin worm-like pipe fishes already mentioned with the eel-like butter fish. But, once secured, there should be no difficulty in deciding that, despite a somewhat unusual shape, this must be a fish with the various fins and the gill openings behind the head as the most characteristic features. Fish are vertebrates and known scientifically as the *Pisces*.

CLASSIFICATION AND NOMENCLATURE

Since man first became interested in animals and plants he has sought to arrange them in some sort of order. At first, attempts at classification had to be based largely on external appearance and on habits—thus all flying and all aquatic animals tended to be grouped together. Then as the structure of animals, and of plants, became better known classification became more and more a matter of comparative anatomy. It was found that animals of very similar habit and even external appearance—whales and fish for instance—belonged to quite different groups while animals as dissimilar in appearance and habit as limpets and squids were related. On the basis of a series of different structural plans, the animal kingdom is now divided into major groups called Phyla. Each Phylum is usually subdivided into a number of Classes (e.g. Starfishes and Sea Urchins belong to different Classes of the Phylum Echinodermata). Classes may be divided into Sub-Classes but below this into Orders (e.g. barnacles and prawns are members of different Orders of the Class (or Sub-Phylum) Crustacea) and then into Families. These are made up of

Genera which are groups of obviously closely related animals, herrings, pilchards and sprats being all species of the genus *Clupea*. Finally come species which may very generally be defined as groups of animals so closely akin that they interbreed and the product of this union is itself fertile (a horse and a donkey interbreed to produce mules but these are sterile, hence the parent animals are regarded as belonging to different species of the genus *Equus*).

The naming of species—of which in the animal kingdom alone there are in the order of one million is a very important matter. The modern binomial system was established by Linnaeus and all nomenclature dates from publication of the tenth edition of his *Systema Naturae* in 1758. The name of an organism contains the name of the genus, which always has a capital letter, followed by the specific, or trivial, name which is always spelt with a small letter, e.g. *Clupea harengus*, the common herring. The generic name is a Latin noun or a latinised word in the nominative case. The specific name may be another noun in apposition or in the genitive or it may be an adjective agreeing grammatically with the generic name.

With the passage of time names have, for various reasons, to be revised or new ones found. Where this has only recently happened, many may be so accustomed to the old names, which appear in all former literature, that the old name has here been printed in brackets after the new one. This applies particularly to the seaweeds which are still in course of major revision. So the plant that used to be called *Dilsea edulis* and is now called *Dilsea carnosa* here appears as *Dilsea carnosa* (= *Dilsea edulis*); or the plant that used to be placed in the genus *Ulva* as *Ulva linza* and is now thought to belong to the genus *Enteromorpha* is written as *Enteromorpha (Ulva) linza*.

The finer technicalities of nomenclature require that the specific name be followed by the name (perhaps abbreviated) of the author who first published it together with the date of publication. Here we have avoided these technicalities as far as possible, never giving the date and only the name of the author if the name in question is *not* contained in the *Plymouth Marine Fauna* (Third Edition, 1957) or *A Preliminary Check-list of the British Marine Algae* by Dr. M. Parke, published in vol. 32 (1953) of the Journal of the Marine Biological Society.

Then there is the question of vernacular names. All birds and most wild flowers have common names by which they are usually known, but only a small minority of shore animals and plants have them. Most of the fishes have common names and also animals such as lugworms, mussels, cockles, whelks, barnacles (in a general way), shrimps and certain crabs. The naturalists of the last century did their best by giving common names to almost all the molluscs and to the sea anemones. But these names were never widely used. In other groups there never have been, and probably never will be, common names. It follows that in this guide we have had no alternative but to use scientific names throughout, giving the common name where one exists. But, of course, the scientific names are internationally used whereas the common names have no such validity.

To those unaccustomed to them these scientific names may look more formidable than they really are. It is perhaps unfortunate that so many of them are polysyllabic and yet, once the fear of them has been overcome, they roll splendidly off the tongue—try once or twice *Polysiphonia fastigiata*, or, better still, *Strongy locentrotus drobachiensis*!

Examining specimens
adapted from *A History of British Starfishes*

PORIFERA
Sponges

ABOUT 250 species of sponges grow in British waters. Primitive animals, they live by drawing in a stream of water through many minute pores, extracting food and oxygen and expelling the waste through a large hole (osculum) which in some species is an outlet shared by a number of associated individuals. The osculum is conspicuous in some species.

Very few occur above mean tide level. They begin to become conspicuous on the lower shore. Most of them form close encrustations on rocks and in crevices and may be confused with some seaweeds, e.g. *Lithophyllum*, or with some sea-mats, e.g. *Flustrella hispida*, or with some encrusting Tunicates. Some are so thin that they feel hard, though most of them have a " spongy " texture; when pressed by the ball of the thumb they usually exude water. None of them resembles a bathroom sponge (but see the egg-case of whelks, p. 217 and pl. xxv).

Identifying sponges is a specialised study, and largely depends on microscopic inspection of the shape and arrangements of minute, hard, splinter-like spicules which give stiffening to the mass of the sponge. For only a very few is identification in the field possible. The last shadow of doubt seldom disappears.

Nearly every species varies widely in colour. The shape of growth also varies, depending on the shape and depth of crevices, shelter from wave action, etc. A big overlap exists between the external appearance not only of related species but even of related genera.

Perhaps partly because identifying sponges is so difficult not much is known at present about their distribution. A small group of solitary sponges has the individuals attached by one end. These primitive " purse sponges " are of more defined shape and less varied colour than the encrusting forms.

PURSE SPONGES

Rather stiff, pale grey, like a cylindrical vase, up to 2 in. long, perhaps on a stalk, several vases springing from a common stem or holdfast. Terminal osculum fringed with stiff, long, hair-like spicules. If the vase is gently rubbed outer layer of " sand " comes away leaving grey, smooth " skin " from which many small hairs project. Low down on middle shore. Under stones, in pools, among seaweed, not much exposed to wave action. Widely distributed. Common.

Sycon coronatum pl. 1

Rather stiff, bushy and may be much branched, looking perhaps like very minute, rough, pale, bunch of bananas. At end of each vase is an osculum, perhaps fringed with hairs. Low down on middle shore. In pools. Widely distributed. Very common. *Leucosolenia* spp.

At least five species are common. One crowds round stems of *Fucus* (p. 226 and pl. xxxii), white, about ¼-in. tall. Another, also white, attached to stones in patches of about 1 sq. in., may be ½-in. high. Yet another, tubes of which twist slightly and are much branched, may be yellow, pink, red, or bluish-grey.

Hanging lankly, attached to rocks, particularly overhangs among red seaweeds *Plumaria elegans* (p. 241 and pl. 38) and *Lomentaria articulata* (p. 248 and pl. 39). Grey to pale yellow flat vases attached by stalk, sometimes in groups, usually oval, with compressed osculum at end, Usually 1 in. long, may be 2 in. Lower shore. Widely distributed. Very common. *Grantia compressa* pl. 1

N.B. Stiff stalked yellowy vases, like grains of wheat, about 3/10 in. tall, abundant on rocky shores, are egg-capsules of common dog-whelk. *Nucella lapillus* (fig. 86c, p. 134).
Stiff, flattened, partly translucent vases, about 3/10 in. tall, often attached to *Fucus*, are egg capsules of netted dog-whelk,

Nassarius reticulatus (fig. 86c, p. 134).

BORING SPONGES

Shells, particularly of oysters, and limestone rocks may be found bored with round holes of various sizes (in shells, usually $\frac{1}{10}$-$\frac{1}{8}$ in.) and in the holes little smooth lumps of pale yellow or yellow-orange sponge. Shells may be attacked from both sides and be riddled with holes. Lower shore. Widely distributed. Common. *Cliona celata*

ENCRUSTING SPONGES

Perhaps the first two sponges cover a greater area of rock than all the rest put together.

Very variable shape. Rough middle-green is commonest colour; may be yellow, orange, etc. Surface usually fairly smooth, patterned with *well developed, more or less regularly placed oscula*, like miniature volcanoes. Fragments begin to appear at mean tide level, in clefts, under thick layers of *Ascophyllum* (p. 227 and pl. xxxii) and *Fucus* (p. 226-7 and pl. xxxii). Commoner on lower shore, under overhangs, on shaded surfaces, amongst holdfasts of seaweeds. Patches may cover 30-40 sq. in. Colour varieties often touching each other. Widely distributed. Abundant. *Halichondria panicea* BREAD CRUMB SPONGE pl. 1

Very variable shape; orange, rich dark orange-red, or occasionally almost scarlet. Surface rough, almost granular, puckered with pattern-less grooves. Oscula small and numerous, arranged without pattern, heighten coarse texture of mass which may cover 20-30 sq. in. Fragments on middle shore but becomes abundant on the lower shore. Under overhangs, in rock clefts, among holdfasts of seaweeds. Widely distributed. Abundant. *Hymeniacidon [sanguinea]* pl. 1

Isolated lumps (patches), perhaps to 6 in. across, coarse, rather massive growth that may be 2 in. thick; often bright orange but may be yellow. Oscula are large, not much raised in mass of sponge and not distributed evenly. Lower shore. On sides of boulders, perhaps more likely where rock gives way in a yard or two to muddy-gravelly sand. Probably widely distributed and not uncommon. Easily confused with *Suberites*. *Myxilla [incrustans]* pl. 1

Growing in lumps and convoluted folds, reminiscent of drawing of brain; may be 6 in. across. Rather smooth surface, without oscula. Usually bright orange; may be yellow. Lower shore. On boulders. Probably widely distributed. Not uncommon. Easily confused with *Myxilla*. *Suberites domuncula* (=*Ficulina ficus*)

Small patches on boulders, not 1 in. across; vivid, real Reckitt's blue. Very thin, rather slimy. No obvious oscula. Lower shore. Uncommon. *Terpios fugax* Duch. & Mich.

Small patches, typically only 2 in. across; very flat and thin; rather smooth shiny surface broken up by well defined oscula, fairly regularly distributed, which have small collar—rather sharp but with shallow uplifted edge. Blood-red. S. coasts. Not common. *Ophlitaspongia seriata* Bow. pl. 1

May be quite small patches on coasts exposed to wave action, on sides of deep overhangs; or may be massive developments under large overhangs and at end of small caves. *Elephant-grey, smooth outside but pale creamy-yellow when broken.* Large lumps may be easily 6 in. deep and as much as 2 ft. across, bridging and filling large cracks. These large lumps often almost inaccessible. Oscula large; to some extent arranged in rows. Lower shore. Locally may be not uncommon. *Pachymatisma johnstoni* (Bow.) pl. 1

Amongst the various other things which may be confused with sponges are:

Long gelatinous lumps, irregularly lobed and fingered into blunt-

43

ended shapes, 4 to 12 in. long. Growing independently or on sea-weeds or hydroids. Greenish-yellow, grey. See

Alcyonidium spp. p. 174 and pl. iii

Smooth, may be gaily coloured, lobes decorated with pattern of stars. In quiet water. See   *Botryllus schlosseri* p. 192 and pl. 29

Rough irregular lumps of coarse " bathroom sponge," pale straw colour. Mostly on strandline. Egg mass of whelk. See

Buccinum undatum p. 217 and pl. xxv

See also the encrusting Polyzoa (Sea-Mats), p. 172 and pl. iii, and some of the Tunicates p. 186 and pl. 29, or even tightly closed Sea-Anemones, p. 56 and pl. 5 and 6, or the seaweed

Leathesia, p. 232 and pl. xxvii

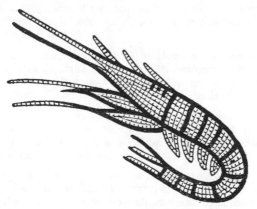

Common Shrimp from a tesselated pavement
reproduced in *A History of the British Stalk-Eyed Crustacea*

COELENTERATA

Hydroids (Sea-Firs), Siphonophores, Jellyfish, Sea-Anemones, Corals, Sea-Gooseberries, etc.

COELENTERATES are amongst the commonest of marine animals; they are very simply constructed but are most diverse in outward appearance. They are typically radial in design and often very like flowers. Many of them live attached like plants, although, apart from sea anemones and corals, they often have a free jellyfish stage in their life history—just as the large jellyfish go through a small attached stage. Many coelenterates form elaborate colonies of individual " flower-heads " (polyps or zooids) attached to a common " stalk." In the hydroids these horny stalks may assume characteristic patterns.

In the middle of the flower-like polyp is a mouth which also serves as an anus; food enters and waste leaves by this one opening. All coelenterates are carnivorous. The tentacles usually associated with the mouth possess stinging cells which paralyse and secure the prey, which the tentacles then pass to the mouth.

HYDROZOA

Hydroids (Sea-Firs)

It is very easy to confuse some of these with the equally common Bryozoa (Sea-Mats), with which they were formerly grouped as Zoophytes (Plant-Animals), or even with dead pieces of calcareous red seaweed, e.g. *Corallina* (p. 250 and pl. 35).

The characters of the species listed below can be seen more readily if a living specimen is placed in sea water, when the polyps may relax and open. But even then a hand lens will often be necessary.

A

" Flower-heads " (zooids) always visible, even when disturbed.

   i. Tentacles knobbed, see fig. 2a.
   ii. Tentacles threads, see fig. 2b.

Fig. 2a. x 10   Fig. 2b. x 10

45

B

" Flower-heads " (zooids) retreat into minute, stiff, translucent cups when disturbed.

   i. Usually rather feather-shaped. Cups on one side of branch only, see fig. 3.

   ii. Cups in rows on both sides of branch.

     (*a*) Cups in closely opposite pairs, see fig. 4.

     (*b*) Cups alternate on each side of branch, see fig. 5.

C

" Flower-heads " (zooids) not in rows, but bell-shaped cups carried at end of relatively long stalks, see fig. 6.

Fig. 3.   Fig. 4.   Fig. 5.
x *c* 1   x *c* 4   x *c* 4

Fig. 6. x *c* 2-4

A. " **Flower-Heads** " (**zooids**) **always visible, even when disturbed**

Fig. 7. Tentacles of
Coryne muscoides,
x 10

   i. Tentacles knobbed, see fig. 7.

Rose-coloured colonies, often with yellow undertones, with deepest colour towards tips; up to 6 in. tall; irregularly but very branched, *stem and branches closely and regularly ringed* (fig. 8). Lower shore. In deep pools; attached to large seaweeds on muddy/sandy flats. Tends to SW coasts. Not very common.

Coryne muscoides fig. 8, pl. i.

Pink and red colonies, with richer shades towards tips. Very like *Coryne muscoides* except that branches tend to come off one side of stem and that *most of length of stem and branches is smooth,*

46

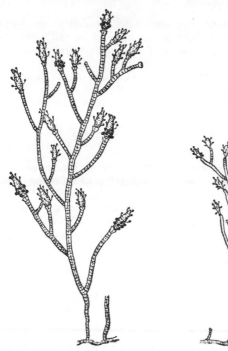

Fig. 8. *Coryne muscoides*, x 2   Fig. 9. *Syncoryne eximia*, x 2

leaving only small ringed sections irregularly placed in colony
(fig. 9). To 6 in. tall, usually only 3 in. Lower shore. Among
Laminaria (p. 225 and pl. xxxi); in rock pools, on rock faces, on
lobster-pot ropes and floats. Widely distributed. Probably common;
less so in Scotland.   *Syncoryne eximia* pl. i.

Head bearing tentacles much the largest part of the colony and may
be 2 in. long, elongated oval coming to sharp point; shape like spike
of cuckoo pint (*Arum maculatum*). Head can contract to about 1/3
length. Except round tip, head covered with small tentacles which
have reddish tips. Head is attached to stones by " roots " springing
out of main base, which is brown. From where head joins main
base are small branches on which may be pink globular sacs. Lower
shore. Under stones. Tends to S. and W. coasts. May be locally
common.   *Myriothela cocksi* pl. i.

ii. Tentacles threads, see fig. 10.

Fig. 10. Tentacles of
Clava multicornis,
x 10

Rich reddish, with tendency to yellow. *Crowded bunches*, about 1 in. tall, rising *from close network of " roots"*; usually attached to brown seaweeds, particularly *Ascophyllum* (p. 227 and pl. xxxii) and *Fucus* (p. 226 and pl. xxxii). " Stalk " thickens towards end. Where one cluster is found probably plenty more are close by. Low on middle shore. Perhaps commonest on S. and W. coasts.

Clava squamata pl. 2.

Smaller than *C. squamata*, rarely more than ¼ in. tall. Rose-pink " stalks," rising perhaps singly, and *not in crowded bunches, from open pattern of " roots*." On stones and seaweeds; in pools. Common in S.W., becoming scarcer northwards. *Clava multicornis* pl. 2.

Colony may be 3 in. tall, based on dull yellow strong stem which thickens towards base and is much branched. At least lower branches bear branchlets ending in pale pink cups. On stones, on pieces of shell, holdfasts of seaweeds. Lower shore. Probably widely distributed.

Bougainvillea ramosa pl. i.

Pale pink *patch on snail shell, inhabited by hermit-crab*, most often round the shell mouth. Lens will show mixture growing, of white stalks not more than ¼ in. tall crowned with zooids, and shorter pink stalks which may have minute oval-globular sacs attached towards end. Usually on lower shore of sandy flats. Widespread. Common.

Hydractinea echinata pl. 2.

Brown stems, rising from twisted interlocked system of "roots", *very little if at all branched* (see fig. 11). Up to 6 in. tall, each crowded with minutely stalked rose-pink to deep red zooids that have *one drooping row of white tentacles* as fringe all round and stiffer shorter row sticking up round centre. On rocks on lower shore. Widely distributed. Probably not uncommon. *Tubularia indivisa* pl. 2.

Pale horn-coloured or yellow stems, 1-2 in. long, *usually, and sometimes very, branched; fairly regularly* separated sections ringed (see fig. 12); pale red zooids, minutely stalked, having *outer drooping fringe of white tentacles* and scarcely visible inner stiff short circle of tentacles. On rocks of lower shore; on buoys. Widely distributed. Probably common. *Tubularia larynx* pl. 2.

Fig. 11. *Tubularia indivisa*, x c 1

Fig. 12. *Tubularia larynx*, x c ?

B. " Flower-Heads " (zooids) retreat into minute, stiff, translucent cups when disturbed

i. Usually rather feather-shaped. Cups on one side of branch only. See fig. 13, p. 50.

White or pale yellow fronds rising in small groups of 4-10 to about 5 in. tall, from open interlacing of short " rootlets " attached to shells or stones or seaweeds, particularly large brown seaweeds. Joined branches alternate along stem, with up to 7 *zooids confined to the side of branch nearest tip of frond, one at each joint.* In close double row up part of main stem may be found minute pear-shaped vases (part of reproductive system), see fig. 13a. Lower shore. In pools, on flats, piles, etc. Widely distributed. Common.

Kirchenpaueria (=*Plumularia*) *pinnata* pl. i.

Like *K. pinnata*, except that pale brown vases occur only on one side of stem and are sharply beaked; *branches have alternate long and short joints, with zooids always on long ones,* see fig. 13b. Lower shore. On weeds, rocks and other hydroids. Widely distributed. Not very common above low water mark. *Plumularia setacea*

As *P. setacea* but at most 1½ in. tall; *irregularly branched, with two joints between each zooid.* Vases often singly, brown, ringed, with wide open top, see fig. 13c. Lower shore. On stones; among sea weeds. Probably widespread and not uncommon.

Plumularia halecioides

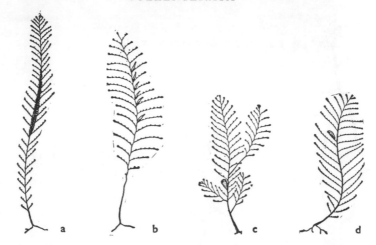

Fig. 13. a. *Kirchenpaueria pinnata;* b. *Plumularia setacea;* c. *Plumularia halecioides;* d. *Aglaophenia pluma.* All x c 1

Curving stems, rising from open system of adhering "rootlets," usually not branched. Dark brown *branches alternate from line down "front"* (all others come from opposite sides). Up to 10 zooids on branch. Vases distributed irregularly, have pronounced stalk to one side and look like minute oval cones, and always *occupy gap left by* absent branch, see fig. 13*d.* Above all on *Halidrys siliquosa,* p. 229 and pl. xxxiii.; on stones and shells. Widely distributed. Common, particularly in W. and S. *Aglaophenia pluma*

ii. Cups in rows on both sides of branch

(*a*) *Cups in closely opposite pairs,* see fig. 14*a* and *b.*

From open network of thread "rootlets" stems rise to 2 in. tall, branches usually opposite, but often of unequal length, and may carry branchlets. Also regularly found only ½ in. tall, not having developed any branches at all, being only stiff little stems. Vases distributed irregularly, smooth, pear-shaped. Cups small, *in pairs* on every joint of stem and branches, giving total effect of a series of articulated triangles, see fig. 14*a.* Middle and lower shores. Pale dirty grey colourless. On rocks; above all on *Fucus* (see p. 226 and pl. xxxii). Widespread. Abundant.

Dynamena (=*Sertularia*) *pumila* pl. i.

Fine, hair-like stems, up to 8 in. long, but usually 4-6 in., forming rather lanky tangles, alternately branched and many times divided again. Cups minute but shaped essentially as in *D. pumila*, see fig. 14*b*. Whole effect is of hair-fine, serrate delicacy; pale cream colour, sometimes tinged with red. Vases distributed irregularly, smooth, pear-shaped. Lower shore and downwards. On *Fucus* spp. (see p. 226 and pl. xxxii) and, particularly, on stems of *Laminaria digitata* (see p. 225 and pl. xxxi). May be rare in Scotland, but becomes not uncommon towards S.W. coasts.

Sertularia operculata pl. i.

Several species of *Sertularia* grow abundantly just off-shore. They have the same basic pattern as the two described above and may be cast ashore in quantities. Known commercially as " White Weed," a species of *Sertularia* is collected from moderate depths, especially off Harwich, dried and stained and sold for decorative purposes.

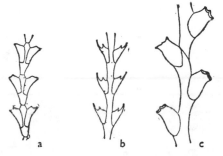

Fig. 14. Sections of stems of a. *Dynamena pumila;* b. *Sertularia operculata;* c. *Sertularella polyzonias.* All x c 4

(*b*) *Cups alternate on each side of branch*, see fig. 14*c*.

Stems irregularly branched, all rather obviously jointed, an impression heightened by zooids occurring alternately throughout and being placed immediately below joints, see fig. 14*c*. Bright straw colour; usually about 2 in. long. Vases may occur irregularly, like ringed and minutely stalked cones. On stones, shells and seaweed. Said to be generally distributed round coast.

Sertularella polyzonias

C. " **Flower-Heads** " (**zooids**) **not in rows, but bell-shaped cups carried on end of relatively long stalks, see fig. 15.**

Relatively thick stem, up to about 3 in. long, irregularly branched. Overall pattern reminiscent of plant horsetail (*Equisetum*) is given by *stalks of zooids coming off in whorls* of 4 to 6, each ringed particularly just below cup. Vases on main stems, with tapering tops, and hardly stalked, see fig. 15*a*. Lower shore. On shells and stones. Probably widely distributed and common. *Campanularia verticillata* pl. i.

Fine stem, about 1 in. tall, fawn-yellow, irregularly branched. From stem and branches, nearly always alternate, come *long ringed stalks of zooids;* just above point of junction are a few rings on stem or branch, Elongated, smooth, open-ended vases, on short, ringed, stalks, irregularly scattered in points of junction between branches, fig. 15*b*. Middle shore to deep water. On rocks, sides of pools, under and on weeds, among stones and mud and on buoys. Very widely distributed. Very common, particularly in summer.

Laomedea (=*Campanularia*) *flexuosa*

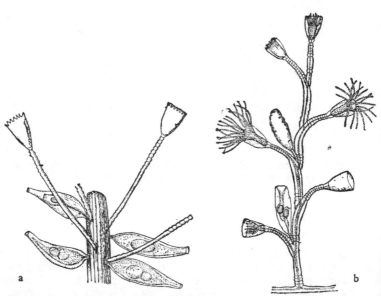

Fig. 15. " Stalks," " cups " and " vases " of
Campanularia verticillata, x *c* 10;
b. *Laomedea flexuosa*, x 2-4;

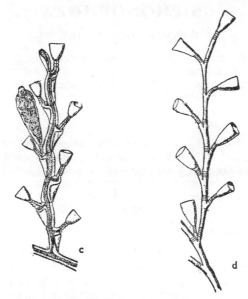

Fig. 15. " Stalks," " cups " and " vases "
c. *Obelia geniculata,* d. *Obelia dichotoma,* both x 2-4

Fine, thin lengths of ramifying " rootlets." Stem irregularly branched, up to 3 in. tall, *markedly zigzag.* At each joint cup on ringed stalk. Grecian-urn-shaped vases from joints of zigzags, fig. 15c. Middle and lower shore. On weeds, particularly on *Fucus* spp. (p. 226 and pl. xxxii) and on *Laminaria* (p. 225 and pl. xxxi). Widespread. Very common.

Obelia geniculata pl. i.

Stem rarely more than 3 in. tall, irregularly branched, and branches often with branchlets, *only slightly bent at joints, sometimes virtually straight,* with few rings immediately above each joint. From joints come cups on ringed stalks, see fig. 15d. Middle and lower shore. On stones, rocks, weeds and other hydroids. Widely distributed. Common.   *Obelia dichotoma*

Other species of *Obelia* grow in shallow water and may break away to be found cast ashore. They have same general pattern, and may be as much as 1 ft. long.

53

SIPHONOPHORA

Portuguese Man-o'-War, etc.

These are hydrozoans which consist of a complicated colony composed of individuals of different kinds, some for feeding, some for attack and defence, some for reproduction, some for suspension or for movement. The two mentioned below float on the surface of the sea, but all those parts which hang down from the floats may be missing from specimens cast ashore.

Elongated-oval, thin, gas-filled, bladder about 6 in. long; pale blue, sometimes shot with pink, with crenated pink-coloured crest. From float hangs down complicated mass of tentacles and individuals to many feet long. The stinging cells are very powerful and living specimens should not be touched with naked hands. An inhabitant of the open Atlantic, this animal only appears on our S.W. coasts after prolonged S.W. winds when it may be very locally abundant and then may be absent for several years.

Physalia physalia PORTUGUESE MAN-O'-WAR pl. 3.

Flat oval membrane with a diagonally set stiff sail, about 4 in. long. Deep blue round margins. Beneath the float hangs down a central mouth surrounded by rings, first of reproductive individuals, then of tentacles. After persistent S.W. winds may be common on S.W. coasts.

Velella spirans BY-THE-WIND-SAILOR pl. 3.

SCYPHOZOA

Jellyfish

Only about half a dozen species occur along British coasts, usually in summer when they may be left stranded by the ebb tide or may be seen from rocks or piers slowly pulsating in the water. The mouth is bordered by four long lips, often subdivided, which trail behind the animal as it swims, but may be missing from jellyfish cast ashore. The number of individuals varies greatly from year to year.

Usually 3 to 8 in. across, but may be 15 in., with rather frilly edge. Watery-colourless with 4 *pale violet crescents* (*sometimes almost circles*) round centre. Widespread and much the commonest jellyfish.

Aurelia aurita pl. 4.

Usually 4 to 8 in. across, but may be 18 in.; skim-milk-white. Lobed edge, each lobe with a dark brown spot from which hang down 24 long

tentacles. Brown spot in centre of umbrella, with 24 *brown triangular patches* radiating from it. Mostly S. and W. coasts. Not very common.
Chrysaora isosceles pl. 4.

Usually about 3 in. to 1 ft. across, but may be much larger. Rim divided into large lobes with 8 bunches of tentacles hanging down. These can sting human beings. Wonderful shades of blue and violet. Not usually very common, eexcpt perhaps E. coast. *Cyanea lamarcki*

As *C. lamarcki* but brick red to yellow. Mostly S.W. coasts. Rare.
Cyanea capillata pl. 3.

Regularly up to 2 ft. across, rather massive. Grey or pale green, darker round margin. Seen from below are four spaces in the umbrella.*
Mouth lobes fused, forming heavy bunched mass with many minute openings leading into stomach. Purple edge of bell divided into many small lobes but no tentacles on these. Mostly S. and W. coasts. Sometimes locally very abundant. *Rhizostoma octopus* pl. 4.

Perhaps 3 to 6 in. across, purple or red-brown, spotted. Frilled edge from which hang 8 thin tentacles. Heavy mouth divided into 4 lobes hangs down from centre. *Strongly phosphorescent.* Gives off phosphorescent slime which clings to one's hands. W. and S.W. coasts only. Very rare. *Pelagia noctiluca*

LUCERNARIDAE

Stalked Jellyfish

These small, rather trumpet-shaped little animals, very easily confused with plants, cling by a basal sucker to seaweeds, eel-grass and stones. The margin of the bell or trumpet is lobed. At no stage do they swim although they move about on the surface.

At every 45° round rim of umbrella obvious bunches of tentacles. On membrane between each bunch *dark spot " anchor."*† Up to ¼ in. tall, rose-red or green, with 8 pale lines from stalk, each to a group of tentacles. Lower shore. Attached to *Laminaria* (p. 225 and pl. xxxi), *Rhodymenia* (p. 238 and pl. 39), *Zostera* (p. 254 and pl. 40), and other

---

*Associated with these large jellyfish, particularly *Rhizostoma octopus*, and often alive within the hollows of the umbrella, may be found the green-eyed amphipod *Hyperia galba*, see p. 109 and pl. x.

†The anchors are used for temporary attachment when the animal moves enabling the sucker at the base of the stalk to establish itself in a new position, cf. movement of a looper caterpillar.

plants. Very rare or absent in N. becoming common in S.W.

Haliclystus auricula pl. 2.

As *Haliclystus*, but without " anchors." May be pale green but usually deep cherry-red. *Lucernaria campanulata*

As *L. campanulata*, except that bunches of tentacles arranged in groups of two. On W. coasts. Very local and rare. *Lucernaria quadricornis*

General shape as *H. auricula*, but " anchors " are horseshoe-shaped, 4 between each group of tentacles. Indeterminate brown in colour. Lower shore. On weeds and undersides of stones. Rare generally but locally may be common. *Depastrum cyathiforme*

ANTHOZOA

Sea-Anemones and Corals

A
Animals solitary without skeleton, i.e. sea-anemones.

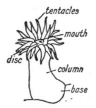

Fig. 16. The parts of a sea-anemone

i. Column smooth.

ii. Column with vertical rows of warts.

iii. Column sticky, lined or dotted.

iv. Anemones associated with hermit crabs.

v. Small anemone not included under i to iv.

B
Animals single with cup-shaped skeleton, i.e. corals.

C
Animals colonial (or apparently so) without external skeleton.

A. ANIMALS SOLITARY without skeleton, i.e. sea-anemones.

Identification of sea-anemones is difficult and certainly often depends on highly technical dissection. Colours and even shapes are variable and individuals may not always resemble the illustrations here given; even taken with the text identities may be difficult to determine. Those marked * are the most easily and certainly recognised.

i. Column smooth

Usually seen when tide is out, when contracts to rounded flat-topped mass of stiff jelly, $\frac{1}{2}$-$1\frac{1}{2}$ in. high; usually brown-red but may be cherry-red, brownish-green, green, yellow-brown, or crimson strawberry-colour with green spots. Blue line along under side of edge of base. When expanded about 200 tentacles in 6 circles, which fold in quickly when touched. Round inside of *top margin of column* 24 *clear blue spots.* Middle and lower shore. On rocks and in pools. Widely distributed and abundant.

Actinia equina BEADLET ANEMONE pl. 5.

Column about $1\frac{1}{2}$ in. tall, rather squat and flaccid, smooth and even shiny, with base splayed out and irregular. About 200 *tentacles 2 in. long, wavy, sticky, unable to contract.* Whole animal usually dull khaki, but may be pink or soft apple-green with ends of tentacles shading into beautiful tinge of violet. In quiet, sunny, shallow pools, often in rows along water's edge. Also on rocks; on brown seaweeds, particularly *Laminaria* (p. 225 and pl. xxxi). Middle and lower shore. Not on E. coast; all down W. coast; on W. half of S. coast; becoming common in S.W.

Anemonia sulcata SNAKELOCKS ANEMONE pl. 5.

Column slimy, 2 to 5 in. tall. Pale brown, orange, salmon-pink, cream or white. Disc very wide and *deeply lobed* into about 6 to 8 curving sections. *Tentacles exceedingly numerous,* slender, pointed, to some extent translucent, giving very *feathery appearance.* Disc and tentacles same great variety of colours as column; usually tone with column unless it is white or olive or brown. Lower shore. Rock overhangs, clefts, under stones and pier piles. Widely distributed. Common; locally abundant.

Metridium senile PLUMOSE ANEMONE pl. 6.

ii. Column with vertical rows of warts

Very broad base, may be 4 in. across, from which squat column rises only 2 in. Rounded and, with tentacles withdrawn, well formed lip round rather flat top. Column covered in grey, *sticky warts to which pieces of shell and gravel adhere,* often thoroughly disguising animal against background. If poked will squirt water and contract still further. Column usually shades of crimson or green, but may be very pale grey; many colours may be found in same column. About 80 *blunt, short tentacles, thickening towards base,* banded in pale shades of translucent colour; tentacles extend widely, well beyond top of column, to show considerable central area of disc to be without tentacles. At centre, mouth. Middle and lower shore. In shaded pools and cracks in rocks; under *Laminaria* (p. 225 and pl. xxxi) and stones. Widely distributed. Common.

Tealia felina DAHLIA ANEMONE pl. 6.

When closed—and it closes tight—about 1 in. across, leaving small circular lip in middle; flat-based, round-topped, *pink column* up which run *about* 6 *rows of white wartlets*. About 50 tentacles, including inner row of 6, stick out stiffly when open, translucent, delicately banded, from flat, rather greenish disc. Column up to 2 in. tall. Middle and lower shore. Often along edges of small, shallow pools, with column sunk into crack; under stones. Isle of Man round to Channel Isles. Commoner towards S.W.

Bunodactis verrucosa WARTLET OR GEM ANEMONE pl. 6.

Column nearly always greenish, paler lower down. Size and shape as *Bunodactis* but dark *warts in about* 30 *vertical rows*, becoming much larger at top, to form knobbly lip, and fewer and smaller towards base. Tapering tentacles, rather stiff and pale-translucent. Middle and lower shore. Pools, which may be small, shallow and sunny; may be in colonies; under stones. W. and S. coasts, but even in S.W. not very common. *Anthopleura thallia* (Gosse) pl. 6.

Column may be pink, brown, orange, etc. often paler higher up; up to 2 in. tall, but single animal varies greatly by extension. *Wartlets in* 48 *vertical rows*, much larger near lip than on middle of column, and are *spotted with crimson. Tentacles not readily retractile*, may be translucent, near-colourless, or brown, or even iridescent green. Middle and lower shore. In pools; under large seaweeds and stones. S. and W. coasts. Not common. *Anthopleura ballii* (Cocks)

iii. Column sticky, lined or dotted

Column variously shaped, usually dotted. May be slender stalk, 4 in. or more tall. May be trumpet-shaped. Either of these may retract into squat, round tentacle-fringed mass. Base is wider than bottom of column; may be flat or frilled. *At least* 300 *tentacles*, may be 700, rather short and limp. Colours variable, pinks, browns, creams, violets. No marked patterning. Throat usually pale. Tentacles may be ringed, spotted or plain. Lower shore. Either in rock pools, where column may be sunk into cracks, or else in muddy gravel sticking to dead shell or stone 3 in. deep, with tentacles open and flush with surface even when exposed by tide; but closes up and draws down into mud when disturbed. Possibly violet hues of column occur more commonly in mud. W. and S. coasts. Widely distributed. Common, except on E. coasts where may be absent.

Cereus pedunculatus pl. 7.

Individual animals change shape; round squat circles to trumpets 2½ in. tall. *Not more than* 200 *tentacles*. White stinging threads may be emitted from column if disturbed. Wide range of usually bright colours, sometimes patterned, sometimes not. Middle and lower shore. In pools; on vertical rocks; in crevices. " In some districts hundreds may be seen under overhanging rocks during the period of low water, protruding from their holes with a drop of water depending from their nearly closed apertures." Widely distributed. Common. Locally abundant. *Sagartia elegans* pl. 7.

A number of varieties have been separated:

Colours of disc and tentacles contrasting but not patterned.

(a) *column and disc usually orange* but may be buff; tentacles nearly white. var. *venusta* pl. 7.

(b) *column variously coloured;* disc and tentacles white. var. *nivea*

(c) *orange-drab disc;* pink or magenta tentacles. var. *rosea*

Colours of discs and tentacles not very bright, but arranged in patterns.
usually browns or creams, with either radial patterns or rings of contrasting shades; tentacles fitting into overall pattern.
var. *miniata* pl. 7.
Patterns may be faint. Orange tentacles may lie over patterned discs. Very complicated!

Very like *S. elegans*, but not brightly coloured or boldly patterned; may have wide range of colours that are rather sombre. (Green as colour for column, disc or tentacles does not occur in *S. elegans*.) Pieces of shell and fine gravel commonly adhering to column. Two rather distinct size groups; overall diameter either about 2 in. or only $\frac{1}{2}$ in. Middle and lower shore. Larger ones tend to be buried in mud or sand, among mussels, in rock cracks, in pools that are partly filled with sand or mud. Smaller ones in cleaner places, cracks in shallow pools, under rock overhangs, under large seaweeds. Widely distributed. Probably very common N. coasts; becoming less common towards S.W. *Sagartia troglodytes* pl. 7.

Even less than $\frac{1}{2}$ in. across base and about as high. When tide is out appear as soft, very pale, translucent-near-white jelly blobs, with delicate vertical lines, greens and pale buffs. White threads often lying on column. About 100 white tentacles. Lower shore. May occur in numbers on rock overhangs on rather exposed coasts amongst sponges and sea squirts. Also singly under stones. Distribution is to S. and W. No records for Scotland. May be very common locally. *Sagartia (Actinothoë) sphyrodeta*

No adherent base. Column appears smooth until touched. Up to 4 in. long, can elongate. Often with bulb below constriction towards base. Pale browny-pink, rather speckled, may have brown blotches round base, with 12 *fine vertical lines. About* 12 *tentacles*, translucent and usually patterned in contrasting shades of pale brown. Lower shore. Makes *burrows in sand* and is usually about 3 in. below surface. Widely distributed. Not common. *Peachia hastata* pl. 5.

iv. Anemone associated with hermit crab

Tough column up to 4 in., buffs and pale browns to cream colour, with *vertical lines* which may be faint if column is also spotted; spots dark. About 300 *translucent tentacles*, pale grey to straw-coloured, may be faintly spotted. Nearly always on shell of whelk *Buccinum undatum* occupied by hermit crab *Eupagurus bernhardus* (p. 116 and pl. 15). Lower shore. Not common. *Calliactis parasitica* pl. 6.

Base wrapped around snail shell inhabited by hermit crab Eupagurus prideauxi (p. 117); convoluted and edges fuse where they meet one another on far side of shell. Column pale fawn, suffused pink-purple which pales towards tentacles to be creamy white. Spotted all over with *garish magenta spots*, largest round middle of column. Disc and tentacles white. Small anemones may have more conventional shape. Those too large for shell secrete horny membrane under base effectively to increase capacity of shell and so remove necessity for crab to find larger shelter. Lower shore. On sandy flats where hermits are exposed. Widespread. Common.

Adamsia palliata pl. 6.

v. Small anemone not included under i to iv.

Column when extended only ½ in. tall and not more than ¼ in. thick. Translucent, tinged pink or pale blue. *Gut visible in middle as scarlet line, leading to scarlet mouth.* 28 tentacles, long, delicate, translucent, pink or scarlet, may be banded. Lower shore. In small pitted holes in rocks; on steep overhangs. W. coasts. Local; not common.

Milne-Edwardsia carnea pl. 5.

B. ANIMALS SINGLE with cup-shaped skeleton, i.e. corals.

Limy skeleton in form of flat-topped cup about ½ in. high and a little wider than high, with numerous radiating ribs which fill cavity and curl over rim of cup. Usually pure white, may be pink. Disc white with chestnut circle round mouth; about 50 tentacles with brown markings and usually opaque white tips. Animal can contract tightly within cup or expand clear of it when it may be taken for an anemone. Lower shore. Occurs singly or in groups together. On overhangs; in deep cracks, etc. S.W. coasts. Rare but locally common.

Caryophyllia smithii DEVONSHIRE CUP CORAL pl. 7.

Skeleton superficially resembles that of *C. smithii* and about the same size. Animal bright scarlet or orange with transparent tentacles dotted with bright yellow patches or warts, tips rounded and transparent. Lower shore. In deep and sheltered rock pools. S.W. coasts. Very rare and local. *Balanophyllia regia* SCARLET AND GOLD STAR CORAL

C. ANIMALS COLONIAL (or apparently so) without external skeleton.

Small anemone (actually more nearly related to corals) which grows in numbers together so that adjacent columns appear united. These thin and delicate, $\frac{1}{2}$ in. high, $\frac{1}{4}$ in. across, usually *clear grass-green* but may be orange, grey, scarlet, or pink. About 100 translucent tentacles with *dark knobs on tips*. In crevices, on overhangs, etc. Lower shore. S. and W. coasts. Locally may be common. *Corynactis viridis*

Colonies consisting of rounded tough masses, flesh-coloured when out of water (hence common name). Under water outline softened by emergence of numerous minute colourless polyps each with 8 feathery tentacles. Colonies usually up to 6 in. tall but small ones sometimes in pools. May be dead white, yellow, orange or pink. Substance of colony stiffened by little limy spicules within it. Lower shore. Rocky coasts, in sheltered places such as under pier piles. Widely distributed. Locally common. *Alcyonium digitatum* DEAD MEN'S FINGERS; ALCYONARIAN OR SOFT CORAL pl. 5.

CTENOPHORA

Sea-Gooseberries or Comb-Jellies

Small rounded or oval " jellyfish " characterised by 8 rows of swimming plates arranged like meridians of longitude on a globe. Each consists of many small beating combs (or ctenes) highly iridescent in life. They differ from the other Coelenterates in having no stinging cells, but they are equally carnivorous, catching prey by means of " lasso " cells. They may be seen in the surface waters from boats or piers or may be stranded or viewed in pools. Numbers vary greatly from year to year but they may be very common. Two are widespread.

Animal oval-spherical (like gooseberry) about $\frac{1}{2}$ in. across and $\frac{3}{4}$ in. long; in addition to combs are one pair of very long, branching tentacles which may be completely withdrawn. Commonest in late spring and in late summer and early autumn.
Pleurobrachia pileus SEA-GOOSEBERRY pl. 2.

Animal up to 2 in. or more long, thimble-shaped with slight waist and large internal cavity. Swimming plates obvious; no tentacles. Colourless or pale pink. Spring to autumn. *Beroë cucumis* pl. 2.

PLATYHELMINTHES

TURBELLARIA
Flatworms

The simplest worms, with a common mouth and anus on the under side. Small creatures that flow gently along the underside of rocks with a movement that continues inexorably although no muscle-flexing is visible to the naked eye. Waves of movement pass along the flat body and the animal advances. Few are as long as $\frac{1}{2}$ in. Most are coloured much as the ground on which they live and are easily overlooked. Many are probably widespread and common. One or two are well known.

Body $\frac{1}{8}$-$\frac{1}{4}$ in. long, dark grey or nearly black, streaked. Constrictions at neck. Two rounded horns. Two eyes. Under small stones at mouth of fresh-water streams. Upper and middle shore. Locally very common. *Procerodes* (=*Gunda*) *ulvae* pl. ii.

Body nearly $\frac{1}{2}$ in. long, oval, with tail that may trail out to a point when animal moving. Two sharp horns and many eyes. Translucent creamy-white, with red or brown markings.
Oligocladus sanguinolentus pl. ii.

Body may be more than 1 in. long, round-oval, fluted *wavy edges. Rich cream background along which are dark lines*, the outer ones being continuous round tail. Lower shore. Under stones, particularly those resting on muddy gravel. May be limited to S.W. Not uncommon locally. *Prostheceraeus vittatus* pl. ii.

NEMERTINI

Ribbon Worms

THE NEMERTINES are unsegmented worms, i.e. the body is not divided transversely into a series of compartments as it is in the commoner Annelid worms (p. 66). The body, usually smooth and slimy, can be extended until it is very long and thin or be contracted into a fraction of that length. Hence it is impossible to do more than suggest the length of the species described below. The mode of movement is so typical that this alone is an aid to identification. Small waves flow along the body towards the head; in the longer animals several waves may be travelling forward at the same time, one behind the other. The animal glides along slowly and smoothly, the swellings running rhythmically forward.

Nemertines are carnivorous and have a proboscis which is thrust forward from an opening above the mouth. In some it is armed with a thin stylet or needle.

A	B
With eyes.	No eyes.

i. Four eyes placed at corners of oblong.

ii. More than four eyes.

A. WITH EYES

i. Four eyes placed at corners of oblong

Body about 1½ in. long, flattened. Pale cream with pink down middle which does not run into bluntly rounded head. Lower shore. In pools; among weed and shells; under stones. Widely distributed. Common. *Nemertopsis flavida* pl. 8.

Body rounded, less than one inch long, brown or yellowish, darkening towards *pale, fairly wide stripe*, right along middle of back. Thin dark thread along each flank. Head with near-white, rather square-cornered end, with dark line across it behind the two rear eyes. *Tail white, bluntly pointed.* Lower shore. Under stones; amongst *Laminaria* (p. 225 and pl. xxxi) or *Zostera* (p. 254 and pl. 40). Widely distributed. Common. *Oerstedia dorsalis*

About ½ in. long, delicately pink or grey, with rather translucent edges. Four very small eyes. Lower shore. Among seaweeds; in pools; under stones. Widely distributed. Not common.

Prostoma flavidum pl. 8.

N.B. Several other species with four eyes occur occasionally.

ii. More than four eyes

Eyes in four groups, row on either side of front of head, and two clusters farther back and towards middle of head. Body 1 to 3 in. long; flattened, bluntly rounded tail. Shades of white or pink, with two darker *pink patches at base of head;* translucent, rather irregular line down middle of back. Shallow constrictions at base of head to form a " neck." Has proboscis as long as body. Lower shore. Under stones; amongst *Laminaria* (p. 225 and pl. xxxi) and shingle. Widely distributed. Common. *Amphiporus lactifloreus* pl. 8.

Eyes more or less all round edge of head, but tending to groups. Very thin, almost string-like, usually 6-8 in. long, but may be 18 in.; flattened. If disturbed when extended, contracts quickly and remarkably thoroughly. Out of water it writhes. Dull olive or grey-green above, with sharply contrasting near-white underside. " Neck " is not pronounced and has pale fawn bar across it. Lower shore. Under stones; among *Laminaria* (p. 225 and pl. xxxi). Perhaps only in S. and W. Not common.

Eunemertes gracile (Johnston) (=*Emplectonema gracilis*)

Eyes numerous and tend to be in two clusters, but often hard to see because of texture of head colour. Worm usually 4-6 in. long, but may be 12 in. Rounded over back, but flat below. Brown above, with lengthwise streaks, possibly faint purple iridescence; sharply contrasting off-white below. Pale streak across " neck." Round-pointed head, with slit at tip. Writhes and wriggles in coils. Middle and lower shore. Under stones; in gravel. Widely distributed. Common. *Eunemertes neesii* (Oersted) (=*Emplectonema neesii*) pl. 8.

Eyes in two lines of about three to six in each, on forward sides of head, sometimes hard to see. Body 3-9 in., flattened, reddish-brown, paler below. Head swollen just forward of distinct " neck." Middle and lower shore. Under stones on rather muddy gravel. Often several together. Widely distributed. Common. *Lineus* spp.

There are two species which are not distinguishable if colour is reddish-brown. But if colour is definitely pinkish

Lineus ruber pl. 8.

If colour is green *Lineus gesserensis* O. F. Müller.

Eyes numerous on each side of head, but hard to see. Worm

Ophlitaspongia seriata

Grantia compressa: PURSE SPONGE
with *Plumaria elegans* × 1

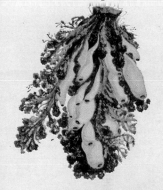

Syton coronatum × 1

Myxilla [*incrustans*]

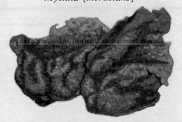

Hymeniacidon [*sanguinea*]

Halichondria panicea
BREAD-CRUMB SPONGE

Pachymatisma johnstoni

SPONGES : PORIFERA

1

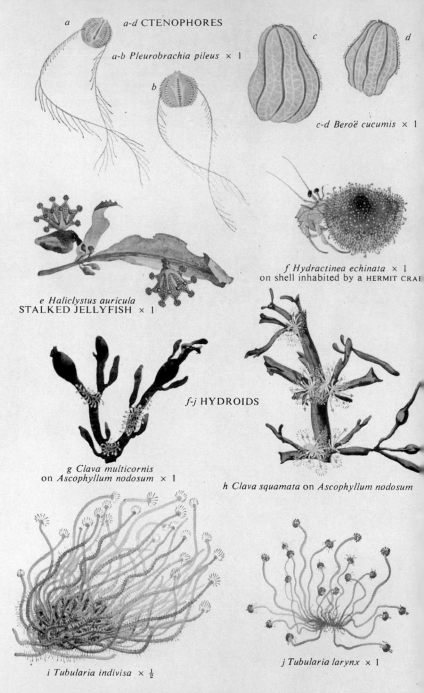

a-d CTENOPHORES

a   *a-b Pleurobrachia pileus* × 1

b

c   *d*

c-d Beroë cucumis × 1

f Hydractinea echinata × 1
on shell inhabited by a HERMIT CRAB

e Haliclystus auricula
STALKED JELLYFISH × 1

f-j HYDROIDS

g Clava multicornis
on *Ascophyllum nodosum* × 1

h Clava squamata on *Ascophyllum nodosum*

i Tubularia indivisa × ½

j Tubularia larynx × 1

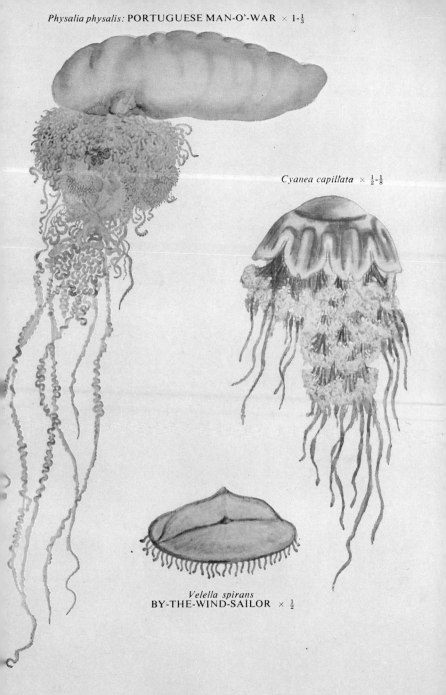

Physalia physalis: PORTUGUESE MAN-O'-WAR × 1-⅓

Cyanea capillata × ½-⅛

Velella spirans
BY-THE-WIND-SAILOR × ½

SIPHONOPHORES & JELLYFISH : COELENTERATA

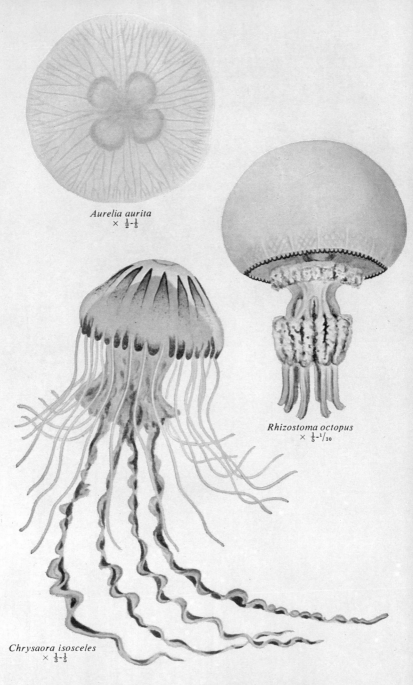

Aurelia aurita
× ½-⅕

Rhizostoma octopus
× ⅕-¹/₁₀

Chrysaora isosceles
× ⅓-⅕

JELLYFISH : COELENTERATA

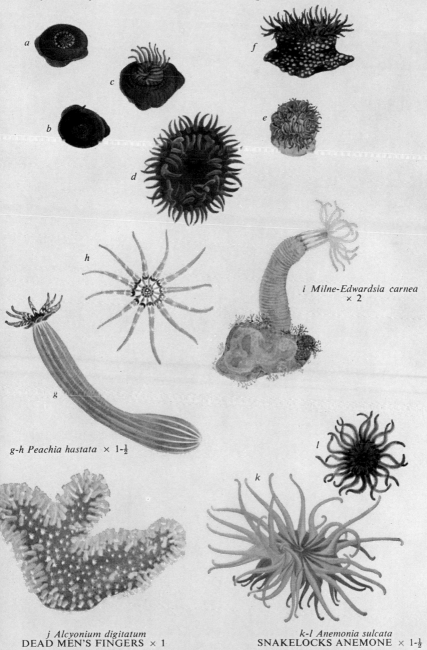

a-f Actinia equina: BEADLET ANEMONE × 1-½

a

b

c

f

e

d

h

i Milne-Edwardsia carnea
× 2

g

g-h Peachia hastata × 1-½

l

k

j Alcyonium digitatum
DEAD MEN'S FINGERS × 1

k-l Anemonia sulcata
SNAKELOCKS ANEMONE × 1-½

SEA-ANEMONES : ANTHOZOA

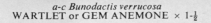

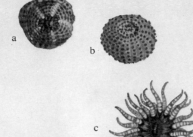

a-c Bunodactis verrucosa
WARTLET or GEM ANEMONE × 1-½

a

b

c

d *Adamsia palliata*
on shell occupied by a HERMIT CRAB × 1-¼

e *Calliactis parasitica* × ½-¼

f Tealia felina: DAHLIA ANEMONE × 1-¼

g *Anthopleura thallia* × 1-½

i

h

h-i Metridium senile
PLUMOSE ANEMONE × 1-½

6   SEA ANEMONES: COELENTERATA

Sagartia elegans
var. *venusta* × 1

Sagartia troglodytes
× 1-½

a

a-b Cereus pedunculatus
× 1-⅛

b

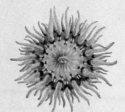

Sagartia elegans var. *miniata* × 1

Caryophyllia smithii
DEVONSHIRE CUP CORAL
× 1

Sagartia troglodytes
× 1-½

SEA ANEMONES & CORALS : COELENTERATA   7

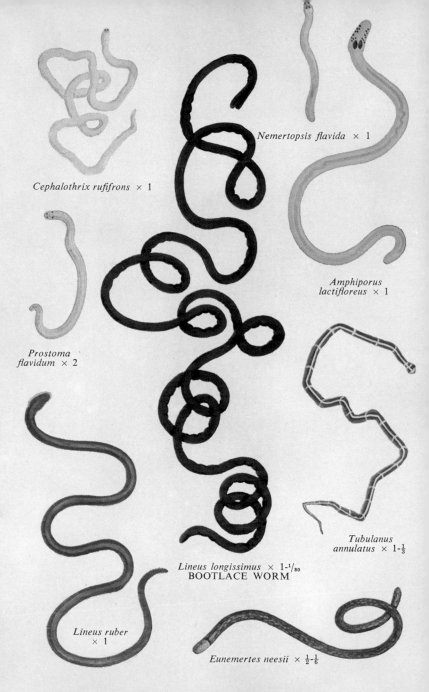

Cephalothrix rufifrons × 1

Nemertopsis flavida × 1

Amphiporus
lactifloreus × 1

Prostoma
flavidum × 2

Tubulanus
annulatus × 1-⅓

Lineus longissimus × 1-¹/₃₀
BOOTLACE WORM

Lineus ruber
× 1

Eunemertes neesii × ½-⅙

RIBBON WORMS: NEMERTINI

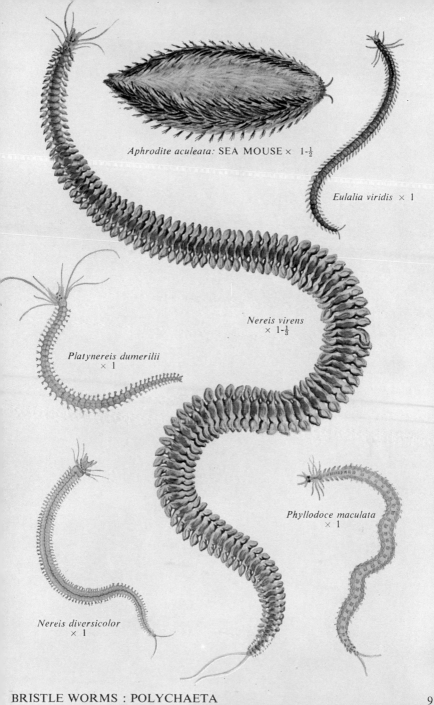

Aphrodite aculeata: SEA MOUSE × 1-½

Eulalia viridis × 1

Nereis virens
× 1-⅓

Platynereis dumerilii
× 1

Phyllodoce maculata
× 1

Nereis diversicolor
× 1

BRISTLE WORMS : POLYCHAETA

9

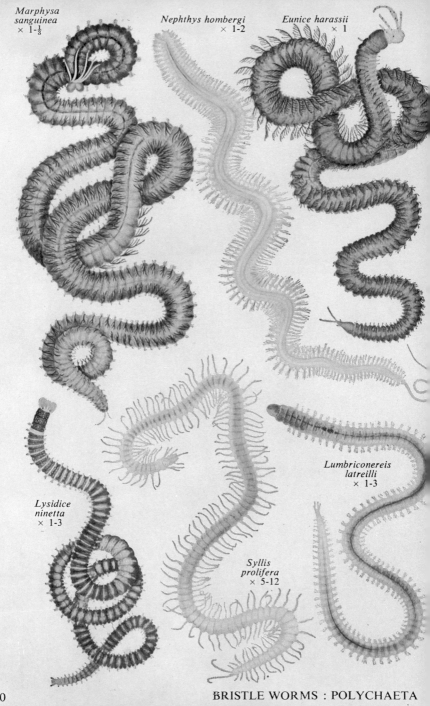

Marphysa sanguinea
× 1-⅓

Nephthys hombergi
× 1-2

Eunice harassii
× 1

Lumbriconereis latreilli
× 1-3

Lysidice ninetta
× 1-3

Syllis prolifera
× 5-12

BRISTLE WORMS : POLYCHAETA

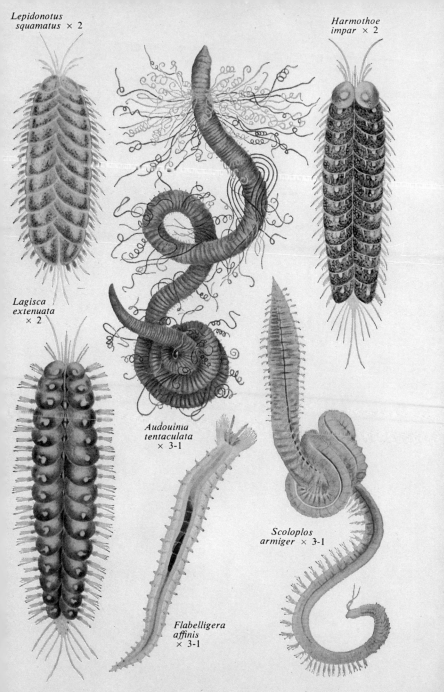

Lepidonotus squamatus × 2

Harmothoe impar × 2

Lagisca extenuata × 2

Audouinia tentaculata × 3·1

Scoloplos armiger × 3·1

Flabelligera affinis × 3·1

BRISTLE WORMS : POLYCHAETA

11

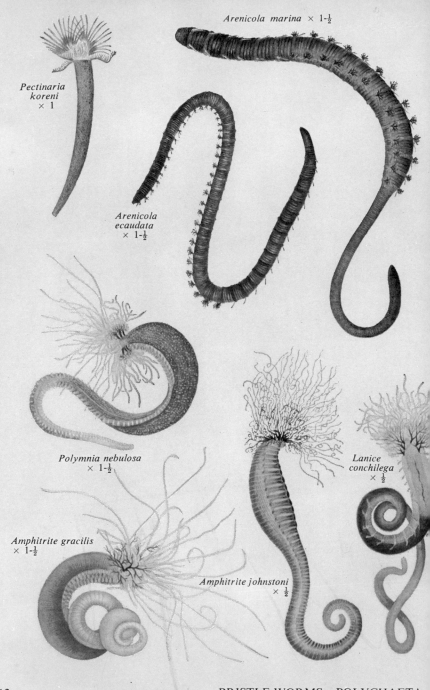

Arenicola marina × 1-½

Pectinaria koreni × 1

Arenicola ecaudata × 1-½

Polymnia nebulosa × 1-½

Lanice conchilega × ½

Amphitrite gracilis × 1-½

Amphitrite johnstoni × ½

BRISTLE WORMS : POLYCHAETA

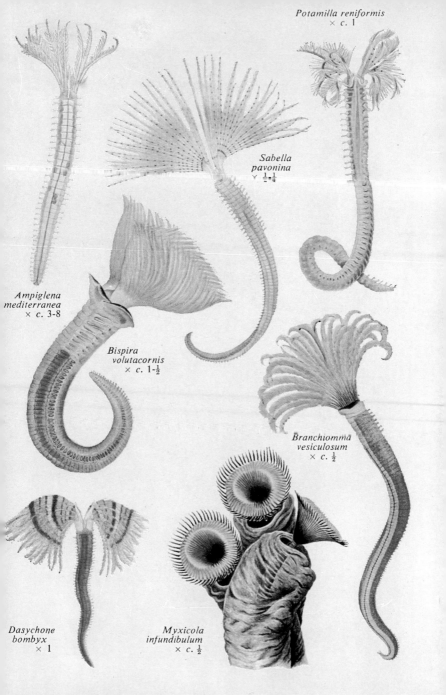

Potamilla reniformis
× c. 1

Sabella
pavonina
× ½ – ¼

Ampiglena
mediterranea
× c. 3-8

Bispira
volutacornis
× c. 1-½

Branchiomma
vesiculosum
× c. ½

Dasychone
bombyx
× 1

Myxicola
infundibulum
× c. ½

BRISTLE WORMS : POLYCHAETA

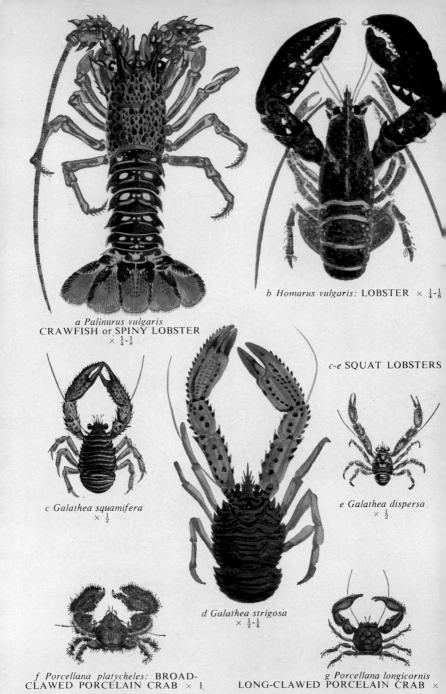

a Palinurus vulgaris
CRAWFISH or SPINY LOBSTER
× ¼-⅛

b Homarus vulgaris: LOBSTER × ¼-⅛

c-e SQUAT LOBSTERS

c Galathea squamifera
× ½

e Galathea dispersa
× ½

d Galathea strigosa
× ½-¼

f Porcellana platycheles: BROAD-
CLAWED PORCELAIN CRAB × 1

g Porcellana longicornis
LONG-CLAWED PORCELAIN CRAB ×

LOBSTERS, SQUAT LOBSTERS, CRABS : CRUSTACEA—DECAPODA

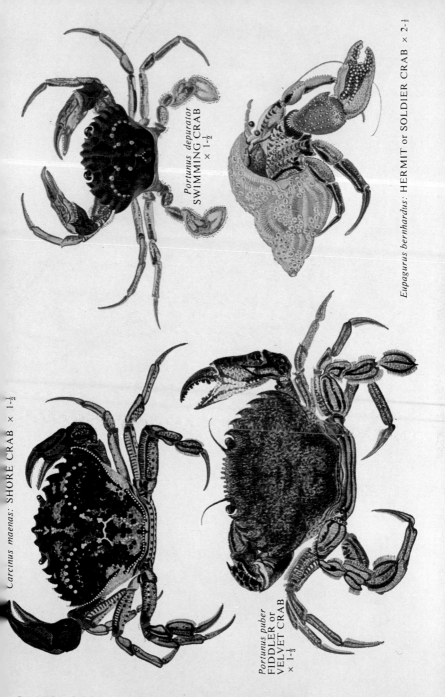

Carcinus maenas: SHORE CRAB × 1-½

Portunus depurator SWIMMING CRAB × 1-½

Eupagurus bernhardus: HERMIT or SOLDIER CRAB × 2-½

Portunus puber FIDDLER or VELVET CRAB × 1-⅓

CRABS : DECAPODA

15

Maia squinado
SPINY SPIDER CRAB × $\frac{1}{2}$-$\frac{1}{6}$

Macropodia rostrata
× 1

Inachus
dorsettensis × 1

Hyas araneus
× 1-$\frac{1}{2}$

Eurynome aspera
× 1

a

b

Pinnotheres pisu.
PEA CRAB
[a] female, [b] m
× 1

a-i ARCHAEOGASTROPOD LIMPETS: *j-n* MESOGASTROPOD LIMPETS

a, j, k, n head end facing bottom of plate; *b-i* facing top; *l, m* facing right

e Acmaea virginea
WHITE
TORTOISESHELL
LIMPET × 1

*c Emarginula
reticulata*
SLIT LIMPET
× 1

j

d Acmaea tessulata
TORTOISESHELL LIMPET
× 1

iodora apertura
WHOLE LIMPET × 1

k

f Patina pellucida
BLUE-RAYED
LIMPET × 1

j-k Calyptraea chinensis
CHINAMAN'S HAT × ½
j outside, *k* inside shell

n Capulus ungaricus
BONNET LIMPET × 1

g-i COMMON LIMPETS

h Patella intermedia
interior of shell
× ½

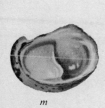

i Patella aspera
interior of shell
× ½

m

l

l-m Crepidula fornicata
SLIPPER LIMPET × ½
l outside, *m* inside shell

a Haliotis tuberculata
ORMER, interior of shell
× ½

g Patella vulgata
interior of shell
× ½

LIMPETS : MOLLUSCA—GASTROPODA

17

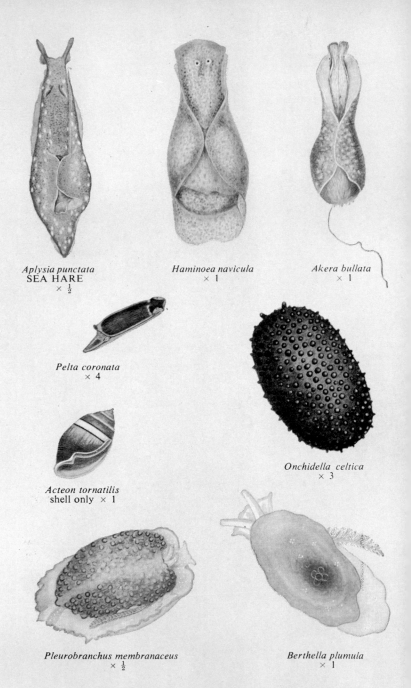

Aplysia punctata
SEA HARE
× $\frac{1}{2}$

Haminoea navicula
× 1

Akera bullata
× 1

Pelta coronata
× 4

Acteon tornatilis
shell only × 1

Onchidella celtica
× 3

Pleurobranchus membranaceus
× $\frac{1}{2}$

Berthella plumula
× 1

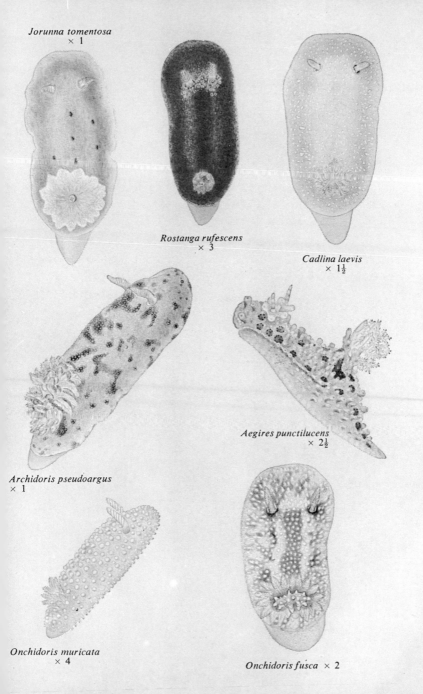

Jorunna tomentosa
× 1

Rostanga rufescens
× 3

Cadlina laevis
× 1½

Archidoris pseudoargus
× 1

Aegires punctilucens
× 2½

Onchidoris muricata
× 4

Onchidoris fusca × 2

NUDIBRANCH SEA SLUGS : MOLLUSCA—GASTROPODA   19

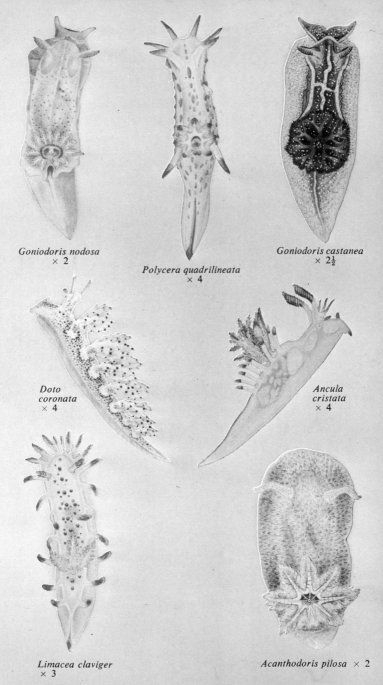

Goniodoris nodosa
× 2

Polycera quadrilineata
× 4

Goniodoris castanea
× 2½

Doto
coronata
× 4

Ancula
cristata
× 4

Limacea claviger
× 3

Acanthodoris pilosa × 2

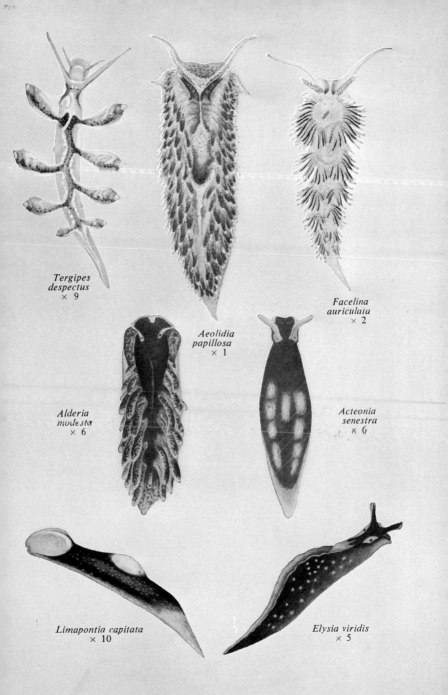

Tergipes
despectus
× 9

Aeolidia
papillosa
× 1

Facelina
auriculata
× 2

Alderia
modesta
× 6

Acteonia
senestra
× 6

Limapontia capitata
× 10

Elysia viridis
× 5

NUDIBRANCH SEA SLUGS : MOLLUSCA—GASTROPODA   21

Modiolus modiolus
HORSE MUSSEL × ½

Mytilus edulis
COMMON MUSSEL × ½

Musculus marmoratus
MARBLED CRENELLA
× ½

Modiolus barbatus
BEARDED
HORSE MUSSEL
× ½

Musculus discors
GREEN CRENELLA
× ½

Modiolus phaseolinus
BEAN HORSE MUSS
× ½

Chlamys tigerina
TIGER SCALLOP
× ½

Chlamys dis
HUNCHBACK SCALI

Pecten maximus
GREAT SCALLOP or CLAM
× ½

Chlamys opercularis
QUEEN
× ½

Chlamys varia
VARIEGATED SCALL
× ½

MUSSELS & SCALLOPS : MOLLUSCA—LAMELLIBRANCHIA

Donax vittatus
BANDED WEDGE SHELL
× ½

b Ensis ensis
× ½

d Phaxas pellucidus
× ½

a Ensis siliqua
× ½

c Ensis arcuata
× ⅔

Gari fervensis
FAROE SUNSET SHELL × ½

Gari depressa
LARGE SUNSET SHELL
× ½

Mya truncata
BLUNT GAPER × ½

Corbula gibba
BASKET SHELL
× ½

e Solen marginatus
× ½

Mya arenaria: SAND GAPER × ½

RAZOR & SUNSET SHELLS, & GAPERS : MOLLUSCA—LAMELLIBRANCHIA

Solaster papposus
COMMON SUNSTAR
× c. ½-¼

Henricia sanguinolenta × ½-⅙

Solaster endeca: PURPLE SUNSTAR ×

Asterias rubens
COMMON STARFISH
× 1-⅙

Marthasterias glacialis: SPINY STARFISH × c. ½-¼

24   STARFISH : ASTEROIDEA

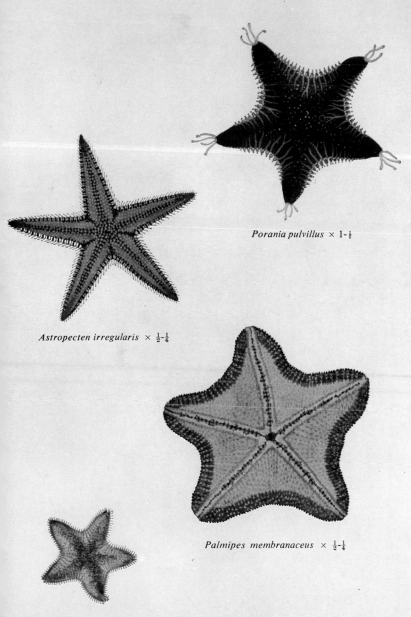

Porania pulvillus × 1-½

Astropecten irregularis × ½-¼

Palmipes membranaceus × ½-¼

ina gibbosa: CUSHION STAR × 1-½

STARFISH : ECHINODERMATA—ASTEROIDEA 25

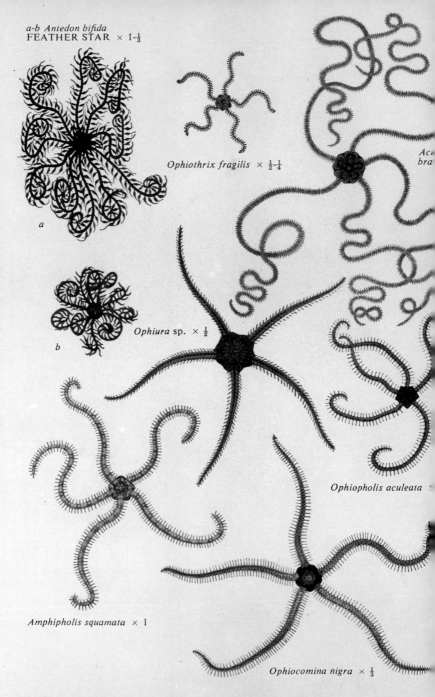

a-b Antedon bifida
FEATHER STAR × 1-⅓

a

b

Ophiothrix fragilis × ½-¼

Ac
bra

Ophiura sp. × ½

Ophiopholis aculeata

Amphipholis squamata × 1

Ophiocomina nigra × ⅓

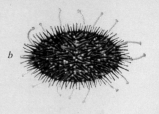

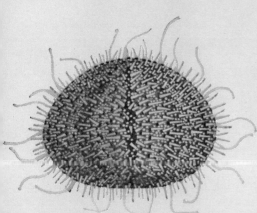

b-c Psammechinus miliaris
side view and under surface × 1-½

a Echinus esculentus
COMMON SEA URCHIN × ½

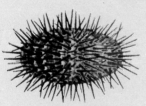

d Paracentrotus lividus × ½

g Spatangus purpureus: PURPLE
HEART URCHIN from above × ½-⅓

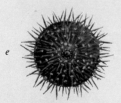

e-f Strongylocentrotus drobachiensis
under surface and side view
× ¼

h-i Echinocardium caudatum: SEA POTATO
from above in life and bare test after spines removed × ½

SEA URCHINS : ECHINODERMATA—ECHINOIDEA   27

e Saccoglossus cambrensis × 4

a-d SEA CUCUMBERS

a Cucumaria normani × ½

b Cucumaria lactea × 1

c Cucumaria saxicola × 1

d Holothuria forskali × 1

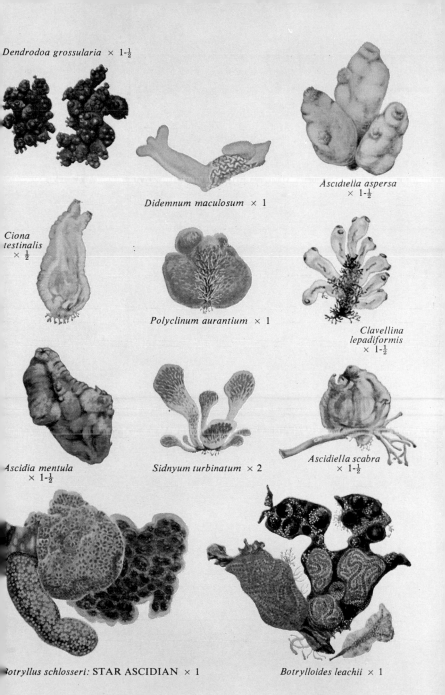

Dendrodoa grossularia × 1-½

Ascidiella aspersa × 1-½

Didemnum maculosum × 1

Ciona testinalis × ½

Polyclinum aurantium × 1

Clavellina lepadiformis × 1-½

Ascidia mentula × 1-½

Sidnyum turbinatum × 2

Ascidiella scabra × 1-½

Botryllus schlosseri: STAR ASCIDIAN × 1

Botrylloides leachii × 1

SEA SQUIRTS : TUNICATA   29

Liparis montagui
MONTAGU'S SEA-SNAIL × ½

Ctenolabrus rupestris
GOLDSINNY WRASSE
× ½

Centrolabrus exoletus
ROCK COOK
× 1-½

Labrus bergylta
BALLAN WRASSE
× ½-¼

Crenilabrus melops
CORKWING WRASSE × 1-

Cyclopterus lumpus:
LUMPSUCKER × ½-⅛

FISH : PISCES

Spinachia vulgaris
15-SPINED STICKLEBACK
× ½

Gasterosteus aculeatus
3-SPINED STICKLEBACK
× 1-½

Blennius montagui: MONTAGU'S BLENNY × 1

Blennius gattorugine
TOMPOT
GATTORUGINE
× ½-⅓

Blennius pholis: COMMON BLENNY, SHANNY × 2-½

Zoarces viviparus: VIVIPAROUS BLENNY, EEL-POUT × 1-⅓

Centronotus gunnellus: BUTTERFISH, GUNNELL × 1-½

FISH : PISCES

Gobius pictus
PAINTED GOBY × 1

Gobius ruthensparri
SPOTTED GOBY × 1-½

Gobius paganellus: ROCK GOBY × 1

Gobius niger: BLACK GOBY × 1

Cottus bubalis: LONG-SPINED SEA SCORPION × 1-⅓

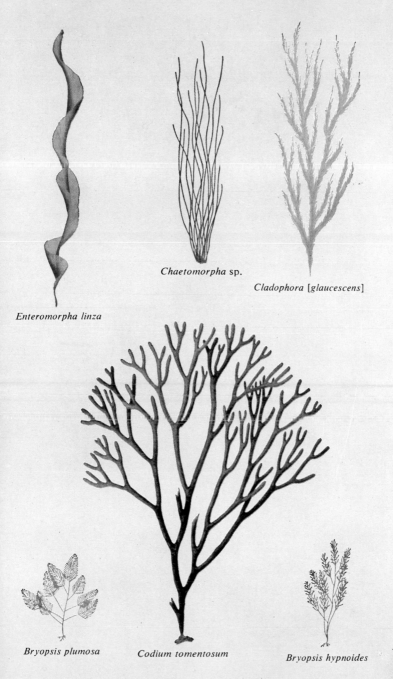

Enteromorpha linza

Chaetomorpha sp.

Cladophora [*glaucescens*]

Bryopsis plumosa

Codium tomentosum

Bryopsis hypnoides

GREEN SEAWEEDS : CHLOROPHYCEAE

33

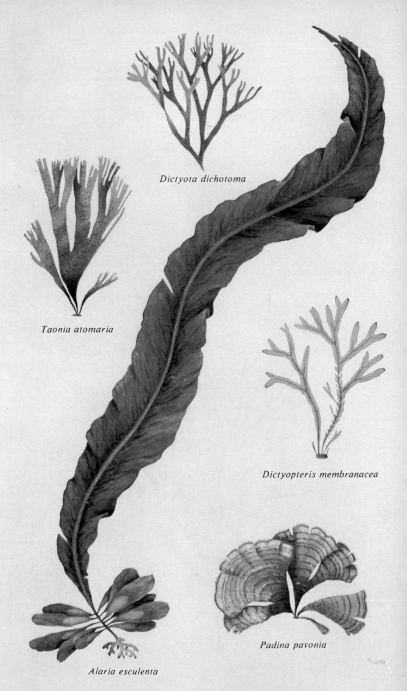

Dictyota dichotoma

Taonia atomaria

Dictyopteris membranacea

Alaria esculenta

Padina pavonia

BROWN SEAWEEDS : PHAEOPHYCEAE

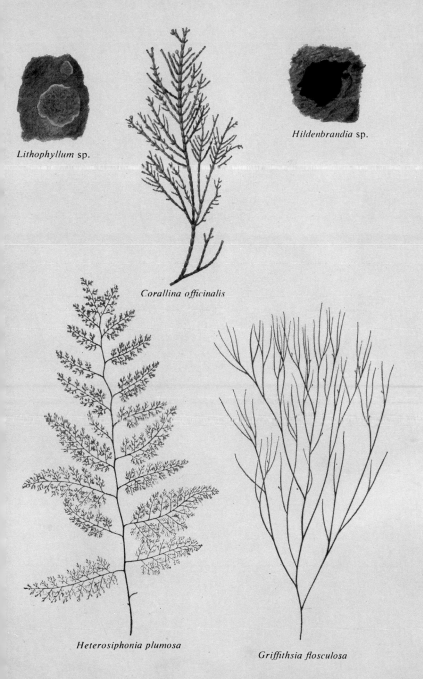

Lithophyllum sp.

Hildenbrandia sp.

Corallina officinalis

Heterosiphonia plumosa

Griffithsia flosculosa

RED SEAWEEDS : RHODOPHYCEAE

35

Delesseria sanguinea

Membranoptera alata

Apoglossum ruscifolium

Hypoglossum woodwardii

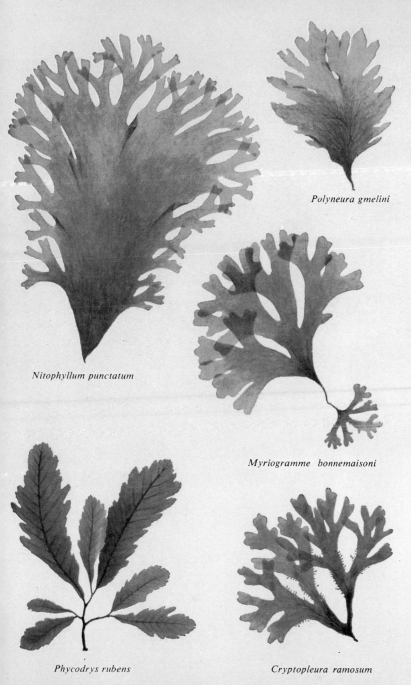

Polyneura gmelini

Nitophyllum punctatum

Myriogramme bonnemaisoni

Phycodrys rubens

Cryptopleura ramosum

RED SEAWEEDS : RHODOPHYCEAE

37

Halurus equisetifolius

Ptilota plumosa

Rhodochorton sp.

Plumaria elegans

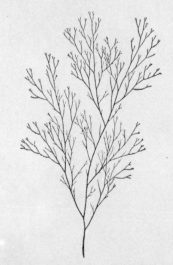

Ceramium rubrum

Chondrus crispus

RED SEAWEEDS : RHODOPHYCEAE

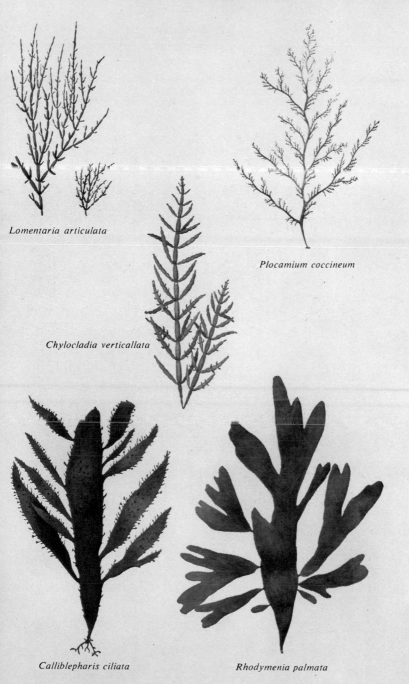

Lomentaria articulata

Plocamium coccineum

Chylocladia verticallata

Calliblepharis ciliata

Rhodymenia palmata

RED SEAWEEDS : RHODOPHYCEAE

39

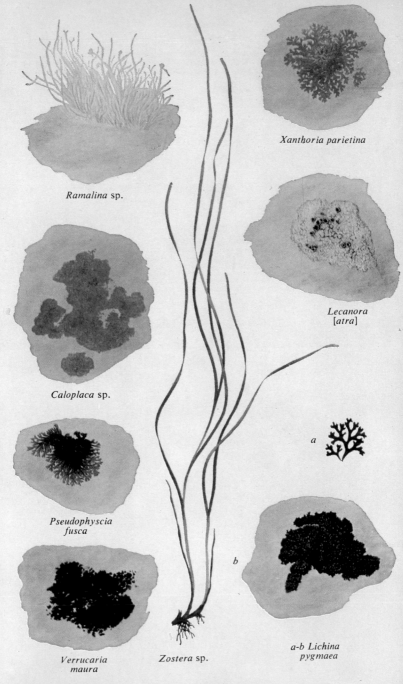

Ramalina sp.

Xanthoria parietina

Lecanora [atra]

Caloplaca sp.

Pseudophyscia fusca

a

b

Verrucaria maura

Zostera sp.

a-b Lichina pygmaea

enormously long; 15 ft. is commonplace and " once 30 yards were measured without rupture, and yet the mass was not half uncoiled." Blackish-brown, except for pale end of head, with purple reflections; slimy. In coiled lumps under stones that rest on muddy shingle. Lower shore. Widespread. Common in N.; uncommon in S.

Lineus longissimus BOOTLACE WORM pl. 8.

B. NO EYES

Beware *E. neesii* and *Lineus* spp. above.

Body about 3-6 in., up to 18 in., pinkish-brown, paling towards tail. *Two pale cream stripes right down middle of back, divided only by hair's breadth of main colour.* Blunt end of head divided into two shallow lobes. Lower shore. Under stones; in sand and fine mud. Probably widespread. May be locally common. *Lineus bilineatus*

Body rounded, 6-20 in. long. Brick-red or brownish-red, paler below, overlaid with square network of white stripes. Lower shore. Under stones; on sandy flats. Widespread. Not uncommon.

Tubulanus annulatus (= *Carinella annulata*) pl. 8.

Body about 4 in. long. Can stretch to thread or contract to thick worm. Pointed head and tail. Pale cream, with darker, perhaps reddish, patch at end of head. Pale line may run down middle of body. Lower shore. In clean sand; among *Corallina* (p. 250 and pl. 35); among shells. May be many together. Widely distributed. Probably locally common. *Cephalothrix rufifrons* pl. 8.

ANNELIDA
Segmented or Bristle Worms

POLYCHAETA
Marine Bristle Worms

THE POLYCHAETES are the most numerous and the most diversely specialised in form and habit of the various groups of marine worms. Like the common earthworms (also Annelids), the body is segmented, i.e. divided transversely into many small compartments. On each side of these segments paddles or " parapodia " with projecting bristles occur in the more active species, but bristles are always present.

Polychaetes may be divided, conveniently rather than scientifically, into two groups: (1) those that move about freely either swimming or crawling—the *Errantia*; and (2) those that live within a tube of their own construction, the majority never voluntarily moving out of this—the *Sedentaria*. The tube may be limy or of parchment-like consistency or made of mucus or consolidated grains of sand or particles of mud. In some cases it is so delicate that it is destroyed in collecting the worm which occupies it.

Each group is divided into families, whose characters are usually well defined, but the distinction between genera and species often depends on very small differences which cannot be described here and which would, in any case, need careful examination under the microscope. Many worms are to be found on the shore, of which, without a microscope, one can say only that they are Errant or else Sedentary; indeed for some of the very small thread-thin worms it may be difficult to go even as far as that.

ERRANT POLYCHAETES
Segmented worms that move about more or less freely

A
Having interlocking pairs of hard scales covering at least part of back. Generally flattened. Family *Aphroditidae* Scale Worms

i. 12 pairs of scales.
ii. 15 pairs of scales covering whole length of body.
iii. 15 pairs of scales covering only front part of body.

iv. 18 pairs of scales.
v. 156 pairs of scales.
vi. Scales hidden by mat of fine hair.

B

Worm eventually rolls out proboscis on which are black hooked jaws, when held in hand; either two large jaws reminiscent of jaws of a stag-beetle, or four smaller jaws, or a single large jaw. This unrolling may occur several times in quick succession. It may be encouraged by light pressure by finger and thumb behind head.

i. Large, active worms, brightly coloured, having four eyes, two antennae, several pairs of feelers and two large, black jaws. Fig. 17.
Family *Nereidae* Ragworms

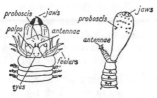

Fig. 17   Fig. 18

ii. Small, thin worms, tapering both ends, much ringed, with four minute antennae and four jaws. Fig. 18.
Family *Glyceridae*

iii. Small delicate worms, those over ¼ in. long with four eyes, three antennae, two pairs of feelers and one large black jaw. Fig. 19. Family *Syllidae*

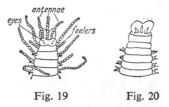

Fig. 19   Fig. 20

iv. Large worms with first two segments without bristles. One black jaw below and series of paired pieces above. Fig. 20. Family *Eunicidae*

C

Proboscis not armed with jaws. Body not covered by scales.

i. Green or blue worms with paddle-shaped lobes folded from sides on to back. Family *Phyllodocidae* Paddle Worms

ii. Large flattened worms, living in sand, whose body shines with pearly radiance; single long tail thread. Small head with four antennae so short as to appear as sharp points; without visible eyes. Very active and moving with characteristic lateral waves passing quickly down body.
Family *Nephthydidae*

A. HAVING INTERLOCKING PAIRS OF HARD SCALES
covering at least part of back. Generally flattened. Pl. 11.
Family *Aphroditidae* SCALE WORMS

N.B.—These scales are readily thrown off when the worm is handled. It is necessary to count the number of pairs at once and to notice whether or not the tail was covered by them.

i. 12 pairs of scales

Worm about 1 in. long. Whole body covered by scales which are clearly *not round*, and *overlap each other* and are roughly spotted. Usually brownish; may be yellow. Middle and lower shore. Under stones; among seaweeds. Probably widely distributed. Certainly common in S.W. *Lepidonotus squamatus* pl. 11.

As *L. squamatus* but *scales round, smooth*, colour-patterned, not meeting each other across back and not covering tail. Abundant in S.W. Not on E. coasts. *Lepidonotus clava*

ii. 15 pairs of scales covering whole length of body

Worm less than 1 in. long, *almost colourless*, with dark band running down back. Scales delicate, *transparent*, rounded, not meeting across back. Lower shore. *Only on sea-urchin Echinus esculentus* (p. 181 and pl. 27). Widely distributed. Not uncommon. *Scalisetosus assimilis*

Worm about 1 in. long, rather more pointed at tail than at head. First pair of scales round, rest rather kidney-shaped and overlapping; brown, grey or may be variegated with yellowish fleck near centre, *clearly fringed with hairs* and scattered sparsely with *dotted granular knobs*. Active creature that breaks up when molested. Middle and lower shore. Under stones; among seaweeds. Widely distributed. Common. *Harmothoë impar* pl. 11.

As *H. impar*, but about ½ in. long. Scales with pale patch in middle, *fringed with fine hairs, and along back edge row of tiny dark spots*. *Harmothoë imbricata*

As *H. imbricata* but scales patterned dark, sometimes with circles, on less dark background; often brown or red; *not fringed with hairs*. *Harmothoë lunulata*

iii. 15 pairs of scales covering only front part of body

Thin worm, 2-5 in. long, usually glistening and iridescent. Back reddish and may shine through scales, which may have grey metallic texture and pale centres with dark outer edge. Variable! On each of the *about* 50 *uncovered segments* three spots, usually brown. Lower shore. In worm tubes, especially *Polymnia* (p. 80 and pl. 12), cracks in rocks and muddy sand. Probably widely distributed but nowhere very common. *Polynoë scolopendrina*

Worm about 1½ in. long, tapering gradually from middle to tail. Scales variable in colour, often grey-brown, usually with pale patch. *About* 10 *uncovered segments*, each of which may be marked with spots. Lower shore. Under stones; in cracks in rocks. Widely distributed. Common. *Lagisca extenuata* pl. 11.

iv. 18 pairs of scales

Semi-transparent worm, 2-4 in. long. Scales over whole body are irregularly shaped, grey or translucent purple or brown; yellowish body may show through. Lower shore. Under stones; among *Laminaria* (p. 225 and pl. xxxi). Widely distributed. Not uncommon. *Halosydna gelatinosa*

v. 156 pairs of scales

Worm 4-8 in. long, thin. Scales usually greyish but variable, tough; are not thrown off; overlap quite widely. Lower shore. In sand; under stones. Widely distributed. Not uncommon. *Sthenelais boa*

vi. Scales hidden by mat of fine hair

Body 3-4 in. long, elongated oval, back covered by felt of fine grey hairs. On flanks " gorgeously iridescent green and golden hairs and lustrous brown spines." Lives normally offshore but after storms or even normally at extreme low water of springs on sand. Widely distributed. Not uncommon on shore.

Aphrodite aculeata SEA-MOUSE pl. 9.

B. Worm eventually rolls out proboscis on which are black hooked jaws when held in hand ; either two large jaws reminiscent of jaws of stag-beetle, or four smaller jaws, or a single large jaw. This unrolling may occur several times in quick succession. It may be encouraged by slight pressure by finger and thumb behind head.

i. **Large active worms, brightly coloured, with large head,** having four eyes, two antennae, several pairs of feelers and two large black jaws. Fig. 21. Family *Nereidae* RAGWORMS

Fig. 21

The sub-division of the family used to be based on relative lengths of parts of the head and some other parts, but the French zoologist Fauvel has shown that these parts themselves vary. They may be contractile and some may even be sloughed and regrown. An important character is the arrangement of the teeth on the proboscis

—the little black dots between the head and the jaws (Fig. 22). This character is rather fine for a lens.

So we are reduced to describing one or two common animals with the old warning added that identification from the characters which we list cannot be certain.

This superb worm, small at 8 in. long, is commonly more than 1 ft. and may be 3 ft. and as thick as a finger. At first sight mistaken for a Phyllodocid (Paddle-Worm) (see p. 73) because of the lines of flattened lobes that fold on to back from each side. But it has jaws. Overall colour is green, but back has iridescent glints of purple, while lobes may also glint except from fawn border. Underside is pale iridescent pinkish. Colours darken as animal contracts. Mostly on N. and W. coasts. May be locally common.

Nereis virens (Sars) pl. 9 and fig. 22*a*.

Body 3-4 in. long, 90-120 segments with bristles. *Very small antennae*, mere stubby processes between palps. Colour varies, but often yellowish-brown shading to green along sides. Blood-vessel makes *red line all down back*. Middle and lower shore. In sand and mud where salinity low; associated with brackish water, i.e. estuarine. Widely distributed. Common. *Nereis diversicolor* pl. 9 and fig. 22*b*.

As *N. diversicolor* except that it is typically bronze-brown, and nearly always brown tinged, with tendency to green flanks. Lower shore. On rocky shore, among seaweeds and shells. Widely distributed. Perhaps commoner in N. than in S. *Nereis pelagica* fig. 22*c*.

As *N. diversicolor*, 4-10 in. long. When proboscis out, *two dark rows of teeth shaped like a pair of eyebrows* may be seen behind jaws. Green glinting bronze particularly in middle. Lower shore. In

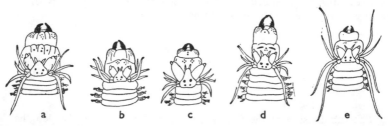

Fig. 22. Heads and " teeth " in the Nereidae; a. *Nereis virens;* b. *Nereis diversicolor;* c. *Nereis pelagica;* d. *Perinereis cultrifera;* e. *Platynereis dumerilii.* All x *c* 5-8

gravelly mud or sand; under stones; in pools. Widely distributed. Common. *Perinereis cultrifera* fig. 22*d*.

Worm 1-2½ in. long, excluding feelers which reach back at least quarter length of worm. When proboscis out usually impossible to see teeth. Variable colour, usually yellowish-brown, but it may be green or shades of red. Lower shore. Among *Laminaria* holdfasts (p. 225 and pl. xxxi), where it may make tough tubes. Widely distributed. Probably common. *Platynereis dumerilii* pl. 9 and fig. 22

ii. **Small thin worms, tapering both ends, much ringed,** with four minute antennae and four jaws. Fig. 23.

Worms 1-4 in. long, thin and tapering to both ends, looking extremely ringed, each of about 150 segments having two or three lines round it. At head end is a much ringed pointed prolonged conical prolongation that bears four tiny antennae arranged crosswise on tip. From base of this cone a pear-shaped proboscis is rolled out; on flat end are four small black teeth arranged crosswise. On each side of two segments nearest head is a tiny single tuft of bristles; all segments lower down bear two tufts on either side. These worms may be pale yellow or grey, nearly transparent or pink. Often rolling up into coils when touched. Lower shore. In sand, gravel or mud. Widely distributed. Common.

Family *Glyceridae* figs. 23 and 24.

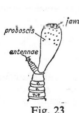

Fig. 23   Fig. 24

In *Glycera convoluta* the pointed conical prolongation carrying the antennae, see fig. 23, has 14—16 rings; in *G. capitata* 8; in *G. lapidum* 11.

Fig. 25

iii. **Small delicate worms;** those over ¼ in. long with four eyes, three antennae, two pairs of feelers and one large black jaw. Fig. 25.

Large family of small delicate worms up to 2 in. long. Those above ¼ in. have four eyes, *three antennae,* two pairs of feelers that both

71

come from the segment next behind the one that bears eyes. Body segments have long bristles which, with antennae and feelers, are for most species repeatedly ringed. Most have *one large black jaw* on proboscis but one genus has semi-circle of teeth. Middle and lower shore. Among seaweeds; under stones; in sand. Widely distributed. Common.   Family *Syllidae* pl. 10 and fig. 25.

iv. Large worms with first two segments without bristles. One black jaw below and series of black pieces above. Happily several species can be identified without seeing jaws.   Family *Eunicidae* fig. 27, p. 73.

Worm 6-8 in. long, *five pale yellow barred antennae, middle one the longest* and ringed. *One pair of inconspicuous feelers* that are well back from antennae (fig. 27a). Red gills developing from vestiges on about fourth segment to feathery combs further back. Two long threads from point of tail and one tiny one from each side. Body brownish-red. Lower shore. Under stones; in cracks in rocks. Widely distributed. Rare.   *Eunice harassii* pl. 10.

Worm 1 ft. or more long, fat; rather as *E. harassii*, but has *no feelers* (fig. 27b) and red *gill filaments arise as bunch*, see fig. 26a. Greenish-brown, shot with reddish tints, iridescent, with green line down back. Lower shore. In rock crevices. S. coasts, particularly Channel Islands. Very rare on W. coasts. Locally common.
                                    Marphysa sanguinea pl. 10.

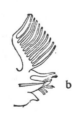

Fig. 26. Gill filaments of a. *Marphysa sanguinea*, x 6; b. *Marphysa bellii*, x 12

Much as *M. sanguinea*, 6-7 in. long, thin. *Gill filaments in combs*, see fig. 26b, *only from about 12th to 35th segments*, without even vestiges towards head or tail. Reddish at head end, iridescent fawn at tail end, with broad purplish line down length of back. Lower shore. In sand among *Zostera* (p. 254 and pl. 40); under stones. S. and possibly W. coasts. Local and probably rare.
                                    Marphysa bellii fig. 27c.

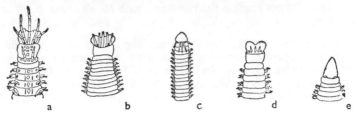

Fig. 27. Heads and anterior segments of a. *Eunice harassii*, x c 3; b. *Marphysa sanguinea*, x 1; c. *Marphysa bellii*, x c 5; d. *Lysidice ninetta*, x 4; e. *Lumbriconereis latreilli*, x 12

Worm 2-6 in. long, round. *Three inconspicuous antennae* between one pair of eyes. *No feelers* (fig. 27*d*). Four pointed processes on tail, inner pair even shorter than outer. First three segments deep brown with pale spots; fourth is pale grey-brown; rest of body brown tinged purple and iridescent. Lower shore. In rock fissures; in muddy sand. S. coasts, locally not uncommon. Very rare elsewhere. *Lysidice ninetta* pl. 10.

Worm 2-6 in. long. *No eyes, antennae or feelers.* Head simple, short, blunt cone (fig. 27*e*). Rather slender tail ending in a fork on either side of which are two bristles. Reddish-brown with some iridescence, with redder line down back. Lower shore. Under stones. Most likely to be found on S. coasts.

Lumbriconereis latreilli pl. 10.

N.B.—Other species of this genus which might be found are very like *L. latreilli*.

C. PROBOSCIS NOT ARMED WITH JAWS. Body not covered with scales.

i. **Green or blue worms with paddle-shaped lobes folded from sides on to back.** Can swim as well as crawl.

Family *Phyllodocidae* PADDLE-WORMS

Head longer than broad (fig. 28*a*). 6-18 in. or more long, more than 400 segments. *Four antennae.* Back iridescent bluish, with shining green paddles, paler at edges. Smaller ones less brightly coloured and blue may have brown tints and paddles yellowish. Lower shore. Under stones; among *Laminaria* (p. 225 and pl. xxxi). Widely distributed. Not common. *Phyllodoce lamelligera*

Head broader than long (fig. 28*b*). Very like *P. lamelligera*. 6-24 in. long. Iridescent blue back banded with green and brown. Rather pink below. Paddles olive-green. *Phyllodoce laminosa* Sav.

73

N.B.—Do not confuse the two above with *Nereis virens*, p. 70 and pl. ix.

Head heart-shaped (fig. 28c). 2-4 in. long. Four antennae. Body yellow or greenish, sometimes deep, with line of three brown spots or bars on each segment. Paddles brown. Lower shore. On cleanish sand; under stones. Widely distributed. Not common, but less uncommon in summer.   *Phyllodoce maculata* pl. 9.

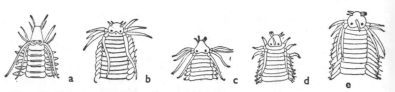

Fig. 28. Heads and anterior segments of a. *Phyllodoce lamelligera*, x 5-10; b. *Phyllodoce laminosa*, x 5-10; c. *Phyllodoce maculata*, x c 15; d. *Eulalia viridis*, x c 15; e. *Eulalia sanguinea*, x c 15

Head bluntly rounded in front (fig. 28d). *Five antennae.* 1½-4 in. long. Beautiful shining deep green, paler towards head and on pointed paddles. Middle and lower shore. On rocks, particularly in spring and summer. Widely distributed.   Abundant. *Eulalia viridis* pl. 9.

Head wider than long and heart-shaped (fig. 28e). 1-2½ in. long. Variable colours. Light greenish-brown or sandy, becoming light brown towards tail. Faint yellow line down back. Underneath may show pink tinges. Paddles may be pale green, grey or sandy. Very active creatures, with constrictions appearing and disappearing at various points in body as it moves. Lower shore. In *Laminaria* holdfasts (p. 225 and pl. xxxi); under stones. Widely distributed. Locally common.   *Eulalia sanguinea*

ii. **Large flattened worms living in sand or mud whose bodies shine with pearly radiance;** single long tail thread. Small head with four antennae so short as to appear as sharp points; without visible eyes. Very active and moving with characteristic lateral waves passing down body.   Family *Nephthydidae* pl. 10.

Three species are common and superficially very alike, being divided largely by structural details of the bristles and proboscis.

Body 3-10 in. long, typically 5-6 in. 90-150 segments. Pearl-grey, with pink or brick-red tints; smooth surface all down back and front. Bristles soft, tend to be yellowish. A really meaty large *Nephthys* is most likely to be this species. Middle and lower shore.

In sand, often with *Arenicola* (lugworms) (p. 256 and pl. 12). Widely distributed. Common. *Nephthys caeca*

Body 3-4 in. long, up to 8 in. 90-200 segments. Iridescent pinkish, shading to bluish-white. Wide line down back. Bristles rather dense and short. Middle and lower shore. In sand and muddy gravel. Widely distributed. Very common. Locally abundant.

Nephthys hombergi CATWORM pl. 10.

Body 2-4 in. long. 90-95 segments. Bristles yellow; some are bent. Body shining pale sandy. Lower shore. In sand. Widely distributed. Not common. *Nephthys cirrosa*

SEDENTARY POLYCHAETES
Segmented tube-dwelling worms

A

Hard, pale coloured, calcareous tube.
   i. Very small tubes spirally twisted.
   ii. Large elongated tubes.
   iii. Thread-fine tubes aggregating into twisting lumps.

B

Tube of mud sticking out of ground, or at least level with surface. *Crown of feathery tentacles* protruded only when animal is under water. At low tide worm is withdrawn deep into tube and seldom seen. Family *Sabellidae*

   Fan or Peacock Worms, pl.13.
   i. Tube upright in mud, sand or gravel.
   ii. More or less horizontal tube under stones or in *Laminaria* holdfast.
   iii. Tubes in or on rocks.

C

Tube of mucus and material so fine that it is destroyed by collecting worm; or may be of fine mud to which so many small stones adhere as almost to cover it; may be mere tunnel in mud which if carefully excavated is slimy and encrusted with sand. Worms with *crown of orange thread tentacles*, from head only, which writhe sinuously and extend surprisingly far in a jar. Obvious *red gills, usually branched, just behind head.*
Family *Terebellidae*.

   i. Three pairs of gills, fig. 29.
   ii. Two pairs of gills, fig. 30.

Fig. 29   Fig. 30

D

Tube firm, of sand only.

i. Single, narrowly conical tube, open at both ends.

ii. Many tubes, 1/5 in. diameter, fused together into honeycomb lump.

iii. Minute tubes, 1/10 to 1/20 in. diameter, appearing out of rocks.

E

Tube a U-shaped gallery in sand, ½ in. diameter, lined with near-white leathery membrane. *Large worm in three distinct parts.*

F

Tube a slimy channel in muddy gravel under stones. Worm without crown of tentacles. Red gill-threads on at least some parts, see figs. 34, 35, p. 83. Family *Cirratulidae*

G

Worm in translucent mucus case, showing green crown of tentacles and red line of stomach.

H

Mucus tube a mere burrow in mud or muddy sand.

i. Red, round worms without any large appendages, looking like earthworms, with the first 9 to 14 segments swollen and in contrast to longer, thin remainder. Family *Capitellidae*.

ii. Burrow in area of little mounds topped with worm casts. Worms fat; greenish- or yellowish-black. Family *Arenicolidae* Lugworms.

I

Thin, pink worms, 2-6 in. long. Burrow in sand. Body in two distinct parts. Two rough tentacles more than half length of body.

J

Small, almost thread-thin worms, living in sand or mud.

i. With coiled "horns" on their head, see fig. 38, p. 86.

ii. Sharply pointed head, without antennae or feelers.

A. HARD PALE COLOURED, CALCAREOUS TUBE

i. Very small tubes spirally twisted

Very small, off-white tubes, *without longitudinal ridges*, rolled in *clockwise coil* as seen from above as it grows, usually less than two complete rounds, together about ⅕ in. across. Worm inside rarely seen unless placed in water; *green* tentacles. Middle and lower shore. Fronds of *Fucus* (p. 226 and pl. xxxii) may be covered with them; on *Laminaria* (p. 225 and pl. xxxi) and other seaweeds; on stones and rocks. Sometimes in immense numbers. Widely distributed. Abundant. *Spirorbis borealis* pl. iv.

As *S. borealis* but *rolled anti-clockwise* when looked at from above as it grows. Tube shining white, no longitudinal ridges, generally rather translucent. Widely distributed. Abundant in deep water.

Lower shore on stones; on *Laminaria saccharina* (p. 225 and pl. xxxi); on shells lived in by hermit crabs. Not common.
Spirorbis spirillum pl. iv.

As *S. borealis* but tube has *three longitudinal ridges.* Tentacles translucent white or cream. Lower shore. Widely distributed. Abundant. *Spirorbis tridentatus*

As *S. spirillum* but tube dull white, with one to three longitudinal ridges. Middle shore. In damp, dark places; under *Ascophyllum* (p. 227 and pl. xxxii); in cracks in rocks; on shells and stones. Widely distributed. Common. *Spirorbis pagenstecheri*

ii. Large, elongated tubes

Triangular, off-white, irregularly bending tube, usually 2-6 in. long, thickening out from small, thin beginning, with keel along top, ending, if worm alive inside, in fine point at mouth of tube. Under water, crown of tentacles, barred red and white, may emerge. Body purplish-brown, red below in female, white in male. Lower shore. On stones, often small flat stones; on shells. Widely distributed. Common. *Pomatoceros triqueter* pl. iv.

Round tube, 3-4 in. long; pale green and pink; becoming larger towards rather uplifted trumpet mouth, showing ringed ridges of growth. Several tubes may be twined together. Crown of bright red tentacles; body reddish or orange. Lives almost entirely below tide marks but tubes commonly cast ashore on shells, particularly *Pecten maximus* (p. 153 and pl. 22) and on stones. Widely distributed. Common. *Serpula vermicularis* pl. iv.

Smooth, white, thin, delicate tubes, to 1½ in. long, gently bent, lightly ringed with growth marks, and entwined in masses together. On shells and stones cast ashore. Animal lives below tide marks. Widely distributed. Common. *Hydroides norvegica* pl. iv.

Smooth, round, white tubes 3-5 in. long, *attached only by narrow end* to shells and stones, tapering gently to maximum diameter, which may be ¼ in. and that maximum maintained to mouth. Gently bending. Thrown ashore. Widely distributed. Common.
Protula tubularia pl. iv.

iii. Thread-fine tubes aggregating into twisting lumps

White, cylindrical tubes, in irregular twisting lumps, often 3 in. sq. and up to 7 in. sq. Lower shore. Among *Laminaria* holdfasts (p. 225 and pl. xxxi); on piers, breakwaters, and shells. Lumps often thrown ashore. Locally common. *Filograna implexa* pl. iv.

B. TUBE OF MUD STICKING OUT OF GROUND, or at least level with surface. *Crown of feathery tentacles* protruded only when animal is under water. At low tide worm is withdrawn deep into tube and seldom seen. Family *Sabellidae* FAN- OR PEACOCK-WORMS. pl. 13

i. Tubes upright in mud, sand or gravel

Smooth, round tube of fine mud (pl. v), may be 18 in. long and ¼ in. diameter, *sticking 3-4 in. out of ground* at low tide; bending, with open end partly closed by elasticity of structure. Sunken end attached to stones. Worm 4-10 in. long, with 100-600 rather small segments. Body pale grey-green with orange and violet tints towards tail. Crown of *tentacles arises from two semi-circular lobes*, 8-45 on either side, various colours, browns, reds, or violets, banded darker. Lower shore. Muddy gravelly sandy flats. Widely distributed. Common. *Sabella pavonina* PEACOCK WORM pl. 13.

Tube rather leathery in texture, fully 1 ft. long, to which are attached, except for top 4-5 in., pebbles, bits of shell—quite large pieces so that tube is heavy (see pl. v). *Sticks out of mud only about 1 in.*, and, when tide is out, is more or less closed. Worm 4-6 in. long, with 100-200 segments, orange or salmon, dotted all over with white grains. Crown of *tentacles not from lobes*, 18-24, closely feathered, brown, yellow, with violet tints, darker at base. On tip of each, dark eye-spot, *spot on central two being bigger than rest*. Lower shore. In gravelly sand. S. and S.W. coasts. Common.

Branchiomma vesiculosum pl. 13.

Tube 6-9 in. long, thick, composed of many translucent layers of mucus, with hole half as wide again as worm, sunk completely in substrate, slightly coloured grey and fawn, darker towards outside. Worm 5-7 in. long, 100-150 segments, each with two rings, yellow or dull orange, some segments paler, some darker. Crown of tentacles from two fans, 20-40 from each, form kind of chestnut-coloured cup that is shiny outside and velvety inside, rimmed with long purple points. Tentacles forming one-half of cup may move independently of others. Lower shore. Muddy gravelly flats. Locally common. *Myxicola infundibulum* pl. 13.

Tube with coarse *fringed rim* (pl. v) sticking up about 2 in., see
Lanice conchilega p. 80 and pl. 12.

ii. More or less horizontal tube under stones or in *Laminaria* (p. 225 and pl. xxxi) holdfasts

Tube 2-3 in. long, lying more or less horizontally under stones or among *Laminaria* holdfasts, tough, leathery, coated with mud and small stones and bits of shell; perhaps small seaweeds growing on it. Worm 1-2 in. long, about $\frac{1}{8}$ in. across, 50-70 segments. Body yellowish brown or greenish, Crown with 12-18 tentacles *fused in lower half* into fan which is strongly marked with semi-circular patterns. Main *stalk of tentacle projects above fan*. On each stalk are about nine pairs of pale steps with two dark spots immediately above. Tentacles various colours, pale green, orange, purplish-red. Lower shore. Under stones; among *Laminaria* (p. 225 and pl. xxxi). Widely distributed. Probably not very common.

Dasychone bombyx pl. 13

iii. Tubes in or on rocks

Tube, most of which is sunk in crack in rock, is not likely to be seen, 7-9 in. long, almost $\frac{1}{2}$ in. wide at mouth. Flexible, of mucus and fine mud at lower end and becoming tough and semi-transparent at top, which may project about 1 in. out of rock. Several tubes, forming groups, may be contiguous. Worm 2-6 in. long, fat, with about 100 segments; shades of brown, with violet tints going to green. Crown of tentacles arise from two spiral lobes, 45-80 on each side, their *arrangement characteristically spiral, white or very pale.* Lower shore. In cracks; in pools; steep shaded overhangs. Even when tide is out worm may not be withdrawn into tube. Not common, W. and S. coasts. Perhaps absent in N.

Bispira volutacornis pl. 13.

Tube 4-5 in., olive-brown, horny, particularly on exposed parts to which sand adheres. When worm goes in, end of *tube doubles over or even rolls up.* Worm 3-4 in. long, 60-100 segments; 1/3 nearest head green-brown, tail 2/3 orange. About 20 rather short, translucent tentacles, in two groups of 10, with long pale near-white branches. When contracted colour dulls. Towards *base of each tentacle two dark eye-spots.* Lower shore. Fissures and holes in rocks; in caves and shells. Widely distributed. Locally probably common.

Potamilla reniformis pl. 13.

Much as *P. reniformis*, only half the size. Tube does not roll up at tip. Tentacles *brownish or grey. No eye-spots.* Between successive layers of rock, particularly limestone. Lower shore. Widely distributed. Common. *Potamilla torelli*

Tubes membranous and transparent, to 1 in. long and occurring in great colonies attached to rocks or holdfasts of seaweeds. Body about $\frac{1}{4}$-$\frac{3}{4}$ in. long, 29-33 segments. Very pale, perhaps yellow; sides darker than middle; fine dark line down middle of back. 10 tentacles in two bunches of five each, almost colourless but with a faintest green tinge. Worm sometimes leaves its tube and many may be found wandering over tube area. Lower shore. Overhanging rocks; holdfasts of seaweeds; in pools. Widespread. Locally abundant.

Amphiglena mediterranea pl. 13.

C. TUBE OF MUCUS and material so fine that it is destroyed by collecting worm; or may be of fine mud to which so many small stones adhere as almost to cover it; may be mere tunnel in mud which if carefully excavated is slimy and encrusted with sand. *Worms with crown of orange thread tentacles, from head only, which writhe sinuously* and extend surprisingly far in a jar. Obvious *red gills, usually branched, just behind head.* Family *Terebellidae*

i. Three pairs of gills, fig. 31.

Tube almost 12 in. long and $\frac{1}{3}$ in. diameter, encrusted with sand and pieces of shell which vary with size of sand particles and kinds of

Fig. 31. *Polymnia nebulosa*, x 1-2

shell available locally. *Stick stiffly above ground 1-2 in., with prominent fringe round rather knobby open end (pl. v).* Worm 8-10 in. long, 150-300 segments, of which 17 have bristles. Body pink, red, or brown. Tentacles palest pink. Gills dull red. Lower shore. In sand. Widely distributed. Common. Locally abundant.

Lanice conchilega pl. 12.

Tube of sticky slime, under stones, particularly those resting on muddy gravel. When stone is raised, sections of tube are on it, with bits of shell and pebbles adhering. May be 8-12 in. long. Body 3-8 in. long, with about 100 segments, soft, fat at head end, tapering backwards, little-finger thick in middle; *bright orange, dotted all over with white marks. Seventeen segments with bristles* which arise from small warts. Crown of pale orange to white tentacles, which are fragile and go on writhing after they have broken off. Three pairs of red gills, of fine divided threads, marked with white; rather strongly stalked clump, *stalk being different colour* (yellowish) from threads, fig. 31. Lower shore. Under stones and large shells resting on muddy gravel. Widely distributed. Common. *Polymnia nebulosa* pl. 12.

Tube merely hole in sand lined with mucus and is usually quite destroyed in digging up worm. Body 6-9 in., may be 12 in.; 100-150 segments, fat, soft, tapering, usually buff, but may be salmon-coloured or brown, on back perhaps becoming greyish towards head. *No pale dottings. Seventeen segments with bristles which arise from pinheads and not from small warts* (cf. *Polymnia*), and start on segment that carries last gill. Crown of tentacles pale shining yellow-orange. Three pairs of gills, much divided, well stalked; all parts of them deep red. Lower shore. In sand and sandy gravel. S. and S.W. coasts. Locally common. *Amphitrite edwardsi*

Tube as *A. edwardsi*. Body 6-8 in. long, 90-100 segments of which those nearest head appear double-ringed. Fat, soft, tapering; 24 *segments with bristles*. Buff, yellow or brown-buff, with pink tints. Tentacles pale orange or pink. Gills dark red. Lower shore. In sand and gravel; under stones. Widely distributed. Probably common. *Amphitrite johnstoni* pl. 12.

A smaller species might be found. Length to 4 in., 90-100 segments, 19 *with bristles*. Even Fauvel's monograph says " Tube?—Colouration? " Probably only N. coasts. *Amphitrite groenlandica*

ii. Two pairs of gills, see fig. 32.

Fig. 32. *Amphitrite gracilis*, x 4

Tube of mucus. Worm 4-8 in. long, thin, *without marked swelling out towards head*. 100-200 segments, of which 16-18 *have bristles*. Pale fawn, grey or red. Crown of tentacles pale cream or pink, may be translucent. *Two pairs of bright red gills*, fig. 32. Lower shore. In rock cracks; in sand; under stones. Probably only S. and and S.W. coasts. Locally not uncommon. *Amphitrite gracilis* pl. 12.

Tube of mucus to which sand adheres and from which seaweeds may grow; 2-4 in. long, only ⅔ in. diameter. Worm 1-3 in. long, 50-70 segments, 17 *of them having bristles*. Brick-red in colour with *white dots*. Tentacles violet threads. Two pairs red gills, *long branches from relatively stout main stem*. Lower shore. Probably widely distributed. *Nicolea venustula*

Tube as *N. venustula*, attached to hydroids and seaweeds. Worm to 1 in. long; 40-50 segments, 15 *having bristles;* pink or brown with transparent skin showing bright red gut within. *No white spots*. Tentacles violet threads. Two pairs of red gills which are *shortly branched* stumps. Lower shore. Among seaweeds, hydroids and sponges. Probably widely distributed and not uncommon locally. *Nicolea zostericola*

ANNELIDA

D. TUBE FIRM, OF SAND ONLY

i. Single narrowly conical tube, open at both ends

Tubes fragile, rigid, 2-3 in. long, narrowly conical, both ends open, to $\frac{1}{4}$ in. diameter at mouth; either straight or bent, made of grains of clean sand or tiny pieces of shell cemented together into an even shape. Found lying on flats, usually empty, but stopper of stiff golden hairs may show that worm survives still. Lower shore. On and in sand. *Pectinaria* spp. pl. v and 12.

Tube *markedly curved* and thinly tapered, with finer grains of sand at small end than at mouth. Worm $\frac{3}{4}$-2 in. long; 17 *segments with bristles*. Pale pink. Widely distributed. Not uncommon.
Pectinaria auricoma

Tube *slightly curved* and thinly tapered, more or less transparent. Under lens see that grains are cemented facet to facet, showing delicacy of " workmanship " not equalled in other species. Worm 1-2 in. long; 15 *segments with bristles*. Body brownish-pink with red blood vessels. Widely distributed. Common. May be locally abundant. *Pectinaria koreni* pl. 12.

Tube very *nearly straight* and usually $\frac{3}{4}$ in. long. Worm 1-3 in. long, 17 *segments with bristles;* pale pink. Usually in deep water. Widely distributed. Rare. *Pectinaria belgica*

ii. Many tubes, about 1/5 in. diameter, fused together to form honeycomb lump

Tubes grouped in masses, perhaps several feet across, made entirely of sand and so firm as to be like honeycombed, porous sandstone. About middle and lower shore, among boulders with sand in vicinity on shore neither very exposed nor very sheltered; may be in estuaries. Single tubes may be found on shells or stones. Worms 1-1$\frac{1}{2}$ in. long, red or reddish-brown; golden-fringed collar round head; short thread tentacles. Widely distributed. Wherever conditions suitable likely to be abundant. *Sabellaria* spp. pl. v.

iii. Minute tubes, 1/10-1/20 in. diameter, appearing out of rocks

Minute tubes, U-shaped and so seeming to be in pairs, $\frac{1}{10}$-$\frac{1}{20}$ in. in diameter and standing up to $\frac{1}{2}$ in. out of rock cracks, often below surface of pools, perhaps coming through encrusting seaweeds (*Lithophyllum* p. 249 and pl. 35) and would pass unnoticed but for two threads that wave about vigorously, sometimes coiling and uncoiling in water. These are worm's antennae. Also boring into shells and limestone. Widespread. Very common. *Polydora* spp. pl. v.

E. TUBE A U-SHAPED GALLERY IN SAND, in sand, ½ in. diameter, lined with near-white leathery membrane. *Large worm in three distinct parts.*

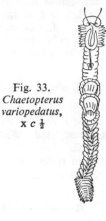

Fig. 33.
Chaetopterus variopedatus,
x c ½

Tubes to 9 in. long, up to ½ in. diameter, U-shaped, in sand or mud, both ends just protruding, dull white-grey, smooth inside but small pieces of shell and gravel adhering outside. Worm unmistakable; 6-10 in. long; pale yellow or green. Body in three parts, nine segments carrying stiff, flattened, spear-shaped bristles; five middle segments carrying total of three plate-shaped fans, constantly in motion in water; about 30 tail segments with bristles and lobes along back. Whole animal very fragile. Phosphorescent. Lower shore and below. Widely distributed. Abundant below tide marks but rare between them.

Chaetopterus variopedatus fig. 33.

F. TUBE A SLIMY CHANNEL IN MUDDY GRAVEL under stones.
Worm without crown of tentacles. Red gill-threads on at least some parts, see figs. 34, 35.   Family *Cirratulidae* RED-THREADS

Worm 3-8 in. long, pointed at both ends; very short segments, to 300 or more. Body yellow-orange, reddish-brown or occasionally bronzy-green. Two bunches of *many more than eight red feelers on about sixth or seventh segments. Red thread gills on most segments* throughout length of worm, except tail 30 or 40 (fig. 34). Middle and lower shore. All threads tend to tight spiral rolling. Widely distributed. Common in S. Rare in N.   *Audouinia* (= *Cirratulus*) *tentaculata* pl. 11.

Fig. 34. *Audouinia tentaculata,* x 1-1/3

Fig. 35. *Cirratulus cirratus,* x 2·½

Worm 1-4 in. long, pointed at both ends, *to* 150 *segments* which in front half of body are clear and *large*. Body yellow-orange or reddish-brown. Two small bunches of *up to eight red thread feelers on fourth or fifth segment*. Red thread gills may occur throughout length of worm, but are largely *concentrated in front third* (fig. 35), and are much less given to tight spiral rolling. Threads may be yellow. Lower shore. In muddy rock clefts as well as under stones. Common in N. Probably rare in S. *Cirratulus cirratus*

G. WORM IN TRANSLUCENT MUCUS CASE, showing green crown of tentacles and red line of stomach.

Worm 1-3 in. long, 30-50 segments, *enveloped in mucus case* through which only tips of bristles protrude. 20-25 tentacles on head. Whole body very pale green with red line of stomach. Lower shore. Under stones; among close-growing seaweeds; in cracks in rocks. Widely distributed. Not common. *Flabelligera affinis* pl. 11.

H. MUCUS TUBE A MERE BURROW IN MUD OR MUDDY SAND

i. Red, round worms without any large appendages, looking like earthworms, with the first 9-14 segments swollen and in contrast to longer thin remainder. Family *Capitellidae*

Body 6-12 in., extremely fragile; 100-150 segments. *Forward part is of 12 segments each with two rings and wrinkled, of which all but first have bristles,* fig. 36. Very large proboscis. Red in front, becoming transparent towards tail. Lower shore. Fine mud; muddy sand. Probably widely distributed, but may be only western. Locally common. *Notomastus latericeus*

Fig. 36. Anterior segments of *Notomastus latericeus*, x 2

Fig. 37. Anterior segments of *Capitella capitata*, x c 5

Body 1-4 in., to 100 segments. *Forward part of nine segments of which first seven carry bristles*, fig. 37. Proboscis small. Blood-red throughout. Middle and lower shore. In black mud; in sand; under stones. Widely distributed. Locally very common.

*Capitella capitata**

ii. **Worms fat, greenish- or yellow-black.** Burrows in area of little mounds topped with worm casts (pl. v).

Family *Arenicolidae* LUGWORMS

Worm 4-8 in. long, body soft, slimy, except stiffer, harder *tail which is without bristles or gills*. 13 *pairs of red gills*. Sandy bays; tidal flats. Widely distributed. Abundant. Best bait for bass.

Arenicola marina pl. 12.

Worm 4-8 in. long, without tail; red gills and bristles going right to end, there being 15 *or* 16 *segments with bristles in front of first pair of gills*. Lower shore. In gravel round or under stones. In rock clefts. Widely distributed. Probably not uncommon.

Arenicola ecaudata pl. 12.

As *A. ecaudata*, and may occur with it, but only 11 *or* 12 *segments with bristles preceding first pair of gills*. S. and W. coasts. Probably not uncommon. *Arenicola branchialis* (=*A. grubii*)

I. **THIN, PINK WORM, BURROWS IN SAND,** 2-6 in. long. Body in two distinct parts. Two rough tentacles more than half length of body. Tentacles and forward part pink, tail grey or greenish. Lower shore. In sand. Widely distributed. Probably common.

Magelona papillicornis

Fig. 37a. *Clymenella torquata*,
Head end *above*. Tail end *below* x 3-5

*Of interest only to those at Whitstable. Tube 5-8 in. long, ⅛ in. diameter, of sand grains and small pieces of shell. Thin worm, 2-6 in long, ⅛ in. diameter, greenish brown to light red, with characteristic head and tail (see Fig. 37a). In all Europe found only at Whitstable, where it is common, having perhaps been introduced in 1936 along with American oysters. *Clymenella torquata* (Leidy)

ANNELIDA

SMALL ALMOST THREAD-THIN WORMS LIVING IN SAND OR MUD

i. With coiled horns on their head

Worm 1-2 in. long, almost thread-thin; 100-150 segments. Two short, thick, pointed tentacles like the nearly retracted horns of a snail, and two long, backward-coiled feelers from side of head (fig. 38a). From point of tail 6-8 lobed processes. Reddish, darker towards head. Middle shore. In black mud, muddy sand. Widely distributed. Locally abundant. *Scololepis fuliginosa*

Fig. 38. Heads and anterior segments of a. *Scololepis fuliginosa;* b. *Nerine foliosa;* c. *Nerine cirratulus.* All x c 12-15

Worm 4-6 in. long, 200-250 segments. *Blunt head.* Two fat feelers coiled like ram's horns (fig. 38b). Gills are red plates that fit on to body as cooling flanges do on to motorcycle cylinder. Red in front tending towards green towards tail. Lower shore. In sand. Widely distributed. Probably not common. *Nerine foliosa*

As *N. foliosa* but only 2-3 in. long. *Sharply pointed head.* Feelers longer and much thinner (fig. 38c). Greenish-blue body. Middle and lower shore. In sand and fine gravel, associated with lugworms (*Arenicola*) (p. 85 and pl. 12). Widely distributed. Common.
Nerine cirratulus

ii. Sharply pointed head, without antennae or feelers.

Worm 2-5 in. long; about 200 segments of which first about 12-20 are fatter than tail on which tufts of bristles more and more point upwards across back. Two thread processes from tip of tail. Bright red, with rosy-orange tints. Middle shore. In clear and dirty sand. Widely distributed. Locally very common. *Scoloplos armiger* pl. 11.

This animal links in habit the sedentary to the errant worms. Although it has no tube it leads a life of little movement and slow steady feeding, rather than the hunting and devouring techniques of the errants.

HIRUDINEA
Leeches

No leeches are really intertidal. But one is such a noticeable animal when seen sticking to a skate or ray that its inclusion is justified.

Body 2-5 in. long, rather fat, particularly to one end. Grey, coarse-skinned and deeply ringed. Well developed suckers at both ends by which it adheres in an arched hoop. Can also move about. On skates and rays. Not uncommon. *Pontobdella* sp.

NEMATODA
Round Worms

ALTHOUGH universally common, worms of this type are never large or conspicuous on the shore. The body is round in section, encased in a firm cuticle and pointed at both ends. These worms can neither " flow " like flatworms nor crawl like annelid worms. They are unmistakable when encountered, and they are common on many seaweeds and also in the gut of shore fishes, should one explore so far. It is extremely difficult to identify species but here, fortunately, that is not necessary. The name of one may, however, be mentioned.

Wart-like branches on the brown weed *Ascophyllum nodosum* (p. 227) due to the presence within the plant of the gall-forming nematode
Tylenchus fucicola

GEPHYREA

More Worm-like Animals

THE GEPHYREA consist of a miscellaneous variety of animals which cannot easily be associated with the other groups of worms. They are not even closely related to each other, so that this group has now been abandoned by zoologists although it remains convenient to use it here.

Most of these animals burrow in mud or sand and feed on detritus. They usually live off-shore and are rare on the shore.

Body about 2-4 in. long, contractile, round, smooth, pointed at both ends most of the time. Pale straw-yellow in middle, medium brown at ends, at tail end for $\frac{1}{2}$ in. and at head for 2-3 in. when proboscis is everted and only briefly when it is not. Lower shore. In sand. Widely distributed. Rare except in scattered places.

Golfingia (=*Phascolosoma*) *elongata* (Keferstein) pl. ii.

Shells of *Aporrhais pes-pelecani*, the Pelican's-Foot (p. 138 and pl. xv) or *Turritella communis*, the Tower-Shell (p. 138 and pl. ii and xv) may be found full of muddy sand with a little round hole in the sand at the mouth of the shell. No more can be seen unless the shell is put into sea-water, when a long pale grey tube may emerge, up to 3 in. long, and quest round irregularly and slowly roll back in again. This is the proboscis of *Phascolion strombi* pl. ii.

Body 1-3 in. long, soft, sausage-shaped, with very contractile fore end, on which is a single pair of bristles. Long grooved proboscis. Body usually covered in slime which, when rubbed off, shows rather rough surface. Bluish or yellowish at head end, grey or pink in middle, dead white tail. Lower shore. In holes in rocks; under stones. S. and W. coasts only. Rare. *Thalassema neptuni*

Body about 3 in. long, fat. Bulbous end which bears longitudinal rows of spines. Rest of body ringed round and carries at end bunch of " ants-eggs." Pink. Lower shore. In dirty mud and muddy-gravel. Apparently not in N. or S.; only E. and W. coasts. Rare.

Priapulus spp. pl. ii.

" Ants-eggs " on one central appendage.   *Priapulus caudatus* pl. ii.

" Ants-eggs " on two appendages   *Priapulus bicaudatus*

ARTHROPODA

THESE ARE the jointed-legged animals, segmented like the annelid worms but with their short paddle-like appendages elongated and divided into sections capable of assuming many forms and serving many functions. The entire body is encased in a protective shell which has to be shed or moulted periodically as the animal grows. In number of species the arthropods outnumber the rest of the Animal Kingdom put together. It is seldom difficult to recognise an arthropod as such, with the exception of certain highly modified, often parasitic, groups. Here are contained the Insects, Arachnids (spiders, mites, scorpions, etc.), Centipedes and Millipedes—all entirely or almost entirely land living—and the Crustaceans which are primarily marine although with numerous freshwater representatives and some that are terrestrial, notably woodlice and, in tropical countries, land crabs.

CRUSTACEA

The most primitive of the existing arthropods and mostly retaining the primitive marine habit, they are distinguishable from other arthropods by possessing two pairs of antennae (insects have one pair, arachnids none) with many other appendages (insects have only six pairs apart from the antennae) and by having some means, such as gills, for obtaining oxygen from water. The body is divided into a head, a thorax and an abdomen (tail region). The first two are difficult to distinguish (unlike the insects where they are often obviously separated by a thin " neck ") but the abdomen is usually distinct. All may bear appendages. They range in size from the excessively minute to large and powerfully armed animals like crabs and lobsters. Representatives of the groups of small crustaceans, notably the copepods (oar-footed), are extremely common in the sea and can be found in pools, but they are too small to be examined by a hand lens and will not be described here, attention being confined to selected representatives of the groups of larger animals starting with the barnacles which do not externally resemble crustaceans, or indeed arthropods, at all.

CIRRIPEDIA
Barnacles

For long barnacles, with their shell of limy plates, were classified with the molluscs. Only when their development was studied were they revealed as crustacea which at a certain stage in development (they start life in the surface waters) fix themselves head downward on to a hard surface such as a rock or under the surface of a ship. They then become protected by a series of plates and use the thoracic appendages—in other crustacea used for swimming or walking—as a means of catching food. These are feathery and extended rather like the bent fingers of a hand, being continually protruded from and withdrawn within the shell. Acorn barnacles are the commonest of all animals on rocky shores.

The three groups of barnacles are readily distinguished.

A

Acorn barnacles form an encrustation covering rocks between tide marks, figs. 39 and 40. They have hard plates and are attached by a broad base. In older individuals the plates are often fused and become difficult to distinguish. Rocks may be completely covered by barnacles, which may be present in concentrations of 30,000 or more to the square yard, giving an overall grey colour to the middle levels of the shore.

those of acorn barnacles but larger and not so hard. The stalk is tough. Fig. 41.

Fig. 39   Fig. 40   Fig. 41

B

Stalked, or ship's barnacles do not normally live between tide marks but may often be found washed up. They attach themselves to drifting wood, to ships or to buoys; some produce a mucus bubble which hardens to form a float from which a group of them may hang. Stalked barnacles have plates similar to

C

The parasitic barnacles attach themselves to another animal when they settle from the sea. This " host " is a shore crab, a hermit crab or some other decapod crustacean. The parasite disappears from view while it extends within the tissue of its host, but eventually a rounded mass, or masses, appears under the abdomen and this represents the sexual organs of the parasite.

A. ACORN BARNACLES; closely encrusting body surrounded by hard grey plates.

i. Four plates, fig. 42.

 Fig. 42. *Elminius modestus*, x 1

Animal pearly-grey, appearing translucent. Four plates easily counted, without tendency to fuse, fig. 42. Leans a little and comes to a point at one side. An Australian barnacle which appeared in S. England towards the end of the war and is now spreading along our coasts and rapidly becoming very common; may soon be the dominant species of barnacle. High on middle shore. Particularly on stones washed by fresh water; not much in exposed water. Common southern half England and Wales, and spreading north. Temperature may eventually limit its distribution.

Elminius modestus DARWIN pl. vi.

No two plates same size; all ribbed longitudinally. *Area in middle not neatly divided by a line into two halves.* Up to ¼ in. across; white; very clean outline to base. Lower shore. Under stones; on shells. Never crowded together. Widely distributed. Not uncommon.

Verruca stroemia pl. vi.

ii. Six plates, fig. 43. Fig. 43. *Balanus balanoides*

All four lateral plates overlap terminals, but when plates are fused together this cannot be seen. *Width across area inside plates greatest nearer to one end,* giving a kite- or shield-shape. See fig. 44. White or pale grey. On exposed shores (kite →wind →exposure). Upper and middle shore, pushing *B. balanoides* lower where the two species

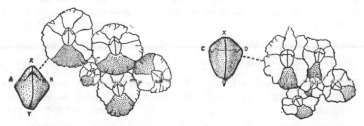

Fig. 44. To show the differences between the acorn-barnacles (*left*) *Balanus balanoides* and (*right*) *Chthamalus stellatus*. Dotted areas are the terminal (rostral) plates, broad in the case of *B. balanoides* because they overlap the laterals; narrow in *Chthamalus* because they are overlapped by the laterals. But in older specimens these plates may be fused together and the differences disappear. In *B. balanoides* the shape of the opening is a diamond, with the greatest width half-way along XY: in *Chthamalus* the shape is a shield or a kite, with the greatest width well towards X on XY. In *B. balanoides* the suture AB usually crosses XY obliquely, at least not at right angles which is the tendency in *Chthamalus*. All these characters vary so much that identity will often require considering all of them, together with the level on the beach, the degree of exposure and the identity of identifiable neighbours

cccur together in comparable numbers. As exposure decreases, range also decreases until the last ones appear at about mean high water of neap tides, always above *B. balanoides*. Southern species. S.W. and W. coasts only; graduating from extremely abundant Cornwall to rare N. Scotland, but spreading northwards.

Chthamalus stellatus pl. vi.

Lateral plates overlap one terminal plate but overlapped by other. When plates are fused this cannot be seen. *Width across area inside plates greatest across middle*, giving diamond shape (see fig. 44). Dirty white. On all coasts. On sheltered shores from below high water neaps to about low water of neap tides; on exposed rocks, where animal may reach $\frac{1}{2}$ in. tall, conglomerated together, at about mean tide level to mean low water springs where *Ch. stellatus* occurs, but in N. from high water neap tides downwards. A northern species graduating from very abundant in N. to common in S.; but absent from tip of Cornwall. *Balanus balanoides* pl. vi, fig. 43.

Purplish-brown, which may be very pale. Biggest acorn barnacle, attaining $\frac{3}{4}$ in. across base and up to $1\frac{1}{4}$ in. tall. Plates may be fairly smooth or vertically lined. They often separate terminally, leaving jagged edge round top of shell. Lower shore. S. coast; W. coast up to St. David's Head. In cracks; on overhangs. Common, but in nothing like the numbers of *B. balanoides* and occupying zone just beneath it. *Balanus perforatus* pl. vi.

Pale grey, often *rather clean*. Plates strongly ridged. Whole animal *tends to lean over to one side* and to have a point on that side. Has hard base often *leaving white ring on rock when removed*. Lower shore. Not on rock surfaces as *B. balanoides* but half under stones or on overhangs; on shells and flotsam. Widely distributed. Common. *Balanus crenatus* pl. vi.

These acorn barnacles are often peppered with minute black pits easily seen through a lens. This is the growth of a lichen *Arthopyrenia* (see p. 255).

B. STALKED BARNACLES, fig. 45. These do not normally live between tide marks, but they may be found cast ashore.

Single individuals or small groups *attached to float* which is whitish and spongy. Plates very thin, brittle, translucent. Stalk of varying length and shape. After prolonged periods of S.W. winds may be found on S.W. shores having sailed from S. Atlantic. Very occasionally in large numbers. *Lepas fascicularis* Linn. pl. vi.

Fig. 45

Numbers *attached to piece of wood*. Plates nearly white, with dark blue translucence. Stalk dark blue-grey or paler.

Lepas [anatifera] GOOSE-BARNACLE

Three other very similar species might almost equally well be found.

C. PARASITIC BARNACLES

Appears as biscuit-coloured structureless mass about $\frac{3}{4}$ in. across and $\frac{1}{4}$ in. long under tail of Shore Crab (*Carcinus maenas*) (p. 117 and pl. 15) and, very rarely, other crabs. Distinguish from eggs, also carried here, because non-granular and occurs in both sexes (i.e. both when under-tucked abdomen of crab is wide and seven-jointed (female) and narrow and five-jointed (male)). Widespread. Common.

Sacculina carcini pl. vi.

Yellowish or possibly orange rolled mass up to $\frac{1}{2}$ in. long, *non-granular*, under tail of hermit crab (*Eupagurus bernhardus*) (p. 116 and pl. 15). (If shell in which crab lives is gently warmed with a match crab will come out undamaged and can be inspected for presence of parasite). Probably widespread and not uncommon. *Peltogaster paguri* pl. vi.

LEPTOSTRACA

Small shrimp-like animals which have eyes on stalks, a rostral spine projecting forward between them. Loosely attached thin shell in two parts meeting in central line of back encloses eight closely set pairs of flat appendages and half covers first four pairs of longer abdominal (tail) appendages; two further pairs of stunted appendages carried on regions not covered by shell. Tail fines away to fork without appendages. Fig. 46.

Fig. 46. *Nebalia bipes*, x c 5

Body $\frac{1}{3}$-$\frac{1}{2}$ in. long, orange- or greenish-yellow with red eyes. Upper pair of antennae with stumpy branch; lower pair of antennae longer than upper; in male being as long as body. Middle and lower shore. Under stones, especially among decaying matter; on bait in lobster pots. Often in great numbers. Widespread. Common.

Nebalia bipes pl. viii.

MYSIDACEA

Opossum Shrimps

These little shrimp-like animals less than 1 in. long may be recognised at once by their appendages. Unlike true shrimps, they have no nippers but have eight pairs of branched swimming legs which come from the segments enclosed by the thin carapace. The long abdomen carries smaller appendages except for the last pair (uropods) which, with the tail segment, form a broad tail fan. The eyes are on stalks and are usually large and black. The whole animal is transparent (Fig. 47).

These are swimming animals often hanging almost vertically in the water. They may be found at the edge of the sea or, better, in pools. Several are phosphorescent; some change colour with changing backgrounds.

Fig. 47. A typical Mysid
(Opossum Shrimp)
Praunus sp., x *c* 1

A
Tail segment with terminal cleft, fig. 47 and 48*a-c*.

B
Tail segment without terminal cleft, fig. 48*d-e*.

A. TAIL SEGMENT WITH TERMINAL CLEFT, fig. 47 and 48*a-c*.

Body less than ½ in. long; *bright red or orange*, but in bright light colour not obvious; large black eyes. Tail segment with deep cleft in tip. Outer half of both edges has about 10 spines with last one on either side much the largest; smaller spines in cleft (fig. 48*a*). Outer section of uropod half as long again as tail; inner section only just longer. Widely distributed. Close to rock overhangs; among *Laminaria* (p. 225 and pl. xxxi). Not common.

Hemimysis lamornae MIDGE SHRIMP

Body ⅘-1 in. long; very variable in colour, from almost transparent-colourless to black; often green. Tail segment with cleft for about 1/6 of its length, with about 20 spines on either edge extending whole length (fig. 48*b*). Inner section of uropod about equal to tail segment; outer section longer. Body markedly bent in middle. In rock pools; among *Zostera* (p. 254 and pl. 40) and seaweeds; in edge of sea over flats; by rocks. Up estuaries. Widely distributed. Abundant.

Praunus spp. CHAMELEON SHRIMPS fig. 47.

Body ⅘ in. long; *glass-colourless but for black eyes.* Tail segment with wavy edges, each with 24-30 spines; triangular cleft at tip, with teeth on edges (fig. 48*c*). In edge of sea; perhaps in pools. Widely distributed. Common. *Schistomysis spiritus* GHOST-SHRIMP

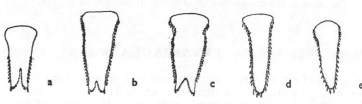

Fig. 48. Tail segments of a. *Hemimysis lamornae*, x 15; b. *Praunus* spp., x 6; c. *Schistomysis spiritus*, x 15; d. *Leptomysis* spp., x 15; e. *Siriella* spp., x 6

B. TAIL SEGMENT WITHOUT TERMINAL CLEFT, fig. 48*d-e*.

Body ½-¾ in. long; colourless, or varied colours—yellowish-red, browns to nearly black. Tail segment toothed all round; at end small spines between larger spines. No cleft in end of segment (fig. 48*d*). Outer section of uropod much longer than tail segment and *fines away evenly to blunt point*. In edge of sea. Widely distributed. *Leptomysis* spp.

Fig. 49. Uropod of *Siriella* spp., x c 6

Body usually ½ in. long; may be ⅘ in. Almost transparent, becoming light reddish-brown towards tail. Tail segment toothed all round. No cleft in end of plate, fig. 48*e*. *Outer section of uropod has joint across it near tip*, with sudden change in shape of outer line, spot being marked with tuft of spines, fig. 49. Edge of sea; among weeds; in pools. Widely distributed. Common. *Siriella* spp.

CUMACEA

The body is compressed from side to side, the anterior part being hooded in a peculiar way by the shield or carapace which covers only about half of it. The uncovered segments carry appendages, but not those of the

Fig. 50. A typical Cumacean

thin abdomen which writhes freely into positions sometimes reminiscent of a scorpion. The last appendages do not form a tail fan although their form often aids in identification of species.

These animals are very small, few of the 72 British species being ½ in. long. Some occur in enormous numbers. Most burrow in sand or mud although sometimes swarms appear in the surface waters near the shore.

No genera are commoner than those illustrated in pl. xiii.

TANAIDACEA

A group of small animals characterised by having bodies which are to some extent flattened from above downwards (cf. Isopods, such as woodlice). Only the first two segments of the middle region of the body (thorax) are covered by the carapace beneath which lies a single pair of nippers. The next six segments carry legs, the short group of abdominal segments bearing swimmerets. There is no tail fan.

Only ⅛-½ in. long, members of the two British families may be separated by their antennae; pl. xiii. Those in the *Tanaidae*, have *no* branch; those in the *Apseudidae* have a branch with the tail appendages divided into two.

They inhabit tubes often within cracks in rocks or in harbour works, in mud amongst the holdfasts of seaweeds, in empty barnacle shells or under rocks. Widely distributed. Common.

ISOPODA
Resembling Woodlice

This is a large and important group with many marine species but also occurring in fresh water and on land, i.e. the woodlice. The body is flattened from above downwards. The inner antennae are inconspicuous, the outer ones very large. The eyes are close set in the head and without stalks. All seven pairs of legs are much the same. The last appendages (uropods) extend back on either side of the tail segment and may be divided. The other abdominal appendages are flattened and lie closely applied to the under surface of the body. They are used for breathing. In the female there is a brood pouch where the young are retained during development.

A

Behind last segment carrying legs appears to be only one more segment (actually consists of several fused into a tail-plate). Apparently no appendages on this tail-plate but these covered by thin membrane. Uropods on either side of tip of tail-plate, each divided into two points which may be minute. Long legs. Fig. 51.

Fig. 51

B

Behind last segment carrying legs about five more segments with minute appendages folded underneath them. Uropods each divided into two plates that spread out and, with tail-segment, form fan. Fig. 52.

Fig. 52

C

Typical woodlice.
Behind last segment carrying legs about five more segments with minute folded appendages underneath them. Uropods each divided

into two long pointed processes. Inner antennae so small as to be easily missed. Fig. 53.

Fig. 53

D

Behind last segment carrying legs one or two more may be indicated by folds part of the way across tail-plate but most of that smooth. No uropods visible from above but from below they appear as single elongated plates hinged at middle of inner edge and folding over abdominal appendages. Long, narrow animals.

   i. End border of tail straight or concave, not coming to a point. Fig. 54.
  ii. End border of tail more or less pointed, certainly produced at centre. Fig. 55.

Fig. 54   Fig. 55

A. Behind last segment carrying legs appears to be only one more segment (actually consists of several fused into a tail-plate). Apparently no appendages on this tail-plate but these covered by thin membrane. Uropods on either side of tip of tail-plate, each divided into two points which may be minute. Long legs. Fig. 56.

Fig. 56

Body ¼-⅓ in. long, oblong-oval; white-grey, *stippled all over dark brown pinpoint-small spots.* First four segments behind head have toothed edges. Outer antennae longer than body. Tail segment with finely serrated posterior edge. Uropods have basal joint as long as the two pieces into which each divides. Middle and lower shore. Under stones; among seaweeds. Widely distributed. Probably not common.

Janira maculosa

Body about ⅙ in. long, oval outline but with pronounced nicks between each segment. Ash-coloured, with *front of head whitish.* Outer antennae ½-¾ length of body. Tail segment wider than long with a dot on either side of the middle line just behind junction with segment in front. Uropods minute. Middle and lower shore. Under stones; among gravel; on weeds. Widely distributed. Common.

Jaera marina pl. vii.

Body about ⅙ in. long, broad-oval, with maximum width well back towards tail. Edge *fringed all round with hairs.* Outer antennae up to 1/3 body length. *Tail segment with semi-circular notch at end* from which uropods extend only just beyond tail, fig. 57. Probably widely distributed and common.

Jaera nordmanni

Fig. 57. Tail segment of *Jaera nordmanni*, x *c* 25

Body about 1/10 in. long; yellow-brown. Large eyes project beyond sides of body. Outer antennae longer than body. First pair of legs short; other *six pairs spidery, long* and bristly. Very active. Lower shore. On seaweeds and hydroids. Widely distributed. Probably not uncommon. *Munna kroyeri*

Fig. 58

B. Behind last segment carrying legs about five more segments with minute appendages folded underneath them. Uropods each divided into two plates that spread out and, with tail-segment, form fan. Fig. 58.

Body ¼ in. long; blue, green or grey. Inner antennae longer than outer, about ¼ length of body. *Sexes widely different* (pl. viii). In male between antennae a pair of large hooked mandibles. Body widest between large eyes, narrowing quickly behind last of five pairs of legs to pointed tail. In female no jaws. Head and first two segments and tail may be spotted. Rest of body covered by thin skin, with one pair of legs at its front corners, one pair in middle and one pair at tail corners and so appears to have only three pairs. Maximum width across middle. Lower shore. In crevices; under stones. Widely distributed. Common. *Gnathia maxillaris* pl. viii.

Body ¼ in. long; rather pear-shaped, with maximum width between third pair of legs; upper side rounded, not flat. Semi-transparent, pale grey; on each segment lines of delicate dots radiating star-wise. Inner antennae very short; outer antennae come from below rather than outside the inner ones and are half body length or more. First three pairs of legs hooked and stronger and shorter than last four pairs which are hairy. Behind last pair of legs, six segments of which last is much the largest and rounded, and from the side of which uropods spread out. Lower and middle shore. In pools and wet sand. Widely distributed. Locally may be very common. *Eurydice pulchra* pl. viii

Body ⅜ in. long, rounded; very pale grey, minutely dotted on first three segments; rear edge of first seven segments marked by transverse line. Inner antennae short; outer antennae not half body length. First three pairs of legs strong and shorter than last four pairs which are hairy. Last of six tail segments triangular and, together with uropods, has hairy fringe, fig. 59. Probably middle and lower shore. In pools. At least S. and W. coasts. *Cirolana cranchi*

 Fig. 59. Tail segment of *Cirolana cranchi*, x c 7

Body ⅕ in. long; parallel sides, smoothly rounded ends. When exposed tends to roll up in ball. Inner and outer antennae much same length; both very short. Last segment of six tail segments rounded and slightly hollow seen from above. Uropods from near front of this segment, spiny. *Burrows into wood in great numbers together;* holes ⅕ in. diameter. Widely distributed. Often in timber cast ashore. Very common. *Limnoria lignorum* THE GRIBBLE pl. viii.

Body ½ in. long, smooth, wide, blunt-ended, oval, ¼ in. across. Rolls up into a ball when disturbed. Grey or whitish, with darker, perhaps reddish, marks. Tail segment rough with perhaps dots and marks of black. Inner antennae half length of outer, which are a third of body length. Seven pairs of legs all similar; behind last of which are indications of further segments but tail segments rounded. *Outer section of uropods with simple unbroken edge.* Swims freely on its back. Widely distributed. Middle shore. In estuaries; saltmarsh pools. Very common. *Sphaeroma rugicauda* pl. viii.

Very much as *S. rugicauda*, but tail segment smooth; *outer section of uropod serrated on outer edge.* Often several together. Among shingle; under stones. S. and W. coasts; perhaps elsewhere. Common.
Sphaeroma serratum

Large difference between sexes (see pl. viii). Females ⅕ in. long, very much as *S. rugicauda*, except reddish, *smooth tail segment which has deep notch;* does not roll into ball. Males ⅓ in. long; grey with reddish or bluish marks. Segment bearing last pair of legs has *two inward bending points sticking backwards.* Whole body rounded. Outer section of *uropods much enlarged,* long-oval. Lower and middle shore. Under stones; in crevices; in empty shells. At least S. and W. coasts. Not uncommon. *Naesa bidentata* pl. viii.

C. Typical Woodlice. **Behind last segment carrying legs about five more segments with minute folded appendages underneath them.** Uropods each divided into two long pointed processes. Inner antennae so small as to be easily missed. Fig. 60.

Fig. 60

Body typically ⅔ in. long, may be well over 1 in.; oval; flattened, greenish-grey with paler dots and markings. Eyes black. Rough texture. Inner antennae vestiges only. Outer antennae stout, about ⅔ body length. Males seven pairs of legs, all the same. Female six pairs. From both sides of tip of tail uropods each of which divides into two long points. Upper shore. Under stones and seaweed; in cracks; in harbour walls. Runs fast. Particularly active at night. Widely distributed. Abundant. *Ligia oceanica* SEA-SLATER pl. vii.

Body to ⅔ in. long; rectangular-oval; varied colour, often lead-grey, may be black or pale yellow. Can roll up, when head and tail fit perfectly together to make globe. Inner antennae too small to see. Outer antennae seven-jointed, ⅓ body length. Hinder edge of last segment but one in tail almost semi-circular and in this space centrally is small triangular last segment with on either side of it flange of uropod, so semi-circular space is exactly filled—at first sight uropods appear to be absent. Upper shore. Under stones, etc. Mixed with *Ligia oceanica.* Widely distributed. Abundant.

Armadillidium vulgare PILL BUG

D. Behind last segment carrying legs one or two more may be indicated by folds part of the way across tail plate but most of that smooth. No uropods visible from above but from below they appear as single elongated plates hinged at middle of inner edge and folding over abdominal appendages. *Long, narrow animals.*

i. End border of tail straight or concave, not coming to a point. Fig. 61.

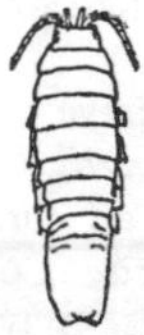

Body to 1 in. long, narrow; each leg-bearing segment considerably wider than long, giving irregular line to sides. Green or brown with lengthwise stripes. *Antennae as long as body. Tail segment with strongly angled corners and no point at tip.* All seven pairs of legs strong, armed with hooks. Lower shore. Among seaweeds and *Zostera* (p. 254 and pl. 40); on drifting refuse. Widely distributed. Not common.

Fig. 61

Idotea linearis pl. vii.

Body in males up to more than 1 in. long, in females to ⅔ in. Males usually uniformly brown, females often with white lateral markings. Oval. *Outer antennae about ⅓ body length. Tail segments with rounded angled corners with, in adults, concave line in between* (but in small specimens this line may be straight). Lower shore. Among seaweed; in pools. Widely distributed. Probably common. May be locally abundant. *Idotea emarginata* pl. vii.

ii. End border of tail more or less pointed; certainly produced at centre. Fig. 62.

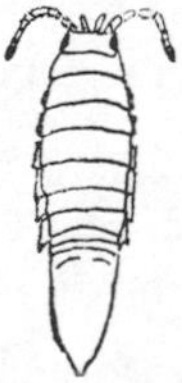

Fig. 62

Body not more than ½ in. long. Dark purple-brown with white marks down central line of back and along sides. *Outer antennae ¼ body length.* All legs with big hooked claw. *Tail plate smoothly shaped to blunt point; no keel to it.* Particularly on exposed shores, among seaweeds and barnacles. Probably widely distributed. Not common.

Idotea pelagica

Body about ½ in. long. Usually uniform green or brown, possibly with pale markings. *Outer antennae half body length. Tail plate with smoothly rounded corners leading to definite point.* High on middle shore. *In brackish pools;* in estuaries. Probably also lower down in seaweed. ? distribution. Probably not uncommon.

Idotea viridis (Slabber) pl. vii.

Body usually ½-¾ in. long. Mostly uniform brown, red or green, sometimes with white markings. *Outer antennae ¼ body length. Sides of tail plate very slightly concave; plate comes to pronounced but blunt point.* Middle shore. Among seaweed, larger ones particularly on *Ascophyllum* (p. 227 and pl. xxxii) and *Fucus* (p. 226 and pl. xxxii); in crevices. Probably widely distributed and not uncommon.

Idotea granulosa Rathke pl. vii.

Body ½-1 in. or more long. Uniformly brownish, may have white marks or marbling. *Outer antennae about 1/3 body length. Tail plate with ridge down middle (keeled), has smooth rounded corners and comes to point,* definite but less than in *I. granulosa.* Lower shore. Among seaweed. Widely distributed. Common; may be locally abundant.

Idotea neglecta pl. vii.

Body ½-1 in. or more long. Uniform green or brown, often with pale spots and lines, particularly at edges. *Outer antennae half body length. Tail plate has two corner-angled points with a longer sharper one in between; has ridge (keel) down centre line.* Lower shore. On seaweed and *Zostera* (p. 254 and pl. 40). Widely distributed. Probably not uncommon.

Idotea baltica pl. vii.

AMPHIPODA
" Sandhoppers "

" Sandhoppers " is an inadequate name for this Order, as comparatively few of them live in sand and fewer still hop. However a large number of individuals live between the tide marks, chiefly under stones and in the rotting seaweed at the top of the beach.

The typical amphipods found on any beach are Gammaridae or Talitridae. They are compressed sideways and typically rather curled up, often with one large one clasping a smaller one. Their eyes are not on stalks. Except for the Caprellidae they have two pairs of hooked nippers, which may be inconspicuous, five pairs of walking legs, three pairs of swimmerets and three pairs of stiff uropods each divided into two which are used to push the animal along or in jumping.

A

Typical compressed curved shape, usually wriggling on their sides. Upper (front) antennae longer than lower and having small branch halfway along which has to be sought with particular care when animal not in water as it then collapses on to antenna and becomes confused with it. Extreme tip of tail and last three pairs of appendages all divided into two. Fig. 63. Family *Gammaridae*.

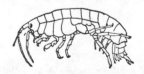

Fig. 63

i. Inner branch of last pair of appendages more than half length of outer branch, see fig. 64a. Spines on three tail segments and on tail.

ii. Inner branch of last pair of appendages less than half length of outer branch, see fig. 64b. Spines on three tail segments and on tail.

Fig. 64. Last appendage of a *Gammarus* sp.; b *Marinogammarus* sp. Both x 10

iii. Inner branch of last pair of appendages less than half length of outer branch. No spines on three tail segments or on tail.

103

B

Upper antennae without branch, only just longer than lower antennae. Last three pairs of legs get successively longer, and are usually bent upwards and backwards. Last three pairs of tail appendages divided into two. Very small red eyes.

C

Jumping animals. Walk and stand upright. Upper antennae without branch and much shorter than lower. Extreme tip of tail and last pair of appendages not divided into two. Fig. 65. Family *Talitridae*.

Fig. 65

i. Upper antennae shorter than large-jointed section of lower antennae.
ii. Upper antennae distinctly longer than large-jointed section of lower antennae.

D

Upper antennae, without branch, shorter than lower antennae. Last three pairs of legs get successively longer, and are usually bent upwards and backwards. Last three pairs of tail appendages divided into two.

E

Body up to ¼ in. long; compressed laterally; living in sand. Upper antennae shorter than lower antennae, and have little branch rising from them. Able to burrow quickly, digging with last three pairs of legs, joints of which are flattened into plates. Fig. 66.

Fig. 66

F

Body not compressed laterally. Lives in U-shaped burrows in mud and muddy sand. Upper antennae shorter than lower which are conspicuously long and heavy. Last three pairs of legs much longer than preceding three pairs. Fig. 67. Family *Corophiidae*.

Fig. 67

G

i. Found on underside of jellyfish. Green eyes.
ii. Found inside dead crabs. Red eyes.
iii. Found on or in pieces of wood, usually bored by isopod *Limnoria lignorum* (p. 99 and pl. viii).

H

Body extraordinarily elongated, string-thin; distinct head; only vestige of tail. Upper pair of antennae longer than lower pair. Moves slowly in loops, legs placed with painful deliberation. May rise feebly on back legs, resembling stick insect. Females have plates below third and fourth segments in which eggs are incubated. Fig. 68. Family *Caprellidae*.

 i. Five pairs of walking legs.
 ii. Three pairs of walking legs, middle body segments being without them.

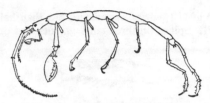

Fig. 68. A typical Caprellid, x *c* 3

A. **Typical Compressed Curved Shape. Usually wriggling on their sides. Upper antennae longer than lower; and having small branch half-way along it,** which has to be sought with particular care when animal is not in water, as it then collapses on to the antennae and becomes confused with it. Extreme tip of tail and last three pairs of appendages all divided into two. Fig. 69. Family *Gammaridae*

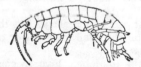

Fig. 69

 i. **Inner branch of last pair of appendages more than half length of outer branch,** fig. 70. Spines on three tail segments and on tail.

Fig. 70

Minute spines along three tail segments and on tail. Second pair of appendages with nippers, short and strong. Each of seven pairs of walking legs become progressively longer, with seventh the longest. Tip of tail divided right to base and so appears double.

Gammarus spp. pl. ix.

Four species not separable within the limits of this list. *G. locusta* is about 1 in. long; variably coloured, often brownish-green with pink patch on each side; abundantly common everywhere under stones on middle and lower shores. *G. zaddachi, G. duebeni, G. chevreuxi* are mainly estuarine but overlap *G. locusta* in habitat. They are good indicators of salinity.

ii. Inner branch of last pair of appendages less than half length of outer branch, fig. 71. Spines on three tail segments and on tail.

Fig. 71

Apart from details in heading indistinguishable from *Gammarus*.

Marinogammarus spp.

Three species are widely distributed and common, and all may enter estuaries. The differences between them are microscopic. *M. marinus* (Leach), abundant under stones, on middle shore, is olive-green or black, about $\frac{3}{5}$-1 in. long.

iii. Inner branch of last pair of appendages less than half length of outer branch. No spines on three tail segments or on tail.

Otherwise as *Gammarus*. *Melita* spp.

None more than $\frac{1}{3}$ in. long. Five species, three of which are probably widely distributed and common.

B. Upper Antennae Without Branch, only just longer than lower antennae, Last three pairs of legs get successively longer, and are usually bent upwards and backwards. Last three pairs of tail appendages divided into two. *Very small red eyes.*

Body $\frac{1}{2}$ in. long. Colour corresponds to colour of seaweeds among which it may be found; may be red, reddish-brown or green. Differs from *Gammarus* in proportions of antennae and in having heavier nippers and eyes small and red. All levels of stony beaches, particularly lower part. Under stones. Widely distributed. Common.

Amphithoë rubricata pl. ix.

B. Jumping Animals. Walk and stand upright. **Upper antennae without branch and much shorter than lower.** Extreme tip of tail and last pair of appendages not divided into two. Fig. 72. Family *Talitridae*.

i. Upper antennae shorter than large-jointed section of lower antennae

Fig. 72

Smooth articulations to small joints at end of lower antennae. Upper antennae hardly reach to last long joint of lower antennae which has spines on its upper edge. *Orchestia* spp. pl. ix.

Two species are widespread and common on either side of average high water level. *O. gammarella* (pl. ix) extends to mean high water of springs; ¾ in. long; reddish- or greenish-brown, perhaps with reddish marks. Among decaying seaweed; in sand; among shingle; places not always damp.
O. mediterranea may be down to mean low water of neaps; ⅗ in. long; often brownish-green. Among seaweed rotting on shingle.

Rough, toothed articulations to small joints at end of lower antennae. Appendages from second segment behind head ends in simple spike; from third segment ends in small claw. ¾-1 in. long. Brownish-grey or green tinged fawn with black line down back. Upper shore. Among rotting seaweed; in sand. Widely distributed. Very common.
Talitrus saltator pl. ix.

Talitrus may be easily muddled with *Talorchestia* but it is nearly always much more common.

ii. Upper antennae distinctly longer than large-jointed section of lower antennae.

Only ¼ in. long. Otherwise very like *Orchestia*. Lower shore. Among seaweeds. Widely distributed. Common. *Hyale* spp.

D. Upper Antennae Without Branch, shorter than lower antennae. Last three pairs of legs get successively longer, and are usually bent upwards and backwards. Last three pairs of tail appendages divided into two.

Body ⅓ in. long. Colour variable. Lower antennae markedly longer than upper and altogether more strongly built. Eyes round, small and dark. First pair of nippers well developed; second pair much larger, varying in shape with sexes, male's being quite characteristic (pl. x). Lower and middle shore. On buoys and ropes; in pools. Widely distributed. Common. *Jassa falcata* pl. x.

Body ⅓ in. long. Translucent whitish, with small chestnut patches. Lower antennae not much longer than upper. Eyes kidney-shaped and not small. Middle of three pairs of tail appendages much shortest. First pair of nippers slightly larger than second. Divided ends of last pair of tail appendages more than twice as long as basal joint. Lower shore. Over and in clean sand. Widely distributed. Common.

Nototropis swammerdami pl. ix.

E. **Body up to ¼ in. long; compressed laterally; living in sand.**
Upper antennae shorter than lower ones, and have little branch rising

from them. Able to burrow quickly, digging with last three pairs of legs whose joints are flattened into plates. Fig. 73.

Fig. 73

Body ⅛ in. long; translucent and almost colourless except for red eyes. Two thick blunt horns stick out beyond eyes which are first joints of upper antennae from which remainder of upper antennae droop; all of which is not longer than large-jointed base segments of lower antennae, whose total length in males equals body length, but in females is only twice length of upper antennae. Low on middle shore. In sand. Widespread and common.

Bathyporeia pelagica pl. ix.

Body ¼ in. long; yellowish, sandy-orange. Might be confused with *Bathyporeia* but upper antennae do not arise from horn and small branch from it comes from near tip. Male lower antennae are as long as body; but female's lower only just exceed length of upper. Main plate of last pair of legs but one has rows of long spines. Middle and lower shore. In sand and shelly gravel. Probably widely distributed and common. *Urothoë* spp. pl. x.

Body ⅖ in. long; sandy colour, matching sand it lives in. Eyes not easily distinguished; head segment projecting forward, cowl-like, from tip of which upper antennae hang. Lower antennae have a base joint flattened and enlarged. Side plates of body progressively larger towards tail. Lower joints of last three pairs of legs also flattened into plates of various shapes. Middle and lower shore. Probably widely distributed and common. *Haustorius arenarius* pl. x.

F. Body not Compressed Laterally. Lives in U-shaped burrows in mud and muddy sand. **Upper antennae shorter than lower which are conlong and heavy.** Last pair of legs much longer than preceding three pairs. Fig. 74. Family *Corophiidae*

Fig. 74

Body ⅓ in. long; sandy-grey. Upper antennae do not reach more than half-way along last large joint of lower antennae, i.e. are half their length. Large joints of lower antennae are as much as half-width of body segments. Colonies of U-tubes about two inches deep in mud, in such numbers that surface may be everywhere punctured with holes about 1/10 in. diameter. Middle shore. Widely distributed. Common; locally abundant. *Corophium* [*volutator*] pl. x.

G. i. Found on underside of jellyfish. Green eyes.

Body ½ in. long; sandy colour, dotted all over red. Large green eyes. Upper and lower antennae minute and rather thick, former just the longer. Found in cavities within umbrella of jellyfish, particularly *Rhizostoma* (p. 55 and pl. 4). Widely distributed. Common.

Hyperia galba pl. x.

ii. Found in shells of dead crabs. Red eyes.

Body not more than ¼ in. long; off-white with large bright red eyes. Upper antennae with branch, hairy; shorter than lower antennae. Upper joints of all legs flattened into plates. Found in dead and cast shells of crabs at edge of sea and left stranded. Possibly only S. and W. coasts. Locally common. *Orchomenella nana* pl. ix.

iii. Found on or in pieces of wood usually bored by isopod *Limnoria lignorum* (p. 99 and pl. viii).

Body ⅓ in. long; light brown. Upper antennae with tiny branch half-way along and are half-length of lower antennae, which have two joints flattened into elongated hairy plates. Second tail appendages reach well beyond tail and finish with long-oval plates, larger in male than in female; third tail appendages flattened into shorter plates (pl. viii). Last tail segment extends centrally into long sharp point. Widely distributed. In drift wood; in piles. Common.   *Chelura terebrans* pl. viii.

H. Body Extracrdinarily Elongated, string-thin; distinct head; only vestige of tail. **Upper antennae longer than lower.** Moves slowly in loops, legs placed with painful deliberation. May rise feebly on back legs resembling stick insect or praying mantis. Females have plates below third and fourth segments in which eggs are incubated.

Family *Caprellidae*

i. Five pairs of walking legs

Body ⅔ in. long; brown or sandy. Upper antennae more than twice as long as lower. Two pairs of nippers, second longer and heavier than first. Five pairs of walking legs of which third is much the shortest. Lower shore. On seaweeds, buoys and floating refuse. Widely distributed. Common.   *Phtisica marina* fig. 75.

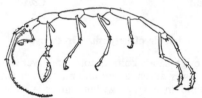

Fig. 75. *Phtisica marina*, x c 3

ii. Only three pairs of walking legs; middle body segments without them.

Body ⅔ in. long; brightly coloured, green, yellow, red, etc. or banded. Lower antennae with scarcely visible hairs near base. Rough tubercles along middle line of back, fig. 76. Lower shore. On seaweeds and hydroids and shells of the Common Whelk, *Buccinum* (p. 140 and pl. xvi). Not common in S. Common in N.

Caprella acanthifera

Fig. 76. Fore-part of *Caprella acanthifera*, x c 5

Body ½-⅛ in. long; light brown or plum-coloured. Lower antennae with hairs below throughout their length. Line of back uneven but not with rough tubercles. Appendage carrying second (large) pair of nippers has top joint almost as long as nipper which is twice as long as broad; fig. 77. Lower shore. Among seaweeds; on hydroids and floating refuse. Widely distributed. Not uncommon.

Caprella linearis pl. x.

Fig. 77. Fore-part of *Caprella linearis*, x c 3

DECAPODA
Shrimps, Prawns, Crabs, Lobsters, etc.

The decapod crustaceans include all the larger members of this great group, from shrimps and prawns to lobsters and crabs. All possess five pairs of " walking legs " carried on the segments of the thorax, i.e. the region between the head in front and the abdomen or tail behind. Head and thorax are covered by a common shield or carapace, which is very well developed in crabs where the small abdomen is tucked underneath. Often there appear to be six pairs of these legs, but then the first pair belongs to the head and is concerned with the feeding mechanism. The first pair of true legs nearly always has nippers, though these may be minute. The abdominal segments behind bear five pairs of appendages, the swimmerets, which are usually much better developed in females because the developing eggs are carried upon them. The first one or two pairs of these appendages in the male are modified in connection with copulation. The last pair of appendages (uropods) are usually different, forming with the tail segment (or telson) a broad tail fan.

NATANTIA
Swimming Decapods; Shrimps and Prawns

A	B
Antennae at least as long as body; with long projection of carapace forming a rostrum which extends forward between the eyes and bears six or more teeth.	Antennae only about half as long as body; rostrum with four or less teeth.

C

Antennae nearly as long as body; no rostrum. Carapace somewhat flattened from above downwards, not laterally as in A and B.

N.B.—Shrimp-like animal, $\frac{1}{2}$ in. long, red eyes. See *Nebalia bipes* pl. viii and p. 93.

TABLE FOR IDENTIFYING COMMON PRAWNS AND SHRIMPS

	Leander serratus pl. xi	*Leander squilla*	*Pandalus montagui* pl. xi	*Palaemonetes varians* pl. xi	*Hippolyte varians* pl. xi	*Hippolyte prideauxiana*	*Spirontocaris cranchi*	*Athanas nitescens* pl. xi	*Crangon vulgaris* pl. xi	*Philocheras fasciatus*
ANTENNAE										
no. of parts of inner pair	3	3	2	3	2	2	2	3	2	2
proportion of length of outer antennae to body length	$1\frac{1}{2}$	$1\frac{1}{2}$	$1\frac{1}{2}$	$1+$	$\frac{1}{2}$	$\frac{1}{2}$	$\frac{1}{2}$	$\frac{1}{2}$	$1-$	$\frac{1}{2}$
ROSTRUM										
no. of teeth										
on tip	2	1	2	1	1	1	2	1		
on upper edge	6-8	7-10	10-12	4-6	2	0	3	0	no	
on lower edge	4-5	3	5-6	2(1)	2	2	0	0	rostrum	
LEGS										
pair with biggest nippers	2	2	2	2	1(2)	1	1	1	1	1
longest pairs	2.3.4	2.3.4	2-5	2 & 5	3	3	2	1	4 & 5	4 & 5

A. ANTENNAE AT LEAST AS LONG AS BODY; with long projection of carapace forming a rostrum which extends forward between the eyes and bears six or more teeth. See Table above.

Body 1-4 in. long, partly transparent, grey, containing purplish dots and lines. Inner antennae in three parts, of which the longest is as long as body. Outer antennae 1½ times as long as body. Between eyes a rostrum which curves upwards, and is divided at tip; has 6-8 *teeth on upper edge, leaving front 1/3 of edge without teeth; 4-5 teeth on lower edge.* Second pair of legs longer than first pair, with heavier nippers. In pools; at edge of sea, particularly among seaweed in Aug. and Sept. on flood tide. S. and W. coasts. In some years abundant, in others only common. Pale green swelling on side of carapace indicates presence within of parasitic isopod *Bopyrus squillarum.*

Leander serratus COMMON PRAWN pl. xi.

As *L. serratus* but only up 2 in. long; rostrum only slightly upcurved, coming to single point; *whole of upper edge occupied by 7-10 teeth; three teeth on lower edge.* Widely distributed. Common.

Leander squilla PRAWN

Body 1-2½ in. long, but usually about 1½ in., reddish-grey, rather transparent, with darker red dots and marks showing through. Inner antennae in two parts, ¼ length of body. Outer antennae much longer than body, and ringed alternately dark and light. Between eyes long rostrum which curves upwards; tip of two points; 10-12 *teeth on upper edge, all on posterior half; 5-6 teeth on lower edge.* First pair of legs without nippers; second pair of legs unequal in length and size, the longer, thinner one having similar (minute) nipper. In pools; at edge of sea. Widely distributed. Great variation in numbers from year to year. *Pandalus montagui* AESOP PRAWN pl. xi.

Body about 1 in. long, almost transparent, with brown-orange lines and dots showing through. Inner antennae in three parts, not as long as body. Outer antennae just longer than body. Between eyes straight rostrum, coming to fine point; with 4-6 *teeth on upper edge and only two, rarely one, on lower edge;* leaving outer 1/3 of rostrum untoothed. First two pairs of legs with nippers, the second pair a little longer and larger. *In brackish water on salt-marshes,* in pools and drainage pans and streams. Widely distributed, but probably not in Scotland. Very common locally. *Palaemonetes varians* pl. xi.

B. ANTENNAE ONLY ABOUT HALF LENGTH OF BODY;
rostrum with four or less teeth. See Table opposite.

Body about ½-¾ in. long. By day commonly clear green, may be reddish- or liver-brown; by night transparent blue. Inner antennae in two parts, very short; outer antennae about half as long as body. Humped back. Between eyes straight rostrum; *on upper edge one tooth near base and another near point; on lower edge,* which is sharply keeled, *two teeth.* First pair of legs very short, with nippers; second pair longer, with nippers, with 3-4 joints to wrist; third pair longest of all. Lower shore. In pools; among seaweed. Perhaps rare in Scotland; common elsewhere. *Hippolyte varians* pl. xi.

As *H. varians*, but may be 1½ in. long; may have white stripe down middle of back. *No tooth on upper edge of rostrum; two teeth on lower edge* are toward tip. S.W. coasts. Not uncommon.

Hippolyte prideauxiana

As *H. varians* but rostrum short and ends in two points, upper one the larger; *three teeth on upper edge; no teeth on lower edge.* Next to nippers on second pair of legs are six joints on wrist. S.W. and S. coasts only. Locally abundant. *Spirontocaris cranchi*

Body ½-1 in. long, red with white stripe down back. Inner antennae in three parts, short; outer antennae about half as long as body. Short rostrum ends in sharp point; *no teeth above or below.* First two pairs of legs equally long; first carry heavy nippers of which one may be larger than other; on second pair, minute nippers. Lower shore. In pools; among seaweed. Often gregarious. W. and S. coasts. May be very common locally. *Athanas nitescens* pl. xi.

C. ANTENNAE NEARLY AS LONG AS BODY; no rostrum.

Carapace somewhat flattened from above downwards, not laterally as in A and B. See Table, p. 112.

Body 1-3 in. long, grey or dark brown, dotted darker or with reddish. No rostrum, but sharp pointed scale just at eye level. Inner antennae in two parts; outer antennae as long as body, rise from tough oval-equilateral plate which is hairy on inner edge. First pair of legs short, heavy, have movable spine that curves across end to meet sharp point —i.e. not typical nippers. Fourth and fifth pairs of legs stouter and longer than second and third pairs. Lower shore. Wherever there is sand; in pools; estuaries, etc. Widely distributed. Locally very abundant. *Crangon vulgaris* SHRIMP pl. xi.

As *C. vulgaris*, only ½ in. long; last third of body suddenly tapers towards tail from level at which broad brown band crosses body. Second pair of legs much shorter than first and third. No point between eyes. S. and W. coasts. Rare. *Philocheras fasciatus.*

Three or four other species of shrimp (*Philocheras*) might be found with various combinations of sharp spines on shell.

REPTANTIA
Walking Decapods, Lobsters, Crabs

A
Lobsters.

B
Squat Lobsters. Abdomen (tail) not reduced but carried tucked under body.

C
Hermit Crabs. Abdomen asymmetrical, not carried under body. Living in snail shells with opening closed with right, and larger, nipper.

Fig. 78

D
Crabs. Abdomen reduced and carried under body.
  i. Small crabs with nippers and apparently only three pairs of legs.
 ii. Typical crabs, with nippers and four pairs of legs.
iii. Dark straw-coloured crab with long hairy antennae; shell longer than broad. In sand.
 iv. Very small crabs, living in mussels or horse mussels, rarely in cockles or oysters.
  v. Spider crabs.

E
Burrowing shrimps. Rather soft, thin carapace, laterally compressed, Large abdomen, broadest about middle of its length, not tucked under body, tail fan well developed. In permanent burrows in sandy mud. Fig. 78.
  i. One nipper much the larger.
 ii. Nippers same size.

A. LOBSTERS

The common lobster hardly needs to be described beyond the reminder that in life it is blue. Length 8-20 in. Among boulders, in crannies; but mostly off-shore. Widely distributed. Not so common as many would wish. *Homarus vulgaris* LOBSTER pl. 14.

Body brown with plum shades; pale-spotted hard spikes. Body 10-24 in. long, with equally long antennae. *No heavy nippers.* Usually below tide marks but also rarely among boulders and in pools. S. and W. coasts only. Not uncommon.
Palinurus vulgaris CRAWFISH OR SPINY LOBSTER pl. 14.

115

B. SQUAT LOBSTERS. Abdomen (tail) not reduced but carried tucked under body.

Body 3-6 in. long, *red with blue lines across it, and dots.* Between eyes short *sharply pointed rostrum with three spines on either side.* Nippers and first three pairs of legs spiny. Fierce. Lower shore. Under stones. Widely distributed. Not common. *Galathea strigosa* pl. 14.

Body usually about 2 in. long, but may be 3 in.; greenish-brown with perhaps little red flecks. Between eyes *rostrum of nine spikes, three large ones almost same size,* hinder pair smallest. *Nippers covered with scaly tubercles and have spines along outside only,* while " wrist and arm " joints have larger spines on inside. Lower shore. Under stones. Widely distributed. Common, particularly in spring.

Galathea squamifera pl. 14.

Body usually under 2 in. long, with nipper-legs adding about another 2 in. Dull red or orange-brown, sometimes uniform, sometimes patterned with pale marks. Between eyes flat rostrum covered with bristles, with *central spike and four on either side.* Nippers hairy. Lower shore. Widely distributed. Not common between tide marks.

Galathea dispersa pl. 14.

Body about ⅓ in. long, nippers another ⅔ in. Bright red with clean blue spots. *Each segment of under-folded tail has single furrow across it.* Between eyes rostrum not sharply pointed, but that point is longer than any of four unequal blunt spikes on either side, last pair of which is very small. Lower shore. Widely distributed. Not common between tide marks. *Galathea intermedia*

C. HERMIT CRABS.* Abdomen asymmetrical, not carried under body. Living in snail shells with opening closed with right, and larger, nipper.

Body usually 1-3 in. long, may be 5 in.; red and yellow dulling towards brown abdomen. Big nipper roughly granulated, with *two rows larger than rest converging towards outer end.* End joint of second and third pairs of legs carrying spines. Small projection of shell between eyes. Lower shore; particularly on sandy flats. Larger ones usually in shells of whelks (*Buccinum undatum*) (p. 140 and pl. xvi), often with anemone *Calliactis parasitica* (p. 60 and pl. 6) on the shell and with the polychaete worm, *Nereis fucata,* also occupying shell. Smaller hermits in variety of shells, e.g. topshells, winkles, small whelks, etc. These, and sometimes the larger, shells may have moss-like covering of hydroid, *Hydractinea echinata* (p. 48 and pl. 2) growing on them. Widely distributed. Very common.

Eupagurus bernhardus COMMON HERMIT CRAB pl. 15.

* To extract hermit crab hold lighted match under edge of shell. Hermit will then release its hold and no harm will be done; they will resist being pulled out direct and break in two.

Under its tail may be a yellowish, *non-granular* lump; see parasitic barnacle *Peltogaster paguri* (p. 93 and pl. vi).

Body 1-3 in. long, light reddish-brown. Big nipper only finely granulated. End joints of second and third pairs of legs without spines and with longitudinal grooves. Front of shell almost straight. Lower shore. Particularly on sandy flats. Usually associated with anemone, *Adamsia palliata* (p. 60 and pl. 6), (rarely with *Calliactis parasitica* (p. 60 and pl. 6), sometimes with *Hydractinia echinata* (p. 48 and pl. 2). Widely distributed but not common between tide marks. *Eupagurus prideauxi*

D. ABDOMEN REDUCED AND CARRIED UNDER BODY

i. **Small crabs with nippers and apparently only three pairs of legs** (fourth pair is much reduced and folds tightly across base of tail).

Body slightly longer than broad, to $\frac{1}{2}$ in. across; broad, flattened, nearly equal nippers another 1 in. Uniformly dirty grey-brown, sometimes reddish-brown. *Hairy*, particularly legs and outer edge of nippers and edge of shell. Middle and lower shore. Under stones, especially where resting on muddy gravel. Widely distributed. Abundant.

Porcellana platycheles BROAD-CLAWED PORCELAIN CRAB pl. 14.

Body almost round, about $\frac{1}{4}$ in. across, with unequal nippers adding another nearly $\frac{1}{2}$ in. Between eyes three lobes, middle one deeply grooved. Fine antennae nearly twice as long as shell. No hairs. Brown, with perhaps red or even yellowish tones and may be patterned. Clean, almost shiny. Lower shore. Under stones; in *Laminaria* (p. 225 and pl. xxxi) holdfasts. Widely distributed. Common.

Porcellana longicornis LONG-CLAWED PORCELAIN CRAB pl. 14.

ii. **Typical crabs with nippers and four pairs of legs**

(a) *Last joint of back legs flattened as a paddle;* may be rounded or pointed.

Shell 1-4 in. across, typically dark green, small ones may be boldly patterned with pale marks symmetrical about middle line. *Three blunt teeth between eyes, which in small ones may be indistinct, and five sharp teeth on either edge of shell* behind eyes. Last joint of back legs flat but sharply pointed. Tail of male five-jointed; of female seven-jointed. Middle and lower shore. On all kinds of beach and up estuaries. Widely distributed. Very common; our commonest crab. *Carcinus maenas* SHORE CRAB pl. 15.

Under tail of both sexes may be biscuit-coloured, *non-granular* mass of the parasitic barnacle *Sacculina carcini* (p. 93 and pl. vi).

Shell 2-5 in. across, reddish-brown with clean *blue joints and lines in legs.* Shell covered with fine pile of hair, giving muddy colour. *Red eyes. Between eyes 8-10 small points of which central pair are longest.* Five large teeth on either side of front edge of shell. Last joint of back legs flat and rounded. Fierce; when disturbed sits back on its tail with nippers held up and out in position of attacking defence. Lower shore. Under stones. S. and W. coasts. Common. *Portunus puber* FIDDLER OR VELVET CRAB pl. 15.

Shell about 2 in. across, reddish-brown, small ones paler; may be rough and scaly, with some hairs. *Between eyes three sharp teeth* much the same size as the five on either edge of shell. At inner corner of eye may be an extra point. End joint of last leg rounded and flat. Lower shore. Widely distributed. Only occasional between tide marks. *Portunus depurator* pl. 15

(*b*) *Pair of back legs not flattened*, but typical rounded walking legs.

Shell 2-10 in. across, roughly oval, uniformly pink-brown except darker claws, rather granular. Between eyes three small blunt lobes and outside eyes 10 large rounded lobes—a pie-crust edge. Middle and lower shore. Particularly rocky shores; under stones and seaweed. Widely distributed. Common.

Cancer pagurus EDIBLE CRAB pl. xii.

Shell 1-3 in. across, surface lumpy. *Between eyes line of shell broken only by groove in middle;* outside each eye four blunt, knobby teeth. Reddish-brown. *Nippers black, moving parts without grooves on surface.* Few hairs on legs. Lower shore. Under stones. S.W. coasts. Locally common. *Xantho incisus* pl. xii.

Shell 1-2 in. across; surface, although divided into parts, is not lumpy. *Nippers brown with grooves on moving parts.* Line of shell *between eyes finely beaded*, and with groove in middle. Legs quite hairy. Colour yellowish-brown, with perhaps red markings. Lower shore. Under stones. Widely distributed. Rare. *Xantho hydrophilus*

Shell to 1 in. across, usually less; brownish-red. Edge of shell between eyes minutely cleft; outside each eye five points on edge of shell, counting angle of eye socket as one. Nippers light brown, unequal, smaller one often with rough surface. Whole *animal hairy.* Lower shore. Under stones; in *Laminaria* (p. 225 and pl. xxxi) holdfasts. S. and W. coasts. Common.

Pilumnus hirtellus HAIRY CRAB pl. xii.

Shell scarcely ½ in. across; variable colours, green, brown or purplish-red, may be mottled. *Between eyes project three points*, outer two triangular and flat, middle one longer and more rounded. *Seven more teeth on either side* of the three. Small nippers. Lower shore. Among rocks; on gravel and seaweeds. Widely distributed. Rare. *Pirimela denticulata* pl. xii.

iii. Dark straw-coloured crab, with long, hairy antennae; shell much longer than broad. In sand

Shell of male 1 in. across and 1½ in. long; of female ½ in. across and ⅘ in. long. Regions of shell clearly defined to form pattern of mask. Between eyes two points; on each side of eye on edge of shell three teeth. Male nippers twice as long as body; in female nippers not longer than body. Lower shore. Widely distributed. Rare in far N. Not uncommon in S.

Corystes cassivelaunus MASKED CRAB pl. xii.

iv. Very small crabs, living in mussels or horse mussels, rarely in cockles or oysters

Shell of male ¼ in. across, female larger. Male is yellowish-grey, with symmetrical pattern. Female slightly translucent, brown above with yellow spot at front, and yellow tail with brown triangle in middle. Shell nearly round, in male tends to blunt point between eyes. Widely distributed. Rare in N., not uncommon S. and W.

Pinnotheres pisum PEA CRAB pl. 16

v. Spider Crabs

Shell 2-7 in. across. Reddish overall, with brown, pinkish, or even yellowish marks. *Between eyes two large points, almost horns; on side of shell about six hard spines and over shell many more, rather shorter but all sharp and hard.* Long, slender, hairy legs. Relatively small nippers. Lower shore. On sandy flats; among rocks and large seaweeds. S. and W. coasts. Common. In some years abundant. Infests lobster pots. *Maia squinado* SPINY SPIDER-CRAB pl. 16.

Shell about ½ in. across, *pale pink with black nippers*. Seven joints to tail. Two strong horns between eyes. About eight strong points and *regular pattern of warts on shell*. Legs rough with warts, particularly first pair which are twice as long as body. Deep-water animal that is rarely stranded on lower shore. Widely distributed.

Eurynome aspera pl. 16.

Shell an elongated triangle, usually 1¼-2 in. across. Dull purple-red. *Between eyes two points that converge and may be touching at tips.* No spines anywhere but body covered with tubercles. Eyes can be withdrawn into sockets. Although thinner than nippers, rest of legs are not much thinner and are longer. *Tail seven-jointed.* Body often almost completely covered with attached seaweeds and hydroids. Lower shore. Widely distributed. In pools; among seaweed. Not usually common. *Hyas araneus* pl. 16

Shell up to 1 in. across, usually less than $\frac{1}{2}$ in., triangular with rounded lower corners. Yellowish-brown. *Across front of shell four small warts; in middle just behind the four one much larger one.* Across base of shell row of three warts, middle one the smallest. Eyes can be withdrawn into sockets. Second pair of legs three times shell length. Other pairs successively shorter and thinner. *Tail six-jointed.* Often covered with seaweed and pieces of sponge. Lower shore. Widely distributed. In pools; among seaweed. Not uncommon. *Inachus dorsettensis* pl. 16.

As *I. dorsettensis* except that *on fore part of shell is a triangle of three warts,* one on each side in front and much larger one further back; and in middle of base of shell a group of three very small warts, not one prominent wart. *Inachus dorynchus*

Shell up to $\frac{1}{2}$ in. across. Usually reddish, but may be yellowish-brown. *Eight definite spines on shell. Eyes cannot be withdrawn into sockets.* Looks really spidery. Four pairs of legs much thinner and longer than first (nipper) pair, second pair being three times as long as body. This pair and third pair have pointed last joints; but *fourth and fifth pairs end in curved hook* (nail). All legs hairy. Lower shore. Under stones; among seaweeds. Widely distributed. Common. (Easily commonest of small spider crabs.)

Macropodia rostrata pl. 16.

E. BURROWING SHRIMPS.

Rather soft, thin carapace, laterally compressed. Large abdomen, broadest about middle of its length, not tucked under body, tail fan well developed. In permanent burrows in sandy mud. Fig. 79.

Fig. 79. *Upogebia* sp., x 1

i. One nipper much the larger

Body to 2 in. long, red or orange-yellow. Carapace smooth. Tail (abdomen) twice as long, second segment being as long as it is wide. Large nipper smooth; may be right- or left-handed; has very thick moving " finger " on which are stiff hairs. Lower shore. In muddy sand. Probably only S. and W. coasts. Locally may not be uncommon. *Callianassa subterranea*

ii. Nippers same size

Body about 1½ in. long. Colour sandy or greenish, may have small orange star-shaped flecks. *Nippers have large moving finger which comes down on fixed one not half the length.* Second pair of legs end in simple point. Lower shore. Burrowing in sand; under *Zostera* (p. 254 and pl. 40) on estuarine mud flats. S. and E. coasts. Locally may not be uncommon. Commensal bivalve, p. 168.

Upogebia spp. pl. xiii.

INSECTA

Insects

Insects are essentially land-living animals, of which only one is known to spend all stages of its life in the sea, and that occurs in the tropical Pacific. Numbers of two-winged flies (Diptera) lay eggs in rotting weed on the strandline. One of these, a midge, *Clunio marinus*, never leaves the shore; the female has no wings and the male appears to use its wings exclusively for skimming over the surface of pools. A few small beetles also live in this weed. On salt-marshes, below extreme high water of spring tides, other beetles, including ladybirds, occur. But only two insects warrant further mention here.

Six legs; no wings

Body to ½ in. long, grey, with dark bands; thin and tapering with hair-like point extending from tail nearly equal to length of body, shorter points either side. Antennae rather longer than body. Upper shore and above. In cracks in rocks; moves fast and can jump when exposed. Widely distributed. Common.

Petrobius maritimus BRISTLE-TAIL pl. xiii.

Body soft-blue, perhaps ⅛ in. long; usually on surface film of rock pools especially where these are small and very sheltered. Upper half of shore, often in groups together; also moving on rocks and weeds. Widely distributed. Common.

Lipura maritima (= *Anurida maritima*) pl. xiii.

CHILOPODA

Centipedes

Centipedes are characteristically land animals with long flattened bodies which are very obviously segmented. The head has a pair of conspicuous

121

feelers and also three pairs of jaws and the first body segment carries a pair of poison claws, all centipedes being carnivorous. The remaining body segments are all alike and each, apart from the last two, has a pair of jointed legs (millipedes have two pairs of legs to each segment).

One typical centipede of the Family *Geophilidae* has invaded the shore from the land. It is generally common on the upper half of the shore living under stones and in crevices and coming out by night to feed on barnacles and rough periwinkles. *Scolioplanes* (*Geophilus*) *maritimus*

PYCNOGONIDA

Sea-spiders

Sea-spiders are arthropods like the true, land spiders and like them they have four pairs of legs. There the resemblance ends. The pycnogonids have excessively thin bodies to the extent that branches of the stomach penetrate into the upper regions of the legs. The abdomen is rudimentary and carries no appendages. The head has two pairs of feeding appendages and also what are called ovigerous legs on which the *male* carries the eggs after they have been laid by the female. Sea-spiders are carnivorous, usually feeding on sea-anemones and other coelenterates. They are not common animals except in polar and deep seas.

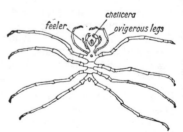

A
Feelers and chelicerae present.

B
No feelers or chelicerae.

Fig. 80. A sea-spider, *Nymphon* sp., x 3

A. FEELERS AND CHELICERAE PRESENT

Very *long and slender* creatures; body $\frac{1}{6}$-$\frac{1}{3}$ in., legs $\frac{3}{4}$-1 in. long; red or perhaps pinkish-yellow. *Chelicerae armed with nippers. Feelers with five joints.* Abdomen very small. Middle and lower shore. Under stones; among seaweed. Widely distributed. Common.

Nymphon spp. fig. 80.

B. NO FEELERS OR CHELICERAE

Rather knobby looking creatures, $\frac{3}{8}$ in. long; legs thick and clearly segmented, with strong claws at tips. Prominent conical rostrum. Nine joints to male's very short ovigerous legs. Dirty yellow or pale brown. Sluggish creatures. Lower shore. Under stones; on sea-anemones; among jetsam. Widely distributed. Probably common.

Pycnogonum littorale pl. xiii.

Particularly long-legged creatures. Body only $\frac{1}{8}$ in. long, with legs up to $\frac{4}{5}$ in. Green, brown or red. Lower shore. Among seaweeds and hydroids. May be commoner in S. than in N. *Endeis* sp.

Several other genera with bodies even smaller than $\frac{1}{8}$ in. may be found.

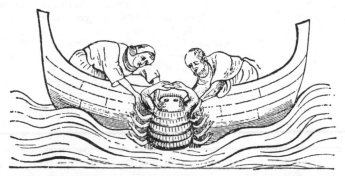

The sign Cancer, from a thirteenth century drawing reproduced in *A History of the British Stalk-Eyed Crustacea*

MOLLUSCA

Chitons, Marine Snails and Sea Slugs,
Bivalves, Elephant's Tusk Shells, Cuttlefish,
Squids and Octopods

THE MOLLUSCA are one of the largest and most important groups of marine animals. Three out of the five classes are confined to the sea, but both bivalves and snails occur in fresh water and the latter, with slugs, on land. Indeed certain snails are characteristic inhabitants of brackish or estuarine waters, so coming between marine and freshwater animals. It is difficult to outline the basic similarities between such externally dissimilar animals as limpets, snails, bivalves and cuttlefish. The original bilateral symmetry has been lost in the twisted and coiled snails. But broadly speaking all molluscs have a muscular organ, the *foot*, on the underside of the body and on or with this most of them either crawl or burrow. Above is the body with a head in front, although this has been lost in the bivalves whose shell encloses the whole animal. Over the back extends a fold of tissue called the *mantle* which forms the *shell*, a characteristic molluscan structure which may, however, be reduced or enclosed within the tissues or even lost altogether as in the sea slugs and the octopods. The shell may assume many forms characteristic of particular groups. Between the mantle and the underlying body there is a space known as the *mantle cavity* which represents the respiratory chamber where the gills are housed; in the land snails these are lost and the cavity functions as a lung. The typical feeding organ, absent only in the bivalves, is a horny lingual ribbon, the *radula*, carried on a muscular pad known as the *odontophore*. The radula bears rows of teeth, which are typically numerous and small in animals which scrape vegetation but few and large in carnivores.

Molluscs occupy every possible habitat in the sea, from burrowing and boring into the ocean floor to swimming in mid and surface waters, and are found from the shore to profound depths. Their feeding and other habits are remarkably diverse. No group of animals is so varied in outward appearance, largely owing to the manner in which the foot, body and mantle with the shell may be modified and their relationships to each other changed; such diversity of form has made possible diversity of habit. The five Classes of the Mollusca may now be considered.

LORICATA (Placophora)
Chitons or Coat-of-Mail Shells

Although often difficult to distinguish because they are small and usually the same colour as the rocks on which they live, chitons (fig. 81) will not be confused with other molluscs because they are flattened and oval-shaped and carry a series of *eight articulating shell plates* along the back. These are bounded by a *girdle* which overlaps the broad foot both laterally and behind and also the head in front (fig. 81). Between girdle and foot is a groove in which lie many small gills. Chitons have the habits of limpets; they occur always on rocks and stones, although sometimes when these are slimy with mud. Owing to the divided and articulating shell they can crawl over and grip irregular surfaces and, if

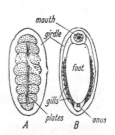

Fig. 81. Chiton ; a. from above, b. from below

detached, curl up (like the terrestrial pill-bug related to the woodlouse). Thus they can be rolled about by the waves and suffer no damage. British species are all small, seldom over ½-in. long; they are inconspicuous because pressed so tightly against the rock surface. Classification is difficult, depending in part on the manner of insertion of the shell plates, which must be removed and cleaned. Only a few species are common.

The Loricata are divided into two Orders but members of only one of these—the Chitonida—will be encountered. Species of three families occur:

Family *LEPIDOCHITONIDAE*

Broad girdle covered with fine granules or acicular spines; broad shell-plates with pronounced central keel.

Valves dull, girdle with minute irregular granules, marginal spines large and cigar-shaped. Red, brown or green. Average length, ½-in.; 16-19 pairs of gills. The commonest chiton, on all rocky shores, generally distributed between tide marks. *Lepidochitona cinereus* pl. xiv.

Valves smooth and shiny, girdle broad (ratio of shell-width to total width 0.6) with lozenge-shaped granules, usually reddish-brown, conspicuous " eyes " on first and last plates and on lateral areas of other plates. Very numerous gills. Lower shore and offshore. Generally distributed, not common. *Callochiton achatinus*

Valves smooth and spiny, girdle narrower (ratio 0.75) with many small ovoid granules fringed with spatulate spines. Gills, 10-15 pairs. Reddish-brown. About ½-in. long. Lower shore and offshore. Widely distributed and common.   *Tonicella rubra*

As preceding but with pale girdle bearing minute widely spaced granules. Reddish-brown with light patches. Gills usually over 19 pairs. The largest British chiton, up to 1 in. long. Lower shore and offshore. Confined to N. rare.   *Tonicella marmorea*

Family *CRYPTOCHITONIDAE*

Fairly broad girdle with spines and 18 to 20 conspicuous tufts of bristles. Plates with pronounced central keel. Gills, 10 to 15 pairs.

With 19 or 20 tufts of bristles, plates with fine round granules. Brown, ⅔-in. long. Lower shore and offshore. Generally distributed, not common.   *Acanthochitona discrepans*

With 18 tufts of bristles, plates with large pear-shaped granules unevenly distributed. Brown, yellow or red. About ½-in. long. Lower shore and offshore. Widely distributed, common in S. and W.

Acanthochitona crinitus pl. xiv.

Girdle very broad (ratio 0.35) with 18 tufts of bristles. Plates with very many minute rounded granules evenly distributed. Length ¾-in. Lower shore. Not common.   *Acanthochitona communis*

Family *ISCHNOCHITONIDAE*

Girdle with complete covering of relatively large smooth granules and fringed with small spines; plates narrow and somewhat glossy, pronounced keel.

Shell yellowish-white. About ⅓-in. long. Lower shore and offshore. Locally distributed.   *Ischnochiton albus*

GASTROPODA

Marine Snails, Limpets, Whelks, Sea Slugs, etc.

The largest of the molluscan classes with also much the greatest range in form and habit among its constituent species. Unlike other molluscs, the gastropods (or univalves) are fundamentally asymmetrical due to *torsion*, i.e. the rotation in an anti-clockwise direction in the horizontal plane, of the body with the mantle and the shell which cover it in relation to the head and the foot. This has occurred in the evolutionary history of these animals; it still takes place in developmental history. One consequence is that the respiratory chamber (mantle cavity) comes to lie behind the head (fig. 82). This is usually well developed and projects well ahead of the shell when the animal is moving; on it are situated the mouth and one or two pairs of tentacles and usually a pair of eyes. The foot is typically broad and used for creeping but it can be variously modified although not strikingly so in the animals here encountered.

The shell is always of one piece (univalve) and typically spirally twisted due to the manner of growth of the margins of the mantle which form it. It is thus asymmetrical but for different reasons than those responsible for torsion. The shell may become a symmetrical cone (after being spirally twisted during development) as it does in the different kinds of limpets or where it is reduced, a process which leads finally to its disappearance (though persisting in development) in the sea slugs which externally (though never internally) become bilaterally symmetrical.

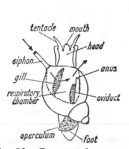

Fig. 82. Gastropod; general view of animal with inhalant siphon, extent of respiratory chamber (mantle cavity) indicated

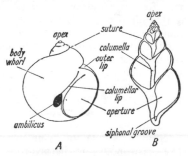

Fig. 83. Gastropod shells; a. with entire aperture and with umbilicus, b. lengthways section through siphonate shell showing columella

Shells are usually right-handed or dextral spirals; a few species are normally left-handed or sinistral and this condition occurs as a rare abnormality in others. (A shell placed with its opening downward and then observed from the summit will show clockwise coiling from apex to aperture if the shell is dextral, anti-clockwise if it is sinistral.) As shown in fig. 83, a shell is composed of *whorls* of which the last, and widest, is known as the *body whorl*. The line of union between whorls is a *suture* and the central pillar around which the shell coils is the *columella;* this may be solid or else hollow, in which case it opens by the *umbilicus*. The animal is attached to the shell by means of a muscle attached to the columella; contraction of this *columellar muscle* causes withdrawal of the animal which is extruded by relaxation of this muscle accompanied by forcing of blood into cavities within the head and the foot, i.e. by hydrostatic pressure. The aperture of the shell may be smooth or *entire* or else be extended into a grooved process, in some cases very long, due to a corresponding extension of the mantle edge which forms a siphon through which water enters the respiratory chamber. The shell aperture is then known as *siphonate*. The aperture of the shell in almost all marine snails, although in very few land ones, is closed by an appropriately shaped horny, sometimes limy, plug called the *operculum* and carried on the upper surface of the hind end of the foot.

Limpets differ from the more usual snail-like forms. The characteristic form and habit of life have been evolved by a number of gastropods quite independently so that there are many kinds of limpets. The cone-shaped shell represents the greatly enlarged last or body whorl, the apical whorls largely or completely disappearing. There is therefore no columella and the animals are usually attached by a horseshoe-shaped muscle leaving the head free to withdraw in front. When disturbed or left dry by the falling tide, limpets grip the rock surface tightly with the rounded foot and pull the shell firmly down around the body. They are then better protected than a periwinkle or a whelk with its operculum closing the opening of the shell.

Despite their name—the land slugs being notoriously unattractive—the sea slugs are amongst the most beautiful of marine animals, delicate in form and vividly coloured. They are common but often very small. The shell is either much reduced and largely or completely enclosed or else, as in the majority, it is absent and the animals have regained, at any rate externally, the bilateral symmetry of their ancestors.

Most gastropods are herbivorous, feeding on the fine vegetation which covers rocks or else browsing on seaweeds. In such animals the radula is broad with many small teeth in each row and it is drawn backward and forward over a muscular pad much as a rope may be moved to and fro over a pulley. The animals may also possess jaws. Other gastropods, including those with siphonate shells, are carnivorous, feeding on either living or dead animals. In these the radula is narrow with few and large teeth while the mouth usually lies at the end of a proboscis which, in one way or another, sometimes after boring through a limy shell, penetrates the body of the prey.

Classification of the Gastropoda is by way of anatomical features which are of little help to the shore naturalist, who in any case may not see the animal expanded; and, as already noted, the possession of a similar type of shell, as in the limpets, is no necessary indication of relationship. Moreover, many shore gastropods are very small, and so must be disregarded here; while some shells common on the shore are not those of animals which live there but must be mentioned because they are so obvious. So attention is confined to animals large enough to be identified without undue difficulty and will include certain shells that have

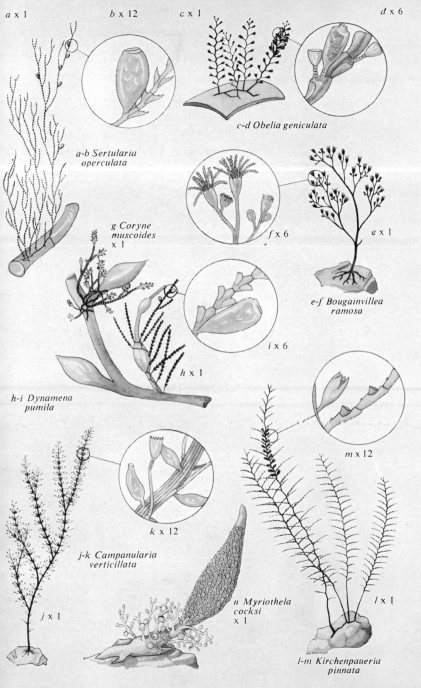

a x 1   b x 12   c x 1   d x 6

c-d Obelia geniculata

a-b Sertularia
operculata

g Coryne
muscoides
x 1

f x 6

e x 1

e-f Bougainvillea
ramosa

i x 6

h x 1

h-i Dynamena
pumila

m x 12

k x 12

j-k Campanularia
verticillata

n Myriothela
cocksi
x 1

l x 1

j x 1

l-m Kirchenpaueria
pinnata

HYDROIDS OR SEA-FIRS: COELENTERATA—HYDROZOA   1

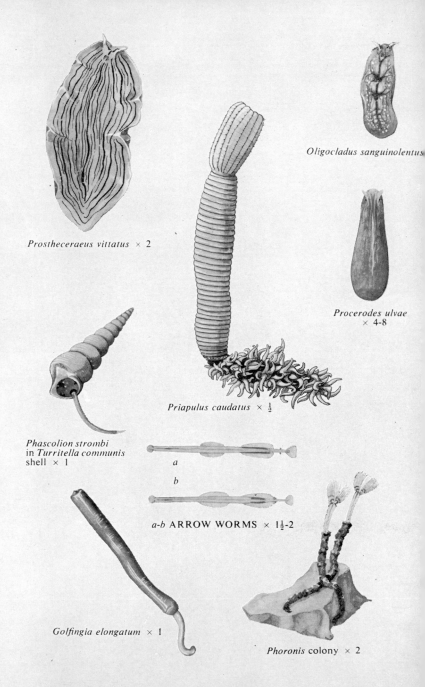

Prostheceraeus vittatus × 2

Oligocladus sanguinolentus

Procerodes ulvae
× 4-8

Phascolion strombi
in Turritella communis
shell × 1

Priapulus caudatus × ½

a

b

a-b ARROW WORMS × 1½-2

Golfingia elongatum × 1

Phoronis colony × 2

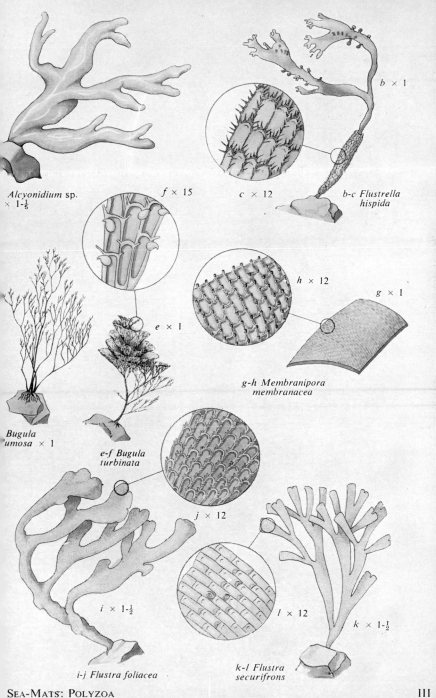

Alcyonidium sp.
× 1-⅕

b × 1

c × 12   *b-c Flustrella*
                    hispida

f × 15

e × 1

h × 12   *g* × 1

g-h Membranipora
membranacea

Bugula
umosa × 1

e-f Bugula
turbinata

j × 12

i × 1-½   *l* × 12   *k* × 1-½

i-j Flustra foliacea

k-l Flustra
securifrons

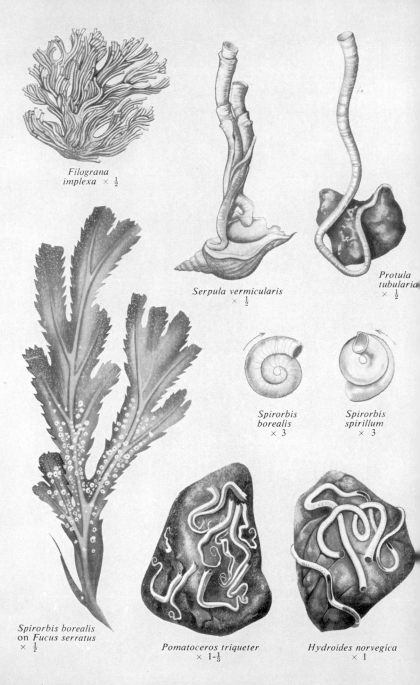

*Filograna
implexa* × ½

Serpula vermicularis
× ½

*Protula
tubularia*
× ½

*Spirorbis
borealis*
× 3

*Spirorbis
spirillum*
× 3

Spirorbis borealis
on *Fucus serratus*
× ½

Pomatoceros triqueter
× 1-⅓

Hydroides norvegica
× 1

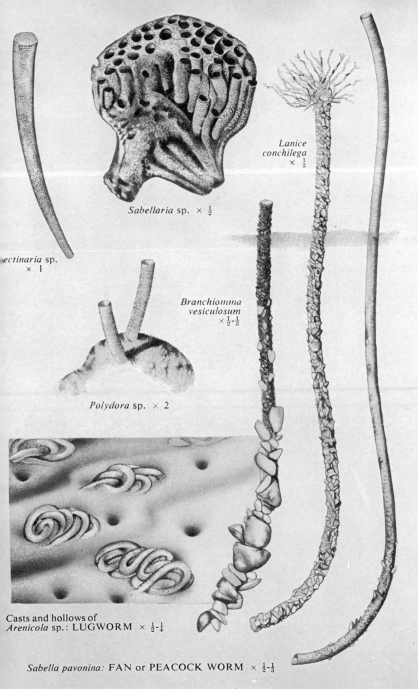

Sabellaria sp. × ½

Lanice conchilega × ½

ectinaria sp. × 1

Branchiomma vesiculosum × ½-⅓

Polydora sp. × 2

Casts and hollows of
Arenicola sp.: LUGWORM × ½-¼

Sabella pavonina: FAN or PEACOCK WORM × ½-⅓

TUBES OF BRISTLE WORMS : POLYCHAETA

V

a Verruca stroemia × 2-3

b Chthalamus stellatus × 2-5

c Balanus balanoides × 2-5

a-f ACORN BARNACLES

d Elminius modestus × 2-3

e Balanus perforatus × 1-2

f Balanus crenatus × 2-5

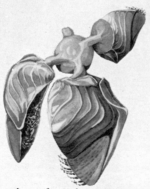

g Lepas fascicularis × 1

i Peltogaster paguri
ON HERMIT CRAB (*Eupagurus bernhardus*)

i-j PARASITIC BARNACLES × 1

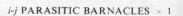

h Lepas [anatifera] × 1

g-h STALKED BARNACLES

j Sacculina carcini
ON SHORE CRAB (*Carcinus maenas*)

BARNACLES : CRUSTACEA—CIRRIPEDIA

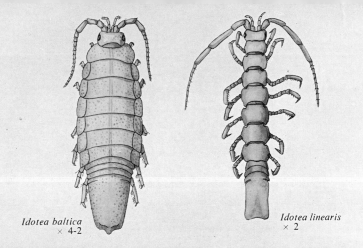

Idotea baltica
× 4-2

Idotea linearis
× 2

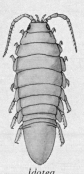

Idotea
neglecta
× 2

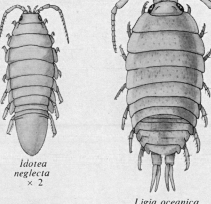

Ligia oceanica
SEA SLATER × 3-1

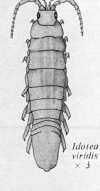

Idotea
viridis
× 3

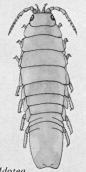

Idotea
emarginata
× 2

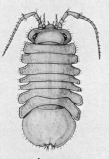

Jaera
marina
× 6

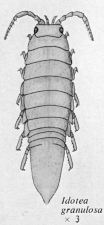

Idotea
granulosa
× 3

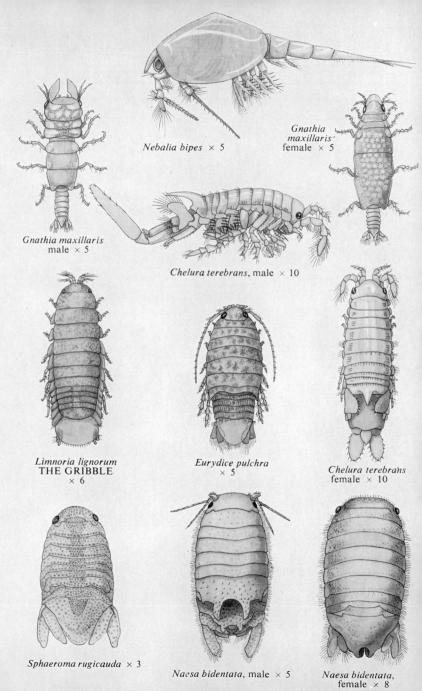

Nebalia bipes × 5

Gnathia maxillaris female × 5

Gnathia maxillaris male × 5

Chelura terebrans, male × 10

Limnoria lignorum THE GRIBBLE × 6

Eurydice pulchra × 5

Chelura terebrans female × 10

Sphaeroma rugicauda × 3

Naesa bidentata, male × 5

Naesa bidentata, female × 8

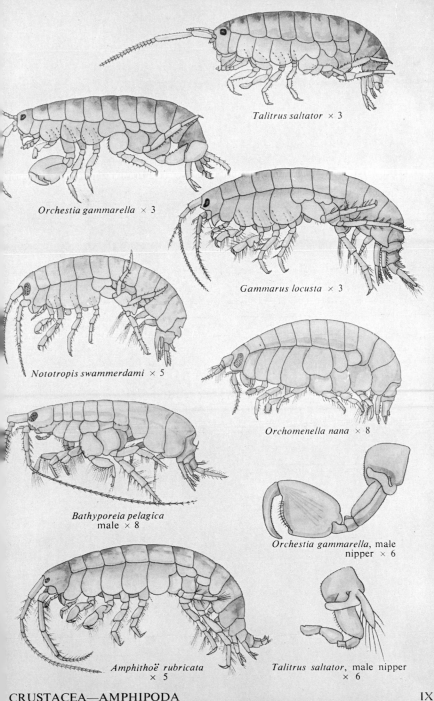

Talitrus saltator × 3

Orchestia gammarella × 3

Gammarus locusta × 3

Nototropis swammerdami × 5

Orchomenella nana × 8

Bathyporeia pelagica
male × 8

Orchestia gammarella, male
nipper × 6

Amphithoë rubricata
× 5

Talitrus saltator, male nipper
× 6

CRUSTACEA—AMPHIPODA

IX

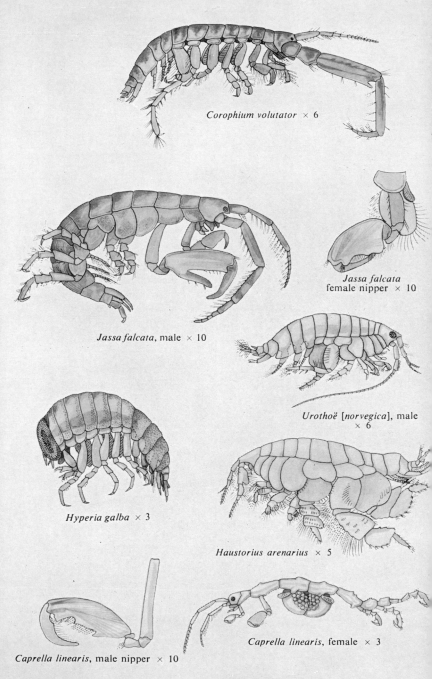

Corophium volutator × 6

Jassa falcata, male × 10

Jassa falcata
female nipper × 10

Urothoë [norvegica], male
× 6

Hyperia galba × 3

Haustorius arenarius × 5

Caprella linearis, male nipper × 10

Caprella linearis, female × 3

X

CRUSTACEA—AMPHIPODA

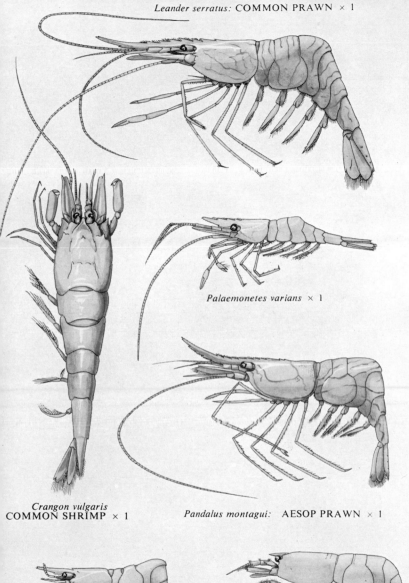

Leander serratus: COMMON PRAWN × 1

Palaemonetes varians × 1

Crangon vulgaris
COMMON SHRIMP × 1

Pandalus montagui: AESOP PRAWN × 1

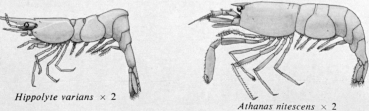

Hippolyte varians × 2

Athanas nitescens × 2

SHRIMPS & PRAWNS : DECAPODA

XI

Xantho incisus × 1-½

Corystes cassivelaunus
MASKED CRAB × ½

Pilumnus hirtellus: HAIRY CRAB × 1

Pirimela denticulata × 2

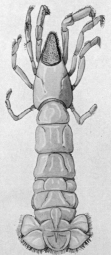

Upogebia [deltaura] × 1

Cancer pagurus: EDIBLE CRAB × 1-⅓

XII   CRABS & BURROWING SHRIMP : CRUSTACEA—DECAPODA

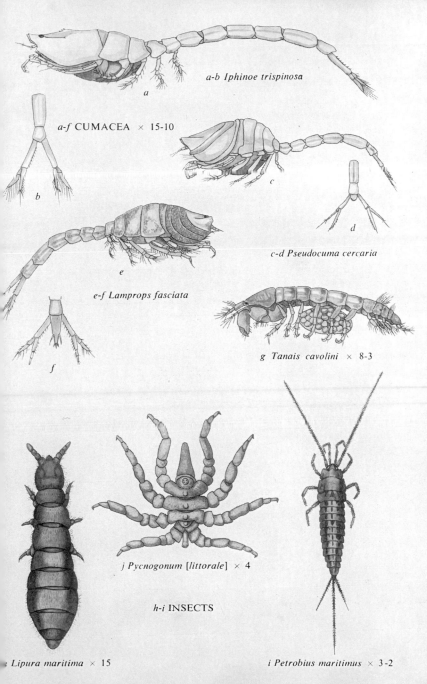

a-b Iphinoe trispinosa

a-f CUMACEA × 15-10

c-d Pseudocuma cercaria

e-f Lamprops fasciata

g Tanais cavolini × 8-3

j Pycnogonum [littorale] × 4

h-i INSECTS

Lipura maritima × 15

i Petrobius maritimus × 3-2

a–d CHITONS (COAT OF MAIL SHELLS)

a–b Lepidochitona cinereus
b shell plate & marginal girdle enlarged

a × 1

c–d Acanthochitona crinit
d shell plate & girdle
with spines enlarged

c × 1

Calliostoma zizyphinum
COMMON TOP SHELL
× ½

Cantharidus striatus
GROOVED TOP SHELL × ½

*Gibbula
lineata*
THICKTOP
SHELL × ½

*Gibbula
magus*
× ½

*Gibbula
cineraria*
GREY TOP
SHELL × ½

*Gibbula
umbilicalis*
FLAT or
PURPLE TOP
SHELL × ½

Littorina littorea
COMMON or EDIBLE PERIWINKLE
× 1

Tricolia pullus
PHEASANT SHELI
× 2

Littorina saxatilis
ROUGH PERIWINKLE
× 1

Littorina littoralis
FLAT PERIWINKLE
× 1

Littorina neritoide
SMALL PERIWINKL
× 2

Lacuna vincta
BANDED CHINK SHELL × 1

Clathrus clathrus
COMMON WENDLETRAP × 1

*Bittium
reticulatum*
NEEDLE SHELL × 2

a-d HYDROBIIDS

*a Peringia
ulvae
× 4*

*b-c Potamopyrgus jenkinsi × 4
c variety with keel*

*d Hydrobia ventrosa
× 4*

e-f Natica alderi
COMMON NECKLACE SHELL × 1
f appearance in life

g Natica catena
**LARGE NECKLACE SHELL
× 1**

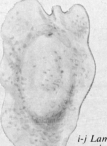

*k Trivia
arctica*

*h Velutina
velutina*
**VELVET
SHELL × 1**
(animal
not shown)

*i-j Lamellaria
perspicua × 1*

i from above

j from below

*l Trivia
monacha*

k-l EUROPEAN
COWRIES × 1

m Ianthina janthina
VIOLET SEA SNAIL × 1

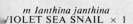

n Aporrhais pes-pelecani
**PELICAN'S FOOT SHELL
× 1**

o Turritella communis
TOWER SHELL × 1

MARINE SNAILS : MOLLUSCA—GASTROPODA   XV

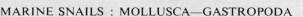

a-b *Nucella lapillus:* COMMON DOG WHELK × 1

a white shell
showing aperture

b brown banded
shell

c Urosalpinx cinerea
OYSTER DRILL
× 1

e Nassarius incrassatus
THICK-LIPPED DOG WHELK
× 1

d Ocenebra erinacea
STING WINKLE
× 1

*f Nassarius
reticulatus*
NETTED
DOG WHELK
× 1

g-h Buccinum undatum
COMMON WHELK × ½
g shell showing aperture
h side view with animal
expanded

g

i Neptunea antiqua: SPINDLE SHELL ×

WHELKS : MOLLUSCA—GASTROPODA

a outside of shell

Glycymeris glycymeris
DOG COCKLE
× ½

c

b inside of shell

e upper valve

e-f Anomia ephippium
SADDLE OYSTER × ½

d

c-d Arca tetragona: ARK SHELL
c inside, *d* outside of shell
× ½

f lower valve

g Monia patelliformis
RIBBED SADDLE OYSTER
upper valve × ½

j Tellina tenuis
× ½

l Ostrea edulis
NATIVE OYSTER
upper valve × ½

h Crassostrea angulata
PORTUGUESE OYSTER
upper valve × ½

l Macoma balthica
× ½

j-n TELLIN & RELATED SHELLS

k Tellina crassa
× ½

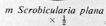

m Scrobicularia plana
× ½

n Pharus legumen × ½

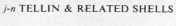

OYSTERS, TELLINS & OTHER BIVALVES : MOLLUSCA—LAMELLIBRANCHIA   XVII

a-d TROUGH SHELLS

a Spisula elliptica
× ½

b Spisula subtruncata
× ½

j Pandora albida
PANDORA SHELL
× ½

c Spisula solida
× ½

i Cardium exiguum
× ½

d Mactra corallina
× ½

g-i COCKLES

e Lutraria angustior
× ½

g Cardium edule
COMMON COCKLE
× ½

e-f OTTER SHELLS

f Lutraria lutraria × ½

h Cardium echinatum
PRICKLY COCKLE
× ½

a Lucinoma borealis
NORTHERN LUCINA
× ½

b Diplodonta rotundata
ROUND DOUBLE TOOTH
× ½

c Dosinia lupinus
SMOOTH ARTEMIS
× ½

e Venus striatula
× ½

d Dosinia exoleta
RAYED ARTEMIS
× ½

f Venus verrucosa
× ½

g–h VENUS SHELLS

g Venus ovata
× ½

i Venerupis rhomboides
× ½

h Venus fasciata
× ½

g–l CARPET SHELLS

l Venerupis saxatilis
× ½

j Venerupis decussata
× ½

k Venerupis pullastra
× ½

a Teredo norvegica: SHIPWORM
× ½

b Xylophaga dorsalis
WOOD PIDDOCK
× ½

c Pholas dactylus
COMMON PIDDOCK × ½

h Gastrochaena dubia
FLASK SHELL
× 1

d Zirfaea crispata: OVAL PIDDOCK × ½

c-j ROCK BORERS

e Barnea parva
LITTLE PIDDOCK
× 1

g Pholadidea loscombiana
PAPER PIDDOCK
× 1

i Petricola pholadiformis
"AMERICAN PIDDOCK"
× 1

f Barnea candida
WHITE PIDDOCK
× 1

j Hiatella arctica: WRINKLED ROCK-BORER ×

XX   BORING BIVALVES : MOLLUSCA—LAMELLIBRANCHIA

Eledone cirrhosa
CURLED OCTOPUS
× c. 1/10

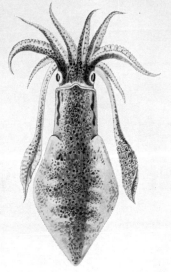

Loligo forbesi
COMMON SQUID
× c. 1/10

Sepiola atlantica
LITTLE CUTTLE × c. 1/2

Octopus vulgaris
COMMON OCTOPUS
× c. 1/10

Sepia officinalis
COMMON CUTTLEFISH
× c. 1/4

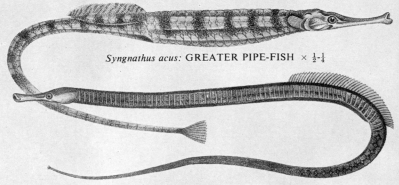

Nerophis lumbriciformis: WORM PIPE-FISH × ½

Syngnathus acus: GREATER PIPE-FISH × ½-¼

Entelurus aequoreus: SNAKE PIPE-FISH × ½-¼

Conger conger: CONGER EEL × ½-¼ [-¹/₁₀]

Anguilla anguilla: COMMON EEL × ½-⅙

Lepadogaster gouani
CORNISH SUCKER × 1-½

Lepadogaster bimaculatus
TWO-SPOTTED SUCKER × 1

Trachinus vipera: LESSER WEEVER × 1-½

Agonus cataphractus: ARMED BULLHEAD × 1-½

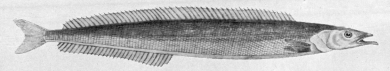

Ammodytes lancea: LESSER SAND-EEL × 1-½

Onos mediterraneus: THREE-BEARDED ROCKLING × 1-½

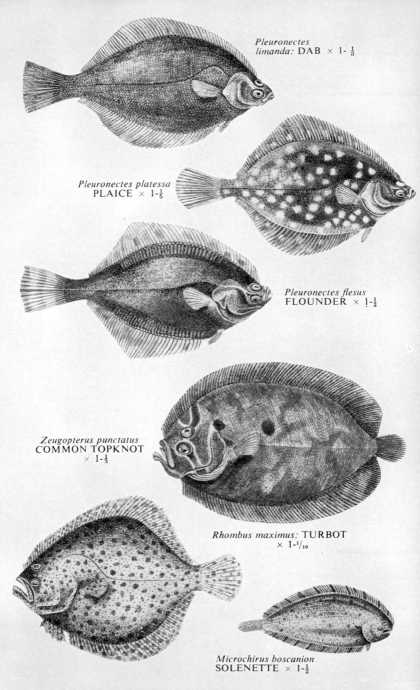

Pleuronectes limanda: DAB × 1-$\frac{1}{3}$

Pleuronectes platessa PLAICE × 1-$\frac{1}{5}$

Pleuronectes flesus FLOUNDER × 1-$\frac{1}{3}$

Zeugopterus punctatus COMMON TOPKNOT × 1-$\frac{1}{3}$

Rhombus maximus: TURBOT × 1-$\frac{1}{10}$

Microchirus boscanion SOLENETTE × 1-$\frac{1}{2}$

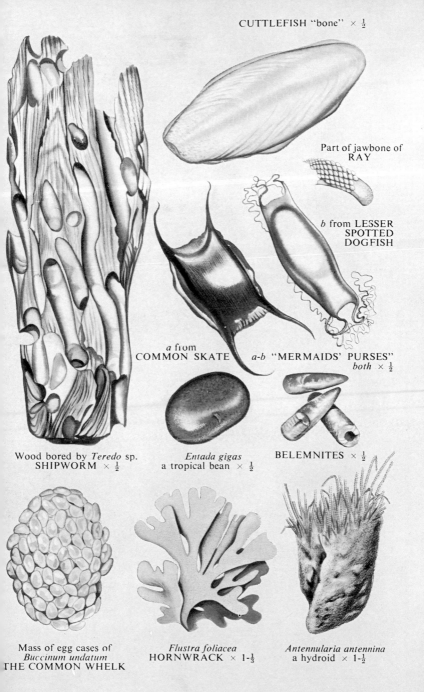

CUTTLEFISH "bone" × ½

Part of jawbone of
RAY

b from LESSER
SPOTTED
DOGFISH

a from
COMMON SKATE

a-b "MERMAIDS' PURSES"
both × ½

Wood bored by *Teredo* sp.
SHIPWORM × ½

Entada gigas
a tropical bean × ½

BELEMNITES × ½

Mass of egg cases of
Buccinum undatum
THE COMMON WHELK

Flustra foliacea
HORNWRACK × 1-⅓

Antennularia antennina
a hydroid × 1-½

THE STRANDLINE

XXV

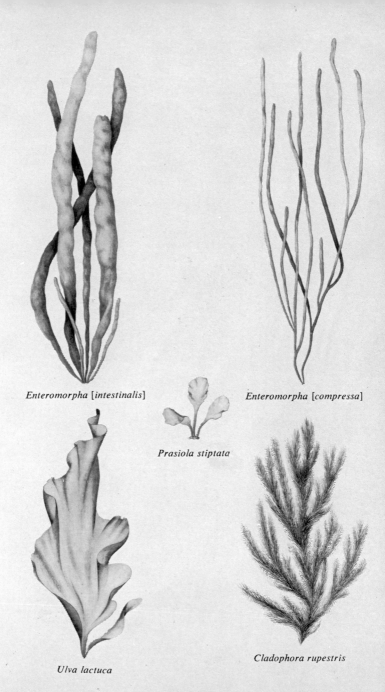

Enteromorpha [*intestinalis*]

Enteromorpha [*compressa*]

Prasiola stiptata

Ulva lactuca

Cladophora rupestris

GREEN SEAWEEDS : CHLOROPHYCEAE

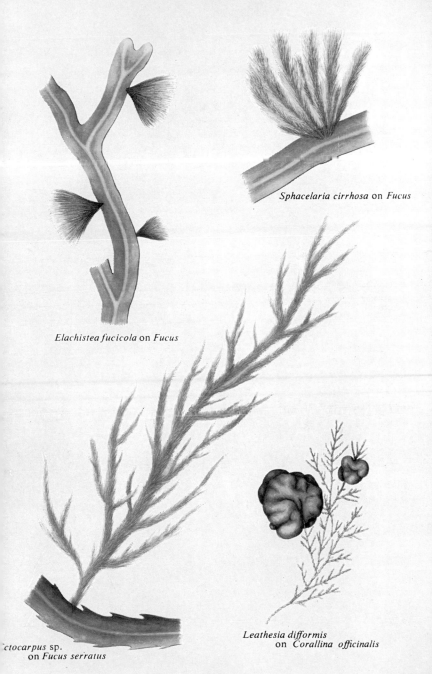

Sphacelaria cirrhosa on *Fucus*

Elachistea fucicola on *Fucus*

Ectocarpus sp.
on *Fucus serratus*

Leathesia difformis
on *Corallina officinalis*

BROWN SEAWEEDS : PHAEOPHYCEAE XXVII

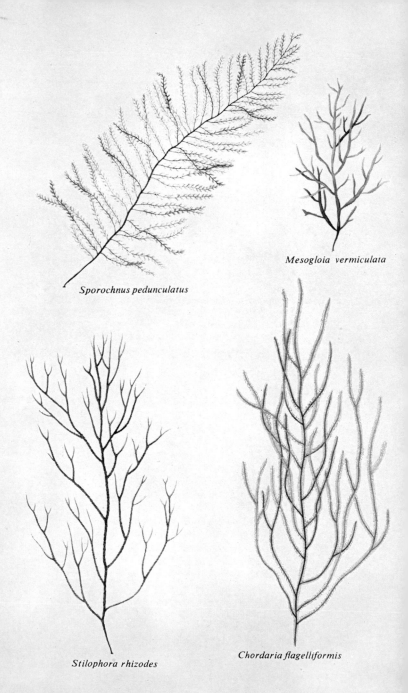

Sporochnus pedunculatus

Mesogloia vermiculata

Stilophora rhizodes

Chordaria flagelliformis

BROWN SEAWEEDS : PHAEOPHYCEAE

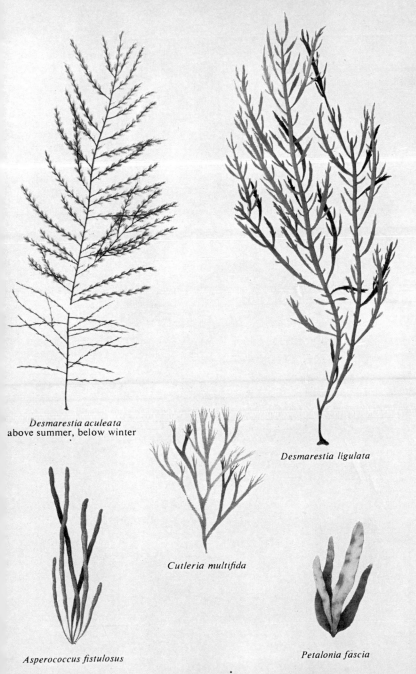

Desmarestia aculeata
above summer, below winter

Desmarestia ligulata

Cutleria multifida

Asperococcus fistulosus

Petalonia fascia

BROWN SEAWEEDS : PHAEOPHYCEAE

XXIX

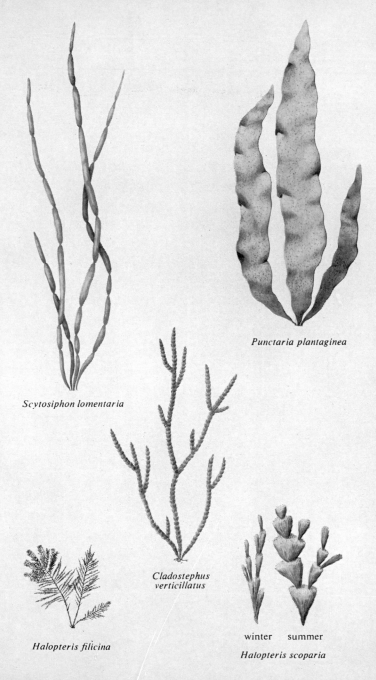

Punctaria plantaginea

Scytosiphon lomentaria

Cladostephus verticillatus

Halopteris filicina

winter   summer

Halopteris scoparia

BROWN SEAWEEDS : PHAEOPHYCEAE

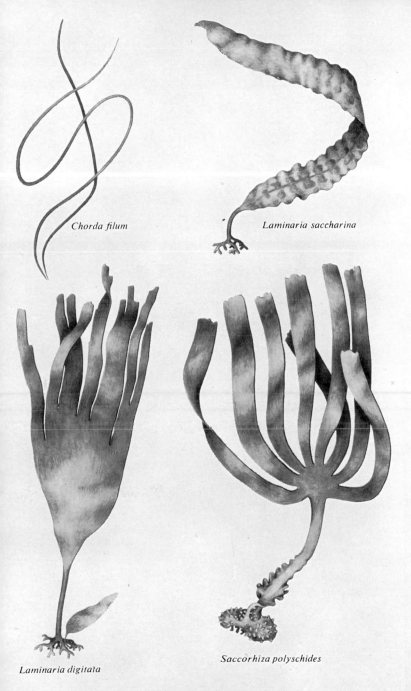

Chorda filum

Laminaria saccharina

Laminaria digitata

Saccorhiza polyschides

BROWN SEAWEEDS : PHAEOPHYCEAE   XXXI

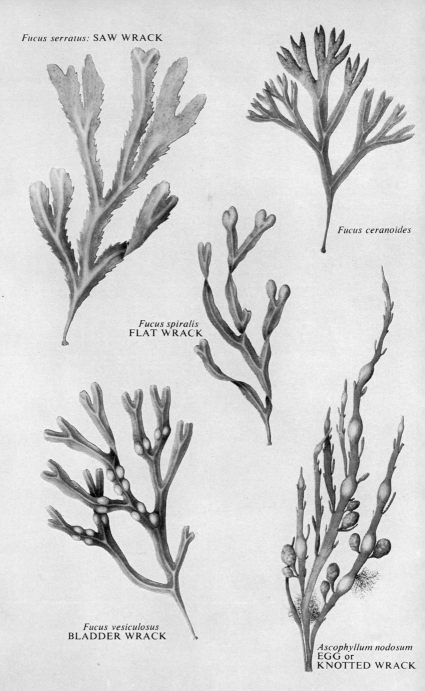

Fucus serratus: SAW WRACK

Fucus ceranoides

Fucus spiralis
FLAT WRACK

Fucus vesiculosus
BLADDER WRACK

Ascophyllum nodosum
EGG or
KNOTTED WRACK

BROWN SEAWEEDS : PHAEOPHYCEAE

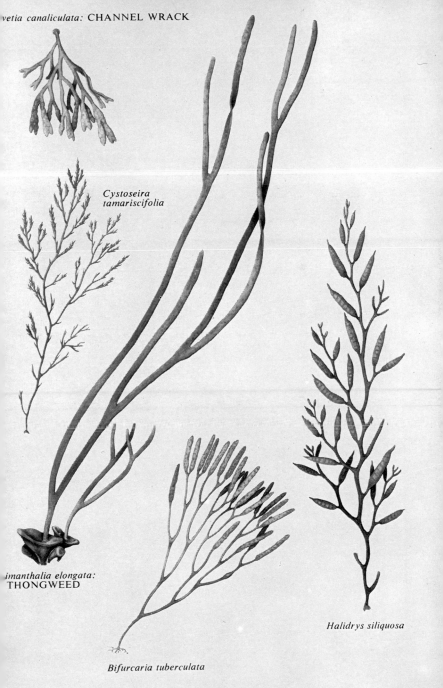

...vetia canaliculata: CHANNEL WRACK

Cystoseira tamariscifolia

...imanthalia elongata:
THONGWEED

Bifurcaria tuberculata

Halidrys siliquosa

BROWN SEAWEEDS : PHAEOPHYCEAE   XXXIII

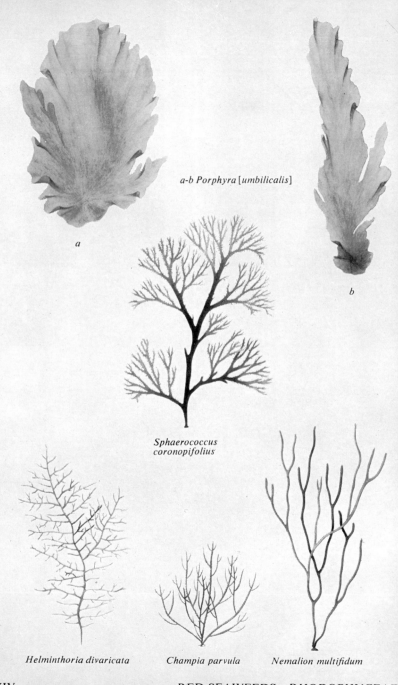

a-b Porphyra [umbilicalis]

Sphaerococcus coronopifolius

Helminthoria divaricata

Champia parvula

Nemalion multifidum

RED SEAWEEDS : RHODOPHYCEAE

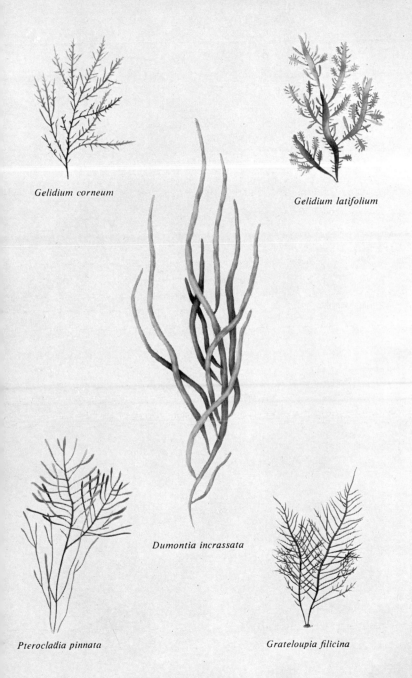

Gelidium corneum

Gelidium latifolium

Dumontia incrassata

Pterocladia pinnata

Grateloupia filicina

RED SEAWEEDS : RHODOPHYCEAE

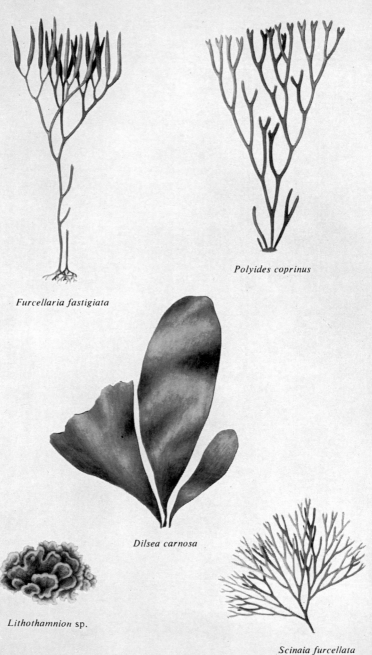

Furcellaria fastigiata

Polyides coprinus

Dilsea carnosa

Lithothamnion sp.

Scinaia furcellata

RED SEAWEEDS : RHODOPHYCEAE

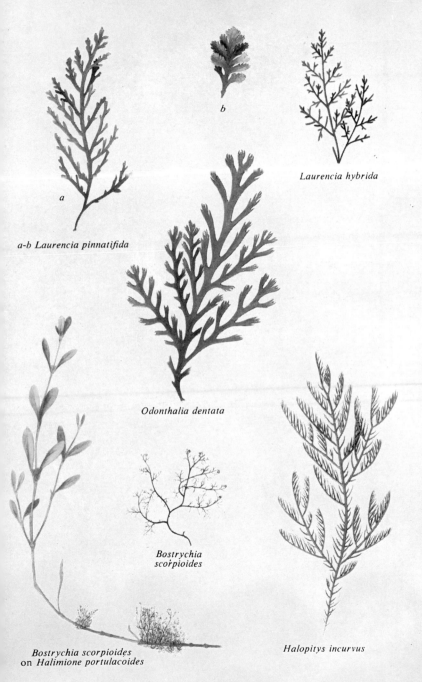

b

Laurencia hybrida

a

a-b Laurencia pinnatifida

Odonthalia dentata

Bostrychia scorpioides

Bostrychia scorpioides on *Halimione portulacoides*

Halopitys incurvus

RED SEAWEEDS : RHODOPHYCEAE   XXXVII

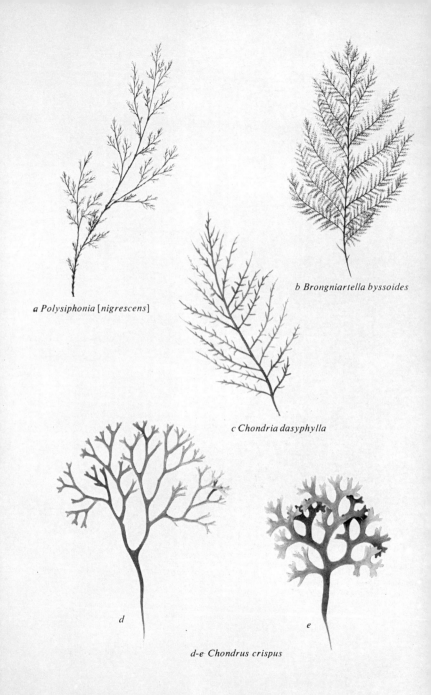

a Polysiphonia [*nigrescens*]

b Brongniartella byssoides

c Chondria dasyphylla

d

e

d-e Chondrus crispus

RED SEAWEEDS : RHODOPHYCEAE

Gigartina stellata

Phyllophora membranifolia

Gymnogongrus griffithsiae

Callophyllis laciniata

Ahnfeltia plicata

RED SEAWEEDS : RHODOPHYCEAE   XXXIX

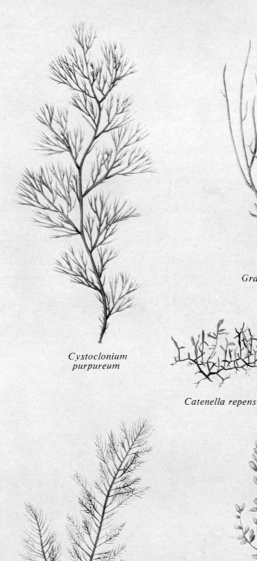

Cystoclonium
purpureum

Gracilaria verrucosa

Catenella repens

Gastroclonium ovatum

Lomentaria
clavellosa

RED SEAWEEDS : RHODOPHYCEAE

housed animals that live on the sea bottom some distance offshore. Using the modern system of classification, the attempt is made to employ characters which can be distinguished by the field naturalist.

Sub-Class PROSOBRANCHIA. Animals with respiratory cavity containing gills in front of body, i.e. showing full effects of torsion. One pair of tentacles on head. Shell, with rare exceptions, large enough for animal to withdraw completely closing aperture with operculum; if limpets then shell can be drawn down over the animal.

Order Archaeogastropoda. Shell spirally twisted or else of limpet form. If the former, aperture smooth and usually round. Always browsing on rocks or stones, never on or in soft substrata of sand or mud. Essentially consist of three groups:

i. Limpets with one or more openings in shell (see Plate 17).
ii. Limpets with imperforate shells, without internal ledge or curved over-arching apex (see Plate 17).
iii. Top shells, i.e. broad based shells, conical or rounded; if surface worn, showing underlying mother-of-pearl (or nacreous) layer. Often with umbilicus (fig. 83); aperture rounded and closed with a horny, or limy, spirally marked operculum. Animal with tentacles on sides of foot, with single feathery gill. Always on clean surfaces, rock or weed.

Order Mesogastropoda. Difficult to define; shell usually spirally coiled, may be rounded and squat or tall and pointed; aperture and operculum vary greatly. Usually broad foot, very varied habits. If limpets, have shelf within shell or else have curved over-arching apex (see Plate 17). Includes winkles, chink shells, necklace shells, cowries, etc.

Order Stenoglossa. May generally be referred to as whelks; aperture siphonate (see Plate xvi); animals usually living in or on soft substrata obtaining clean water for respiration by way of upward projecting siphon. Specialised carnivores with mouth and radula at tip of proboscis.

Sub-Class OPISTHOBRANCHIA. Animals—usually sea slugs—with gills lateral or posterior; shell reduced or absent (present in development); if a shell, rarely an operculum. With two pairs of tentacles, hind pair known as rhinophores and concerned with smell. Often of striking form with feathery gills or other processes on back or sides; usually beautifully coloured. Must be *viewed alive in sea water*, otherwise appear as slimy mass; cannot be preserved to retain appearance in life. Usually crawling, foot broad or narrow. Extremely varied feeding and other habits. Convenient classification is:

i. Shell usually reduced, may be absent, single large gill in reduced cavity (Tectibranch Sea Slugs). (Plate 18.)

(a) Shell external, animal may not be able to withdraw within it.

(b) Shell internal and much reduced: may be detected as a hard lump by gently rubbing along back with finger.

(c) Shell absent.

ii. No shell, numerous exposed gills or other processes on back (Nudibranch Sea Slugs). (Plates 19-21.)

iii. No gills or other processes.

(a) Body elongate and smooth.

(b) Body rounded and tuberculate.

Sub-Class **PULMONATA**. Snails and land slugs, without gills respiratory chamber converted into lung. No operculum.

PROSOBRANCHIA

ARCHAEOGASTROPODA

i. Limpets with one or more openings in shell

The most primitive of existing gastropods because have *two* gills. These are ciliated, producing a water current which enters the respiratory cavity on either side of the head and, after passing through the gills, leaves through the shell openings (fig. 84).

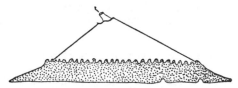

Fig. 84. *Diodora* (Keyhole Limpet); appearance in life, stippled area is the foot which overlaps edge of shell, apical siphon with outgoing current

Shell with series of openings. *Haliotis*

Shell with single apical opening. *Diodora*

Shell with marginal slit. *Emarginula*

Shell very flattened spiral with series of openings, new ones formed as shell grows and oldest ones closed; usually five open and functional. Up to 4 in. long. Lower shore and below. Mediterranean species extending as far N. as Channel Isles, where common.

Haliotis tuberculata ORMER Plate 17.

No trace of spiral coiling, shell ribbed with apical opening. When expanded, mantle tissues extend around margin of shell and obscure head (fig. 84), tubular process protrudes through apical opening. Up to 1½ in. long. Lower shore and below. Not uncommon, widely distributed in S. and W.

Diodora (*Fissurella*) *apertura* KEYHOLE LIMPET Plate 17.

Marginal slit on anterior border of ribbed shell; apex slightly curved. Mantle tissues not extending around shell but tubular process protruding through upper part of slit. About ½-in. long. Lower shore and below. Not uncommon, widely distributed.

Emarginula reticulata SLIT LIMPET Plate 17.

ii. **Limpets with imperforate shells,** without internal ledge or curved over-arching apex.

Shell surface smooth, flattened cone with apex nearer to anterior margin, without ring of gills between mantle margin and foot (fig. 85).
Acmaea

Ditto, but with ring of gills around foot (fig. 85). *Patina*

Shell surface rough and ribbed and margin crenate. Ring of gills round head and foot (fig. 85). *Patella*

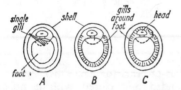

Fig. 85. Limpets viewed from below; a. *Acmaea*, b. *Patina*, c. *Patella*

Flattened, rather delicate shell; usually irregular, reddish-brown markings giving tortoiseshell appearance, hence easily distinguished. Animal with single large gill in cavity behind head. About 1 in. long. Lower shore and below. Common in N. absent in S.

Acmaea tessulata (*testudinalis*) TORTOISESHELL LIMPET Plate 17.

Similar to above but shell off-white with pink or brown rays and more solid. Apex nearer anterior. Under ½-in. long. Lower shore and below, especially among *Laminaria* (p. 225). Widely distributed and common. *Acmaea virginea* WHITE TORTOISESHELL LIMPET Plate 17.

Shell smooth, translucent, characteristic lines of vivid blue spots from apex to margin. Shell becomes more solid with age and loses spots. Under 1 in. long. Lower shore and below, typically on *Laminaria* (p. 225) in depressions eaten out by animal; younger animals on stipe or frond; older in holdfasts. Widely distributed, very common. *Patina (Helcion) pellucida* BLUE-RAYED LIMPET Plate 17.

Patella—much the commonest genus of limpets; found in great numbers on all rocky shores, with rough and ribbed shells. No mistaking *Patella* but careful examination of shell (especially interior as shown in Plate 17) and of animal needed to distinguish between the three species.

Shell typically tall, though variable; internal surface white or yellowish with head scar white to brown. Tentacles fringing mantle (projected around shell when animal moving) transparent. Up to 2½ in. long. Universally common on all rocky shores.

Patella vulgata COMMON LIMPET Plate 17.

Shell flatter with finer ribs and margin marked with dark rays. Interior dark with head scar cream to orange. Foot usually dark. Marginal tentacles opaque. 1½ in. long. Exposed shores only, not so high on shore as *P. vulgata*. Confined to S.W.

Patella intermedia (*depressa*) Plate 17.

Shell even flatter than in *P. intermedia*, apex nearer anterior, marginal rays usually absent. Interior porcellaneous, head scar pale orange to cream. Foot orange. Marginal tentacles cream. Also restricted to exposed shores but lower down than others, high on shore only in pools encrusted with calcareous weeds. S.W., W. and extreme N.E.

Patella aspera (*athletica*) Plate 17.

iii. **Top Shells,** i.e. broad-based shells, conical or rounded; if surface is worn show underlying mother-of-pearl (or nacreous) layer. Often with umbilicus; aperture rounded and closed with a horny (or calcareous) spirally marked operculum. Animal with tentacles on sides of foot, with single feathery gill. Always on clean surface, rock or weed.

Shell sharply pointed cone, large, 10-12 whorls. *Calliostoma*

Shell sharply pointed, small, 6-8 whorls. *Cantharidus*

Shell blunt, deep sutures. *Gibbula*

Characteristically straight-sided shell with flat base, forming regular pyramid, yellow or pink with red streaks; white variety also. The largest top shell, about 1 in. high and broad. Lower shore and below. Widely distributed, common.

Calliostoma zizyphinum COMMON OR PAINTED TOP SHELL Plate xiv.

Somewhat more sharply pointed, higher than broad. Surface with obliquely running ridges, white streaked with red, brown or black. Rare on shore, may be found on eel-grass (p. 254). S.W. only.

Cantharidus striatus GROOVED TOP SHELL Plate xiv.

Three other species of this genus occur but typically below shore levels.

Rounded conical shell of six whorls, grey or greenish with overlying zigzag blackish purple streaks, (cf *Littorina littorea* below). *Aperture of shell mother-of-pearl* curve sweeping round to umbilicus bears *single tooth*. Adult shells have apex always eroded and yellow. Large shell, about 1 in. tall and broad. Middle shore. S.W., between Dorset and Anglesey, locally very common.

Gibbula (Monodonta or *Osilinus) lineata* THICK TOP SHELL OR TOOTHED
WINKLE Plate xiv.

More flattened, very solid shell, eight whorls with irregular ridges and knobs, conspicuous ridge round base, wide and deep umbilicus. Yellow with oblique streaks red or purple. Under 1 in. high, rather broader. Lower shore and below. S. and W., not uncommon.

Gibbula magus Plate xiv.

Less flattened shell, usually seven whorls, lower ones flattened. *Light grey with dark grey narrow stripes*. Umbilicus small. Variable in shape, usually about ½-in. high and broad. Middle and lower shores. Widely distributed, very common.

Gibbula cineraria GREY TOP SHELL Plate xiv.

Resembling above but flatter; *greenish background on which are broad purplish stripes*. About ½-in. high. Middle to top of lower shore. S. and W., locally abundant.

Gibbula umbilicalis FLAT OR PURPLE TOP SHELL Plate xiv.

Shell taller than broad, glossy, last whorl more than half total height, often yellow with reddish lines or spots. Conspicuous *limy* operculum. About ⅓-in. high. S. and W., often common.

Tricolia pullus (Phasianella pulla) PHEASANT SHELL Plate xiv.

MESOGASTROPODA

These gastropods may most conveniently be considered in relation to where they will be found, (i) on rocky shores or on stones, (ii) in sand or washed up on the shore, (iii) or on in estuarine mud.

. **Rocky Shores or Stones**

(a) *Rounded Shells*—Winkles, Chink Shells (Fam. *Littorinidae*). Solid, rounded shells of few whorls, never pearly when worn, operculum horny and ear-shaped. Long head tentacles.

Littorina (Winkles), shell without umbilicus, columella smooth. Commonest genus of intertidal gastropods on rocky shores.

Small, pointed, fragile and smooth shell, dark coloured with bloom on surface reminiscent of that on blue grapes. Up to ½-in. high, a little less in breadth. Largely above upper shore (i.e. in splash zone), especially in crevices on rock (fig. 87). Widely distributed, commonest in the most exposed areas.

Littorina neritoides SMALL PERIWINKLE Plate xiv.

Shell ¼-½-in. high, with 6-9 whorls, *sutures deep.* Very variable in colour, red to black, definitely rough to the touch. As it approaches junction with spire the *curve of aperture of the shell continues and meets the spire at right angles.* Upper and top of middle shore. Widely distributed, very common.

Littorina saxatilis (rudis) ROUGH PERIWINKLE Plate xiv.

Shell seldom as much as ½-in. high; rounded, sometimes *flat-topped not pointed spire;* surface with fine sculpturing appearing initially smooth. Aperture large. Colour most variable, yellow, orange, green, red, purple, brown or streaked. Middle and top of lower shore, especially on *Fucus* (p. 226) on surface of which lays egg capsules (fig. 86). Widely distributed, very common.

Littorina littoralis (obtusata) FLAT PERIWINKLE Plate xiv.

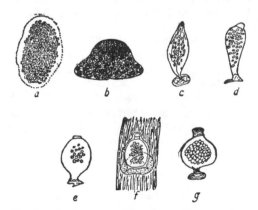

Fig. 86. Attached spawn of common Gastropods; a. *Littorina littoralis* (gelatinous on *Fucus*, etc.), b. *Natica catena* (collar-shaped, gelatinous with included sand grains), c. *Nucella lapillus*, d. *Ocenebra erinacea*, e. *Urosalpinx cinerea* (c.-e. flask-shaped, attached to rock), f. *Nassarius reticulatus* (on eel-grass), g. *Nassarius incrassatus.* Varying magnifications

Shell usually ½-1 in. high, sharply pointed, with marked surface sculpturing, usually dark grey-black or red, always with *concentric* (cf *Gibbula lineata* above) darker lines. Curve of aperture deflected as approaches junction with spire to meet tangentially. Middle shore and below, on rocks and weed. Widely distributed, very common.

Littorina littorea COMMON OR EDIBLE PERIWINKLE Plate xiv.

Small shell of six whorls; pointed apex and with umbilicus; surface semi-transparent and shining yellow usually with conspicuous reddish bands. About ½-in. high. Lower shore and below, on weeds. Widely distributed, very common. *Lacuna vincta* BANDED CHINK SHELL Plate xiv.

Several other species of this genus occur but usually only below tidal levels.

(*b*) *Tall-spired Shells*. A variety of shells of this shape occur, especially low on the shore (these apart from *Turritella* and *Aporrhais* mentioned later among shells that may be found washed up). Two are here described and figured and others are mentioned. They belong to various groups, shape being no necessary indication of relationship.

Small shell in form of high pointed spire, some ½-in. high but only ⅛-in. wide, no umbilicus, almost circular operculum, 15-16 whorls, surface covered with coarse nodules (may be rubbed smooth), reddish-brown if intact. Lower shore and below, on debris, etc. Widely distributed, usually common.

Bittium (Cerithium) reticulatum NEEDLE SHELL Plate xiv. Related species include *Triphora (Cerithium) perversa* with a *sinistral* shell about ⅓-in. long. Confined to south and west.

Shell of 15 whorls with deep separating sutures and very striking ridges crossing each whorl at right angles. Among the most beautiful of British shells, attaining length of 1½ in. Dubiously a true shore species but may occur in extreme low levels of lower shore. Widely distributed. *Clathrus clathrus (Scalaria communis)* COMMON WENDELTRAP Plate xiv.

Other tall-spired shells to be found at the lowest shore levels include the white, smooth-shelled species of *Turbonilla* and *Odostomia*, ectoparasitic, e.g. on oysters and scallops. Over the shore generally are the many species of the *Rissoidae*, most of them with minute shells, among the largest being the banded-shelled *Cingula cingillus* found in crevices or in barnacle shells high on the upper shore (fig. 87).

(*c*) *Limpets*. Representatives of two families of mesogastropod limpets, *Calyptraeidae* and *Capulidae*, may be found. The former have a conspicuous ledge, a modified columella, within the shell, the latter have a higher shell with apex curved like a cap of liberty. In both the gill is enlarged and acts also as the feeding mechanism, filtering fine particles from the water current it creates, i.e. like a bivalve.

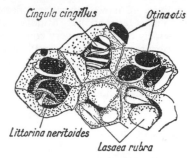

Cingula cingillus *Otina otis*

Littorina neritoides

Lasaea rubra

Fig. 87. Group of small molluscs (three gastropods, one bivalve) in empty barnacle shells from crevice in middle shore.

Shell round with central, low, apex; internal ledge oblique, in posterior half of shell. Smaller male individuals live on shells of larger females; later become females themselves. Lower shore, attached to small stones or shells. SW coasts, locally distributed.

Calyptraea chinensis CHINAMAN'S HAT Plate 17.

Shell oval, up to 1½ in. long, ledge horizontal, brownish. Live in chains (fig. 88) of up to 12 individuals, the oldest being females, the youngest males, i.e. changing sex as they grow. Lower females fertilised by upper males resultant egg capsules deposited within shell of female. Species introduced from North America with oysters about 1880. Enormously prolific and now a major pest on oyster beds round[1] south-east and south coasts to S. Wales; smothers oysters as well as competing with them for food.

Crepidula fornicata SLIPPER LIMPET Plate 17.

Fig. 88. *Crepidula* (Slipper Limpet); chain of eight individuals

Shell with pronounced curved apex and light-coloured, remainder of shell covered with dark horny layer; usually marked concentric growth lines. Only occasionally at lowest levels of lower shore, commoner offshore on rocks but also on scallops and oysters; large individuals females, males probably small and more active. Widely distributed but never common.

Capulus ungaricus BONNET LIMPET Plate 17.

(*d*) *Cowries.* Highly characteristic with body whorl growing over and enclosing all earlier whorls and aperture forming a longitudinal slit along under surface. Mantle tissues when extended cover all the shell and there is a short siphon in front. The numerous, large and brightly coloured tropical cowries are here represented by two very small species.

Shell about ½-in. long, with 20-25 ribs, white in contrast to brightly coloured mantle. On rocks feeding on compound sea squirts on which are deposited vase-shape egg capsules.
With three brownish-purple spots on shell. Lower shore and below. Widely distributed, common.

Trivia monacha (da Costa) (*Cypraea europaea*)
EUROPEAN COWRIE Plate xv.

With no spots, slightly smaller than preceding species. Extreme low levels of shore and below. Widely distributed but less common (less accessible). *Trivia arctica* Plate xv.

(*e*) *Slug-like.* There is a tendency in all groups of gastropods for the shell to be enclosed within the mantle (as it is, although only when mantle is extended, in the cowries). In the family *Lamellariidae*, the shell is reduced and either completely or almost completely enclosed. Unlike the true sea slugs, however, there is but one pair of tentacles, apart from major differences in internal anatomy.

Shell not completely enclosed, oval in shape, of 3½ whorls, body whorl much the largest (i.e. limpet-like), covered with velvety pale brown horny layer. Mantle tissues thick and yellow. Lowest shore levels feeding on *Alcyonium* (Dead-men's-fingers) (p. 61). Widely distributed, not common.

Velutina velutina (*laevigata*) VELVET SHELL Plate xv.

Shell completely enclosed, transparent of 2½-3 whorls; trace only of spire. Animal usually yellow but variable, general form indicated in Plate, where upper and under surfaces shown; head only visible from below. Up to 2 in. long but often smaller on shore. Lower shore and below, under stones feeding on compound sea squirts. Widely distributed but local. *Lamellaria perspicua* Plate xv.

ii. In Sand or Washed up on the Shore

A large family of mesogastropod carnivores, the *Naticidae*, has representatives the world over, all burrowing in sand and feeding on bivalve molluscs, penetrating the shell with a proboscis. All have rounded, very polished shells with a large umbilicus. The operculum is ear-shaped and spirally wound. The foot is very large and reflected over much of the shell (see Plate xv). The egg masses consist of spirally wound collars of jelly with embedded sand grains (figs. 86 and 179).

Shell yellowish-brown with spiral rows of darker or reddish spots, six whorls, large aperture with thick inner lip partly covering umbilicus.

Some ¾-in. in all diameters. Within sand on lower shore and below. Widely distributed and often common.

Natica alderi COMMON NECKLACE SHELL Plate xv.

Shell pale yellow with reddish markings, short spire and seven rounded whorls. Some 1½ in. in all diameters. Within sand on lower shore and especially below. Widely distributed but local.

Natica catena (*monilifera*) LARGE NECKLACE SHELL Plate xv.

Three shells in particular should be mentioned among those which may be found washed up; all are large and of characteristic appearance.

Long tapering shell with up to 19 whorls, the first 10 each with three ridges; up to 2¼ in. long; rounded aperture. Extremely common in muddy gravel at moderate depths, burrowing into this, drawing in suspended material by action of gills. Empty shells often common on shore.   *Turritella communis* TOWER SHELL Plates ii and xv.

Turreted shell with much ornamented whorls and characteristic expanded outer tip of aperture (in fully grown shell) which is bordered by processes or " digitations " giving appearance of pelican's foot. Aperture and so operculum elongate. Also very common burrowing in muddy gravel at moderate depths and empty shells not uncommon.

Aporrhais pes-pelecani PELICAN'S FOOT SHELL Plate xv.

Rounded, snail-like shell, thin end of a beautiful violet colour. May be found washed up on western shores during the summer. Like the siphonophores *Physalia* and *Velella* (see p. 54), this snail lives in the surface waters of the Atlantic, having a float of mucus in which air bubbles are trapped. Rarely intact animals are carried on to the shore.

Janthina janthina VIOLET SEA SNAIL Plate xv.

iii. In Estuarine Mud

An exception is here made by considering animals which are very small but which may be so numerous that the surface of the mud appears granular. These are the hydrobiid snails, three species of which are here considered.

Shell elongate; usually six whorls with shallow sutures, aperture pointed at top. Much the commonest hydrobiid in salt-marshes and estuaries, often eating sea lettuce, *Ulva* (p. 220). Widely distributed.

Peringia (*Hydrobia*) *ulvae* LAVER SPIRE SHELL Plate xv.

Shell more glossy and thick-set; 5½ whorls, last one large, deep sutures. Some individuals with keel (see Plate) running round whorls. Viviparous, also parthenogenetic (no males found). In estuaries higher up, i.e. less saline conditions, than *P. ulvae*. Widely but sporadically

distributed, much commoner in the fresh waters it has recently invaded.
Potamopyrgus (*Hydrobia* or *Paludestrina*) *jenkinsi* (Smith) JENKINS'S
SPIRE SHELL Plate xv.

Shell pointed, 6 or 7 whorls, deep sutures, last whorl not so prominent,
aperture rounded. In all types of brackish and estuarine waters.
Widely but not continuously distributed especially on south and east
but also on west coasts. *Hydrobia ventrosa* (Montagu) Plate xv.

NEOGASTROPODA (STENOGLOSSA)

May be referred to as *whelks*. Shell aperture siphonate with siphon
projecting upward from this (see Plate xvi) so that clean water drawn in
from above mud, etc. Carnivorous with mouth and radula at end of long
proboscis which is extended through opening of "false" mouth. In all
species here described shell thick and sculptured with pointed spire and
oval operculum. Whelks easy to distinguish as such although less easy
to distinguish between different species.

On rocks in barnacle zone, sometimes with mussels, usually very
numerous. Shell a short cone with short siphon and with many flat
spiral ridges. Usually off-white, may be yellow or, where feeding on
mussels, banded with brown (see Plate xvi). Up to 1 in. tall. Egg capsules, like grain of corn (fig. 86, p. 134) attached at one end, common
especially in crevices. Chief predator of barnacles. Widely distributed,
very common. *Nucella* (*Purpura*) *lapillus* COMMON DOG WHELK
Plate xiv.

Shell more pointed, 8 to 10 whorls, up to 2 in. high, well-marked
sutures and rugose longitudinal as well as spiral ridges. Siphonal canal
closed after growth stops (see Plate). Off-white with dark streaks. Feeds
on bivalves including young oysters, also on barnacles, drilling through
shell. On rocks and muddy gravel on lower shore and below but coming
ashore between April and June to spawn characteristic egg capsules
(fig. 86d, p. 134). Pest on oyster beds but exterminated by cold winters
of 1939-40 and 1946-47 along east coast but now returning; common
in south-west and Wales.

Ocenebra (*Murex*) *erinacea* STING WINKLE OR DRILL Plate xvi.

Resembling above but smoother and smaller, 6 to 7 whorls with less
pronounced and more regular ridges. Siphonal canal never closed,
typically twisted. Brownish. Introduced from North America with
imported oysters on young individuals of which it feeds like *O. erinacea*
but more serious pest and more hardy. Similar habits, spawning on
shore in April and May, flask-shaped egg capsules (fig. 86e, p. 134)
usually attached to stones or other objects raised above bottom.
Confined at present to coast of Essex and around Whitstable.

Urosalpinx cinerea AMERICAN OYSTER DRILL Plate xvi.

Nassarius—shells smaller with well-developed spire and only short siphonal canal, so unlikely to be confused with Drills. Same general habitat as these but are scavengers. When foot expanded seen to be divided into two " tails " behind. Two common species:

Shell of ten whorls with network of ridges and grooves, pale brown, up to 1½ in. long, outer lip crenated. Flat egg capsules (fig. 86f, p. 134) laid in rows on eel-grass (p. 254), etc. Lower shore or below, often on sand. Widely distributed, common.

Nassarius reticulatus (*Nassa reticulata*) NETTED DOG WHELK Plate xvi.

Shell about half as high, 8-10 more rounded whorls, pronounced longitudinal ribs. Brownish with dark bands and brown blotch on base. Egg capsules (fig. 86g, p. 134) laid separately. Rocky and stony areas. Lower shore and below. Widely distributed, common. *Nassarius incrassatus* (*Nassa incrassatus*) THICK-LIPPED DOG WHELK Plate xvi.

Larger shell, 7-8 well sculptured whorls with deep sutures, yellow large oval aperture with wide and short siphonal canal (but long projecting siphon). Offshore may reach 6 in., usually much smaller on shore. Egg capsules laid in large sponge-like masses (see Plate xxv). On muddy gravel or sand. Lower shore and below. Widely distributed, common. *Buccinum undatum* COMMON WHELK OR BUCKIE Plate xvi.

Shell of similar size, spindle-shaped, whitish, smooth surface but with very pronounced ridged whorls, aperture with long siphonal canal. Seldom found alive on shore but empty shells not uncommon in north, often occupied by hermit crab. Confined to north (both coasts).

Neptunea antiqua (*Fusus antiquus*) SPINDLE SHELL Plate xvi.

OPISTHOBRANCHIA

1. **Shell usually reduced, may be absent, with single large gill in reduced cavity (Tectibranch sea slugs).**

   (*a*) *Shell external*, animal may not be able to withdraw within it.

   Oval, well-developed shell of seven whorls, pink to brown with white bands. Animal can be completely withdrawn and elongate aperture closed by operculum. When expanded, mantle partly reflected over shell and head lobes, used for burrowing, extended. Lower shore and below, in sandy bays. Widely distributed but local and normally buried although empty shells may indicate its presence.

   Actaeon tornatilis ACTAEON SHELL Plate 18.

   Coiled thin shell with reduced spire and aperture full length of shell, no operculum. Thick fleshy body cannot be withdrawn. Tentacles flattened, large foot with upward projecting lobes (parapodia) used for swimming. On muddy sand usually in deep sheltered bays. Probably widely distributed but very local. Two species:

Oval, very fragile shell with projecting outer lip.
Haminoea navicula (da Costa) (*Bulla hydatis*) Plate 18.

Oblong, more solid shell, outer lip not projecting. *H. hydatis* (L.).

Shell details much as above, animal elongate with better developed parapodia; animal swimming actively especially in spring around breeding season, otherwise wrapped around shell as shown in plate. Long filament projects backward through notch near spire of shell. On mud flats or beds of eel-grass (p. 254). Widely distributed but local. *Akera bullata* Plate 18.

(b) Shell internal and much reduced

Shell thin, translucent, flattened, effectively enclosed and may not be noticed in body, which reaches lengths of 6 in., changing colour with age from red, to brown then olive-green, variously spotted. Ejects purple slime when disturbed. Crawls actively but can also swim with parapodia. Offshore among *Laminaria* (p. 225), etc. but comes ashore to spawn in summer depositing long strings of orange or pink spawn around weed, etc. Widely distributed, may be locally extremely common but varying in numbers from year to year.
Aplysia punctata SEA HARE Plate 18.

Shell entirely enclosed and of no structural importance, large soft body with prominent feathery gill on right side. Broad reddish foot, no parapodia; back reddish-brown and tuberculated, not over-hanging foot. Up to 5 in. long. Feeds on large simple sea squirts. Muddy gravel bottom usually, comes inshore in summer. Widely distributed, locally common in some years.
Pleurobranchus (*Oscanius*) *membranaceus* Plate 18.

Similar to above but less than half its size, body smooth and yellow with white markings, gill free at tip. On rocks and in empty shells, usually below tide levels. In pools and under rocks on lower shore. Widely distributed, not uncommon. *Berthella plumula* Plate 18.

Other Tectibranchs which may occasionally be encountered on the shore include the " lobe shell," *Philine aperta*, with a translucent body spotted with white, about 1 in. long and enclosing a thin white shell retaining an indication of spiral twisting. This animal occurs in quantity on sandy bottoms in shallow water and may be washed ashore after storms.

(b) Shell absent

Elongated, slug-like animal with gill projecting at hind end; tissues smooth, black merging into brown at sides, only ¼-in. long. In rock pools. Widely distributed, locally common.

Pelta coronata (Runcina hancocki) Plate 18.

ii. No Shell, numerous exposed gills or other processes on back (Nudibranch sea slugs)

These naked-gilled sea slugs include the most beautiful animals living on British shores. A selection has here been made of those most likely to be encountered during summer months when they tend to come inshore to spawn and then to die; they are annuals. Care will be needed to find many of them. They are mainly carnivorous although with a great range of feeding habits. All here mentioned are illustrated in colour, these being copied from the figures in the Monograph on British Nudibranchs by Alder and Hancock with supplement by Eliot (see p. 257), the names there used (where different from the modern ones) and the plate numbers being given.

Family DORIDIDAE

The anus lies in the mid-line of the back near the hind end and is surrounded by a *ring of plumed retractile gills*. There are no other processes.

Elliptical in shape, yellowish foot, upper surface tuberculated and yellow blotched with green, pink or brown. Nine large tripinnate gills. Commonest and second largest (2-3 in. long) of British intertidal nudibranchs. Feeds on the bread-crumb sponge, *Halichondria* (p. 42). Lays coiled white egg ribbons about 1 in. wide and 2 in. long. Widely distributed, very common. *Archidoris pseudoargus* SEA LEMON Plate 19

(A. & H. Fam. 1, plate 3 as *Doris tuberculata*)

Smaller, not more than ½-in. long, red with small tubercles and black spots on back, hinder pair of tentacles (rhinophores) yellow, 10 pinnate gills. Feeds on red sponges and difficult to detect. South, not uncommon. *Rostanga rufescens* Plate 19.

(A. & H. Fam. 1, plate 7 as *Doris coccinea*)

Yellowish with scattered brown spots and fine tubercles on back, body depressed laterally, up to 2 in. long and resembling *A. pseudoargus* but with 15 white tripinnate gills. Widely distributed, seldom common. *Jorunna tomentosa* Plate 19. (A. & H. Fam. 1, plate 5 as *Doris johnstoni*)

Dead white, rounded opaque white tubercles with row of yellowish-white spots along each side. About 1 in. long, five small tripinnate gills. May crawl on surface film in pools, but usually under stones. North, commoner on east coast. *Cadlina laevis* (L.) Plate 19.

(A. & H. Fam. 1, plate 6 as *Doris repanda*)

Family POLYCERIDAE

Ring of plumed gills around anus *not* retractile, may be additional lateral processes.

Body elliptical, back with tubercles and handsomely mottled with brown on white background, numerous (over 20) pinnate gills, circle incomplete behind. Feeds on barnacles. About 1 in. long. Widely distributed, common. *Onchidoris fusca* Plate 19.
(A. & H. Fam. 1, plate 11 as *Doris bilamellata*).

Body oval, very small, thin and flat; back with tubercles and yellowish with red and brown spots, radiating lines due to spicules visible through translucent tissues, 10-11 very small gills. Feeds on sea-mat *Membranipora*. Widely distributed, commonest in north. *Onchidoris muricata* Plate 19. (A. & H. Fam. 1, plate 12 as *Doris aspera*)

Body humped and covered with rows of large tubercles, brownish with red spots on each tubercle and large dark areas with brilliant turquoise spot in centre; unmistakable. Three large tripinnate gills with three branched tubercles in front. Widely distributed, never common.
Aegires punctilucens Plate 19. (A. & H. Fam. 1, plate 21)

Body smooth and elongate with pronounced keel down centre, about 1 in. long. Usually pink speckled with white, may be yellow or white; tentacles yellow; 13 large pinnate gills. Feeds on sea squirts and sea mats. Breeding in March. Widely distributed, common.
Goniodoris nodosa Plate 20 (A. & H. Fam. 1, plate 18)

Body reddish-brown with white spots, foot large, conspicuous pale ridge down centre of body; about 1 in. long; 7-9 dark tripinnate gills. Feeds on sea squirts. South and south-east, occasionally common.
Goniodoris castanea Plate 20. (A. & H. Fam. 1, plate 19)

Body translucent white with yellow spots in four lines down sides; occasionally darkly marked animals. Tentacles and additional four head processes all tipped with yellow; 7-9 pinnate gills with backwardly pointed, yellow-tipped processes on each side. $\frac{1}{2}$-$\frac{3}{4}$-in. long. Often on hydroids or sea mats attached to *Laminaria* (p. 225). Widely distributed, only locally common. *Polycera quadrilineata* Plate 20.
(A. & H. Fam. 1, plate 22)

Body elongate and depressed, white with some 24 deep yellow-tipped processes around front and sides and orange-coloured tubercles on back; three long bipinnate gills. Under 1 in. long. Widely distributed, rarely common on shore. *Limacea clavigera* Plate 20.
(A. & H. Fam. 1, plate 20 as *Triopa claviger*)

Body oval and very convex, white to brownish-purple, conspicuous backward pointed tentacles (rhinophores), up to 1 in. long; nine pinnate gills. Feeds on sea-mats *Flustrella* (p. 172) and *Alyconidium* (p. 174). Widely distributed, generally common. *Acanthodoris pilosa* Plate 20. (A. & H. Fam. 1, plate 15 as *Doris pilosa*)

Body elongate, transparent white with yellow markings resembling *Polycera quadrilineata* but 10 orange-tipped tentacles form ring around three large bipinnate gills. Head, tentacles and processes, also hind end of foot coloured. About ½-in. long. Widely distributed, often common in spring. *Ancula cristata* Plate 20. (A. & H. Fam. 1, plate 25)

Body about ½ in. long, yellow to white, 11 pinnate gills. Feeds on sea-mats. Lower shore. Widely distributed except S and SW. *Adalaria proxima* (A. & H. Fam. 1, Plate 9 as *Doris proxima*)

Family IDULIDAE

Slender animals, bearing on the back processes known as *cerata*, in this case elliptical and resembling fir-cones, in a single row down each side of body. These cerata, here and elsewhere, contain stinging cells (nematocysts) obtained from the coelenterates—hydroids or anemones—on which they feed. *No gills* round anus. Rhinophores smooth.

Body pale with crimson markings, about ½-in. long, 5-7 pairs of cerata appearing too large for the delicate body and readily detached. Slender tentacles (rhinophores) arising from large trumpet-shaped sheaths. Feeds on hydroids, especially *Sertularia* (p. 51) growing on fucoids, etc. and lays spawn on them. Widely distributed, seldom common. *Doto coronata* Plate 20. (A. & H. Fam. III, plate 6)

Family AEOLIDIDAE

Very numerous clustered cerata, may extend in front of rhinophores. Anus lateral; foot with lateral processes but short behind.

Body slender and tapering, usually under 1 in. long; rhinophores surrounded with delicate spirally running yellow ridges; 4-6 clusters of cerata, bright crimson tipped with white, in some lights appearing blue. Widely distributed, often common in south and west. *Facelina auriculata* Plate 21. (A. & H. Fam. III, plate 12) as *Eolis coronata;* also as *Eolis drummondi*

Body covered, except in mid-line, by dense mass of brownish-grey or greenish cerata giving appearance of fur. The largest British nudibranch, may exceed 3 in. Between tide-marks usually on underside of stones or below boulders, feeding on sea-anemones; spiral egg ribbons laid within jelly. Widely distributed, very common.

Aeolidia papillosa COMMON GREY SEA SLUG Plate 21.
(A. & H. Fam. III, plate 9 as *Eolis papillosa*)

Family TERGIPEDIDAE

Few and large cerata in single row on each side; foot very narrow and prolonged behind.

Body and cerata transparent with green colour of viscera seen through, large club-shaped cerata with pinkish tips, four on each side, alternating. Only ¼-in. long. On hydroids attached to *Laminaria* (p. 225), etc. Widely distributed, not usually common. *Tergipes despectus* Plate 21.*
(A. & H. Fam. III, plate 36 as *Eolis despecta*)

Family STILIGERIDAE

Cerata more numerous, no jaws but with " ascoglossan " radula, i.e. with one large spoon-shaped tooth in each row. Members of this and of the two succeeding families—which have no cerata—constitute the *Ascoglossa*, all are very small and feed on seaweeds by piercing with the radula and then sucking out the fluid contents; they have been compared to plant bugs among the insects.

Body flattened and small, up to ½-in. long, no head tentacles, some 15 cerata on each side with front and middle regions of body left bare. Olive-green to brownish with white spots. Typical inhabitants of muddy estuaries among eel-grass (p. 254) or in salt-marshes usually on green weed *Vaucheria*. East coast and around Irish Sea, very local.
Alderia modesta Plate 21 (Eliot, plate VII. figs. 3-5)

iii. No Gills or other processes

(a) Body elongate and smooth

Family ELYSIIDAE and LIMAPONTIDAE

Neither cerata nor gills; body smooth.

Elongate body with lateral lobes, dark green with white spots, white along margins of lateral lobes and around eyes; under ¼ in. long. Lives and feeds on *Codium* (p. 223) and other green weeds. Widely distributed on south and west, rare on east. *Elysia viridis* Plate 21.
(Eliot, plate VII, figs. 1, 2).

Body oval, no lateral lobes, light fawn to velvety brown, lighter along sides and around eyes; tentacles present; about ¼-in. long. On green weed in pools. Widely distributed but easily overlooked. *Acteonia senestra* Plate 21. (Eliot, plate VII, figs. 10, 11 as *Cenia cocksii*).

*This figure is a mirror image.

MOLLUSCA

Minute animal, only ⅛-in. long, brownish to black with tentacles reduced to pale coloured crests with eyes in bright patches. In rock pools to top of middle shore feeding on green weed *Clado-phora* (p. 222). Often in large numbers. Widely distributed and locally common. *Limaponta capitata (nigra)* Plate 21.

(*Limaponta depressa* differs in the absence of tentacular crests and may be a little larger; it occurs on salt marshes living on filamentous green weed. Probably widely distributed in such regions)

(b) Body rounded and tuberculate

Animal slug-like, dull greyish colour harmonising closely with rocks on which always found, rubbery consistency; about ½-in. long. No other distinguishing features but unmistakable when once noted. Upper half of shore crawling over rocks when tide is out, but retreating into crevices when becomes too hot and dry. (Was formerly regarded as a Pulmonate; now thought to be allied to Opisthobranchs). Confined to extreme south-west, very local but often abundant on rocks.

Onchidella celtica (Onchidium celticum) Plate 18.

PULMONATA

Very few representatives of this Sub-Class occu·' on the shore, those that do are small; they have a well-developed shell (unlike the Opisthobranchs) but *no operculum* (unlike the Prosobranchs). The three following species, the first two of which belong to the family *Ellobiidae* and the third to the Family *Otinidae*, may be encountered if searched for with care.

Leucophytia: Phytia Fig. 89.

Fig. 89. Shore pulmonate snails; a. *Leucophytia bidentata*, b. *Phytia myosotis* x 3

Pointed solid shell, white, of 6-7 whorls; ¼-in. high, with two ridges on inner wall of aperture. Typical member of crevice fauna on upper shore, especially where some detritus, also in estuaries and salt marshes. South and west, not uncommon.

Leucophytia bidentata (Montagu) Fig. 89.

Shell of same general character and size but thinner and yellowish or

146

brown; may be a third ridge on the inner wall of the aperture, also one or more teeth on outer wall. Commonest in estuaries and salt-marshes. South and west, locally common.

Phytia myosotis (Draparnaud) Fig. 89.

Shell ear-shaped, of two whorls, the second much the larger, the animal being a limpet and incapable of withdrawal into the shell. Reddish-brown to purple shell and white body, only $\frac{1}{8}$-in. long. Confined to crevices and cavities of empty barnacle shells on upper shore. South and south-west, locally common.

Otina ovata Fig. 87 (p. 136).

SCAPHOPODA
Tusk Shells

Fig. 90. *Dentalium* (Tusk Shell); appearance in life with tri-lobed foot and adhesive head processes projecting from wider end of shell

This is much the smallest class of molluscs having characters in common both with gastropods and bivalves and others that are distinctive, notably the tubular form of the shell (fig. 90). This resembles a tusk, being wider at one end (anterior) than the other. In life a trilobed foot projects from the wider end and the animal burrows in sand, etc. while water for respiration is drawn in through the other which projects above the bottom. These animals never live on the shore, only at moderate to considerable depths, but the shell is very solid and resistant and may be found washed up. That of only one species is likely to be found, namely *Dentalium entalis* (fig. 90), which is white and slightly curved. It is commoner on northern than on southern shores.

LAMELLIBRANCHIA
Bivalves

A large and highly successful class in which the body is laterally compressed between two *valves* connected above by an elastic *ligament*, all forming the *shell* (fig. 91). The centre of growth of each valve is known as the *umbo* or *beak*, growth may be symmetrical in front and behind this, when the shell is said to be equilateral; or either the front or more usually the hind portion may be the larger, when it is *inequilateral*. The two valves are usually similar or *equivalve*; if dissimilar they are *inequivalve*. The ligament may be long or rounded and condensed; it may be *internal* or, bulging upward between the umbones, *external*. Beneath lies the hinge usually with teeth, those of one valve fitting into grooves in the other. Their function is to prevent the valves slipping laterally when the shell is closed. *Dentition* is an important feature in the classification of bivalves especially where the body is not available. Teeth may be numerous and similar to one another, i.e. *taxodont*, or be few and differ from each other usually consisting of one central or cardinal teeth with laterals. There are various forms of such *heterodont* dentitions. In other cases teeth are absent.

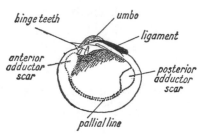

Fig. 91. Lamellibranch (Bivalve); interior of shell (pallial sinus shown in Fig. 98, p. 165)

The shell usually completely encloses the body (fig. 92). There is no head, only a mouth opening and that without a radula. The *foot*, laterally compressed and sometimes absent, may be protruded from between the valves or withdrawn by means of pedal muscles which correspond to the columella muscle of the gastropods. The foot is the organ of movement —except for the scallops which swim by flapping the valves—but in some bivalves it contains a gland producing a horny material which flows along a groove on the hind surface of the foot and is " planted " on to a hard surface forming the tough *byssus* which secures a mussel to rocks.

Food is brought to the mouth (which cannot extend outside the shell to obtain it) by the enormously enlarged gills which extend almost the full length of the animal. Out of the powerful water current they create, particles are sieved and carried to the mouth, guarded on each side by a pair of flap-like *palps* which prevent too much material entering and so blocking the mouth. The organs of respiration have become the organs of feeding, food consisting largely of microscopic plants. Water enters and leaves at the hind end, the *inhalant* opening being below the gills and the *exhalant* opening above them. These openings may be borne at the

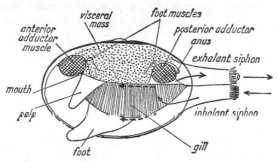

Fig. 92. Lamellibranch; general appearance of animal after removal of left valve, with siphons extended. Arrows show circulation of water for feeding and respiration, broken arrows passage of food along gills to palps and mouth

end of long extensions of the mantle called *siphons* which may be extended —in some bivalves as a single combined structure, in others as separate tubes—for considerable distances. Such bivalves burrow deeply into sand or mud or bore in rock or wood.

Within the valves are *impressions* where muscles are attached. There is a *pallial line* along which the mantle is attached and which is situated a little distance from the margin; if present, siphons are withdrawn into a deep bay or *pallial sinus*. Adductor muscles run between the valves closing the shell when they contract. They work in opposition to the elastic ligament which causes the valves to separate. Usually there are two adductors, one at each end of the pallial line, the *dimyarian* condition; they may be dissimilar in size (*heteromyarian*) or the front one may be lost, the hind one assuming a central position in a rounded shell (*monomyarian*) (fig. 93).

Fig. 93. Dimyarian, Heteromyarian and Monomyarian exemplified by *Glycymeris* (a) with equal adductor muscles, *Mytilus* (b) with reduced anterior adductor, *Pecten* (c) with only posterior adductor. Foot also shown, and byssus in b and c

No entirely satisfactory scheme for classifying bivalves has been produced; features of the body (notably of the gills) and details of the hinge are both used. Neither is of much use to the collector in the field and an arbitrary system is here used relying primarily on habit, i.e.

letting the conditions under which the animal lives and where it may be found by the collector provide initial indication of what it may be. In this way, for instance, all animals that bore into rock or wood are considered together, but similar habit does not necessarily imply close relationship—that can only be determined by discussion of comparative anatomy for which there is here no space.

A

Firmly attached by byssus threads (or unattached on the surface).

i. Elongate shell, not reduced anteriorly (equilateral), similar adductor muscles.
  (*a*) Separated umbones, taxodont dentition.
  (*b*) Umbones touching, shell surface with spines or irregular.
ii. Generally triangular shell, umbones anterior (inequilateral), dissimilar adductor muscles.
iii. Rounded shell, valves usually lying horizontally, single adductor.
  (*a*) Byssus threads issue marginally near hinge, or animal *free* when adult.
  (*b*) Limy byssus passing through space in under

valve (appearing cemented).

B

Cemented to stones or rocks.

C

Burrowing in sand or mud.
i. Two valves similar or almost so (equivalve).
  (*a*) Taxodont dentition.
  (*b*) Heterodont dentition.
    (1) Shallow burrowers.
    (2) Deep burrowers.
ii. Two valves clearly dissimilar (inequivalve).

D

Boring in rock or wood.
i. Rock borers.
ii. Wood borers.

E

Small surface-living bivalves, free and commensal.

A. FIRMLY ATTACHED BY BYSSUS THREADS* (or unattached on the surface).†

i. Elongate shell, not reduced anteriorly (equilateral), similar adductor muscles.

(*a*) *Separated umbones,* taxodont dentition.

The largely and widely distributed family of the *Arcidae* is poorly represented in British seas, with only one species on the shore. The shell is boat-shaped with the umbones far apart—a highly characteristic feature—and prominent ridges radiating out from them;

---

* See also *Venerupis pullastra* and *V. saxatilis* (p. 154), also *Kellia suborbicularis* (p. 167).
† See also *Pandora albida* (p. 164).

up to 1½ in. long. Very firmly attached by a massive greenish byssus extending along much of straight under surface. Shell both difficult to distinguish, often in depression on rock surface, and also to detach. Some 40-50 similar teeth along straight hinge line. Lower shore and below, widely distributed, not common.

Arca tetragona ARK SHELL Plate xvii.

(*b*) *Umbones touching*, shell surface with spines or irregular.

Shell roughly oblong and frequently most irregular, posterior gape (valves not in contact here when adductors contract), external ligament. Moderately long siphons with horny sheath. Foot very small. Attached by byssus threads within crevices among rocks, " nestling." But if rock be relatively soft bores into this (see Rock Borers). Although formerly divided into two species of which only *H. striata* said to bore, it now appears that if two species do exist then both may occur nestling or boring, but always attached by byssus threads. Lower shore and below. Widely distributed, very common.

Hiatella (*Saxicava*) *arctica* and *H.* (*S.*) *striata* (*gallicana*) Plate xx.

ii. **Generally triangular shell,** umbones anterior (inequilateral), dissimilar adductor muscles.

Family MYTILIDAE (*Mussels*)

When opened, the large posterior and very small anterior adductors can be seen, also the extended ligament but no hinge teeth. The strap-like foot is primarily used for placing the byssus threads. The three genera can be distinguished as follows:

Shell pointed, umbo at tip. *Mytilus*

Shell pointed, umbo on upper surface. *Modiolus*

Shell more rhomboidal, striations radiating from umbones. *Musculus*

Shell dark blue, frilled edge of mantle protrudes behind when valves open. Up to 4 in. long (Fig. 93a). A very common shore animal, in dense beds on rocky, stony and also muddy shores where are stones for initial attachment as in estuaries. Also on exposed rocks, where many small ones may settle among barnacles. Middle shore and below. Widely distributed, very common.

Mytilus edulis COMMON MUSSEL Plate 22.

Fig. 93*a*. Side view of shells of Left, *Mytilus edulis;* Right, *Mytilus galloprovincialis.*

Very similar to above but distinguished by more pointed, down-turned umbones, shell higher and less angular on upper margin, longer, up to 5 in. (fig. 93a). Exposed fringe of tissues dark (white to straw-coloured in *M. edulis*). Southern species, dominant mussel in south-west from Lizard to North Devon, less common S. Wales and S. Cornwall. Same habitat as *M. edulis* but not in estuaries.   *Mytilus galloprovincialis* MEDITERRANEAN MUSSEL

The largest British mussel, up to 6 in. long, but usually about 2 in. on shore; shell purplish, thick with horny processes when young, animal dark orange, mantle margin *not* frilled. Commonest offshore but often among holdfasts of *Laminaria* (p. 225), etc. shells frequently washed up. Widely distributed, most abundant in north.
Modiolus modiolus HORSE MUSSEL Plate 22.

Similar to above but not exceeding 2 in. long, shell covered with thick horny layer (periostracum) prolonged over posterior half into thorns serrated on one side. On rocky and broken ground, lower shore and below. Widely distributed, commonest in south and west.
Modiolus barbatus BEARDED HORSE MUSSEL Plate 22.

Much smaller, some ¾-in. long, with thorns but these not serrated. Rounded teeth along hinge. Appears bean-shaped when " thorns " removed. May be covered with shell fragments attached by byssus. Rocky shores. Lower shore and below. Widely distributed, common.
Modiolus phaseolinus BEAN HORSE MUSSEL Plate 22.

Shell oval, rounded and smooth, about ¾-in. long, usually pale green, often with dark mottlings. Difficult to find (though not uncommon) because either embedded in the test of large sea squirts or attached by byssus within dead shells, holdfasts of *Laminaria* (p. 225), etc. Rocky areas. Lower shore and below. Widely distributed, common.
Musculus (*Modiolaria*) *marmoratus* MARBLED CRENELLA Plate 22.

Broader, less angular shell, about ½-in. long, more compressed, bright green, not glossy. Occurs sometimes in numbers together in pools among corallines, etc. Middle shore and below. Widely distributed, common.
Musculus (*Modiolaria*) *discors* GREEN CRENELLA Plate 22.

Family PINNIDAE

Brief reference should be made to the largest British bivalve, shaped like a fan and attaining a length of up to 1 foot and a breadth, at hind end, of 6 in. Occasionally collected on the lower shore in areas of sheltered water on sandy mud. May be common on such bottoms at moderate depths.   *Pinna fragilis* FAN MUSSEL

iii. **Rounded shell,** valves usually lying horizontal, single adductor.

(a) *Byssus threads issue, marginally near hinge,* or animal *free* when adult.

Family PECTINIDAE

These are the scallops, all species of which are attached by byssus threads in early life, some retain this throughout life, one replaces it by a later cementing of the under (always the right) valve to the substratum, others lose the byssus and become free. No trace of anterior adductor, the shell and animal becoming reorganised around the enlarged centrally placed muscle. On either side of the umbones laterally extending " ears " provide extensive surface for ligament attachment. The mantle margins bear numerous tentacles, among them conspicuous opalescent eyes.

Shell inequivalve, right (under) valve convex and left valve flat, nearly circular, 4-5 in. diameter, reddish-brown or yellow. Attached by byssus when very small only, can swim (free margin of valves foremost) by flapping of valves—also sudden escape movement in opposite direction. Very common offshore, shells often washed up, occasional specimen on lower shore.

Pecten maximus GREAT SCALLOP or CLAM Plate 22.

Other British scallops belong to the genus *Chlamys* being equivalve with both valves convex.

Small shell, not more than 1¼ in. diameter, very varied in colour but characteristic markings of stripes and spots. Ears asymmetrical. Free after early life but usually within cavities, under stones, etc. Common offshore, occasionally on lower shore, often washed up. Widely distributed, common.

Chlamys tigerina TIGER SCALLOP Plate 22.

Shell irregular, greatest diameter about 1¾ in., after initial byssal attachment becomes cemented by right valve. With about 70 narrow ribs. Lower shore and below. Widely distributed, common.

Chlamys distorta (*Pecten pusio*) HUNCHBACK SCALLOP Plate 22.

Shell circular, 2-3 in. diameter, colour very variable, some 20 broad, rounded ribs. Free except when very small; active swimmers living in great numbers together on sandy bottom and moving about in shoals. Occasionally on lower shore, shells often washed up. Widely distributed, common.

Chlamys opercularis QUEEN SCALLOP Plate 22.

Shell more oval, greatest diameter 1¾ in., ears asymmetrical, colour variable, 25-30 ribs. Attached by byssus *or* free. Lower shore and below. Widely distributed, common.

Chlamys varia VARIEGATED SCALLOP Plate 22.

Family *LIMIDAE*

Although only occasionally exposed at low water of springs, note should be made of another swimming bivalve which, however, usually occupies a " nest " constructed of byssus threads often among holdfasts of *Laminaria*, etc. In life unmistakable owing to the very long, orange-coloured tentacles which cannot be withdrawn. The shell is white and a broad oval in shape with a rasp-like covering of spiny ribs. *Lima hians* GAPING FILE SHELL

(*b*) *Limy byssus passing through space in under valve* (appearing cemented).

Family *ANOMIIDAE*

In these saddle oysters the opening for the byssus has moved near to the middle of the right valve owing to a deep embayment in this (see Plate xvii). Hence the byssus threads, here impregnated with lime, pass directly down to attach themselves to the rock below (fig. 94). The shell is held so closely to the substratum as to appear cemented to it. As the shell grows, it conforms to the underlying surface, but remains roughly circular. There are several British species, the two commonest and most easily identified being:

 Fig. 94. Saddle Oyster, showing byssal attachment passing through embayment in under (*right*) valve

Shell flat, ½ in. (or less) up to 2 in. diameter, umbo near margin, externally usually dull white, glossy within, three muscle scars on upper valve. On sides of rocks, middle shore and below. Widely distributed, common.

Anomia ephippium COMMON SADDLE OYSTER Plate xvii.

Flatter and smaller shell, about 1 in. diameter, 20-30 ribs radiating from umbo, often with reddish-brown markings; two muscle scars on upper valve. Less common on shore but common offshore.

Monia (Anomia) patelliformis RIBBED SADDLE OYSTER Plate xvii.

B. CEMENTED TO STONES OR ROCKS. Apart from the one species of *Chlamys* already mentioned, this habit is confined on British shores to the true oysters, of which a native and an imported species occur. They may initially attach themselves to a small stone or shell, or be flaked off when small from an artificial " collector," so that most oysters appear free from attachment when fully grown.

Family OSTREIDAE

Shell thick, irregular, rounded or oval, cemented with *left* valve undermost, i.e. inequivalve. Without hinge teeth. Surface marked with usually irregular growth lines representing successive " shoots " by which shell receives sudden, initially very thin, marginal addition.

Shell generally rounded, usually up to 4 in. diameter but can grow much larger. (Especially bigger shells often bored with yellow sponge, *Cliona celata* (p. 42). Occurs naturally in dense beds which can be increased by cultivation. In creeks and estuaries. Widely distributed, commonest in S.E. and S.W. *Ostrea edulis* FLAT OR NATIVE OYSTER Plate xvii.

Larger, more irregular and internally deeper shelled oyster, much broader than long. Imported from Bay of Biscay and relaid on British beds, especially in south-east. Occasionally spawns here and so qualified as member of the British fauna. Same habitat as the native oyster.

Crassostrea angulata PORTUGUESE OYSTER Plate xvii.

C. BURROWING IN SAND OR MUD. This is the habit most extensively, and highly successfully, exploited by the bivalves; they burrow into the protection of sand, gravel or mud by means of the foot which gropes forward, or downward, then anchors itself by terminal distension with blood, the animal pulling forward by contractions of the foot muscles. Contact is retained with the water above by way of the siphons extending from the posterior end. Some bivalves burrow only deep enough to cover the shell and have correspondingly short siphons; others burrow very deeply and have long siphons—with the notable exception of the razor shells which descend deeply for protection, moving with ease vertically up and down in sand. These burrowers all possess two adductor muscles which are usually more or less the same size. There are a very few resembling *Arca* with taxodont dentition, while in some, as seen in *Pecten* and *Anomia*, there are marked differences between the two valves. Apart from these features, it appears most helpful to consider first the shallow and then the deep burrowers, so disregarding classification based on comparative anatomy, but a procedure which leads on to consideration of the more specialised borers in rock or wood.

i. Two valves similar or almost so (equivalve)

   (*a*) *Taxodont dentition*

      Shell almost circular in outline, solid, characteristic brown markings on light background, umbones separated but much less than in *Arca*, up to 2½ in. diameter. Broad hinge plate with, when fully grown, 12 teeth. Lives close under surface of sandy or muddy gravel in moderate depths, only found on shore when washed up; in old shells brown markings may be worn off, but shape and dentition establish identity. Widely distributed, common.

Glycymeris glycymeris DOG COCKLE Plate xvii.

In addition several species of *Nucula*, the Nut Shells, are very common in moderate to considerable depths burrowing in various grades of bottom material. Unless much worn, all are yellow to brown in colour, somewhat triangular in outline and with numerous teeth on either side of a small brown ligament at the apex of the triangle.

(b) Heterodont dentition

1. Shallow Burrowers

Family MACTRIDAE

Trough Shells. These bivalves live in sand or shell gravel, never in mud; short siphons with a horny sheath. The foot is wedge-shaped and white. The shell is triangular and equilateral with a slight posterior gape. There are two cardinal teeth in each valve with four laterals in the right and two in the left. The species are not easy to distinguish. All are much commoner in shallow and medium depths than on the shore where living specimens will only be found at the lowest levels. Empty shells should be found. All are widely distributed and common but not usually on the shore.

Shell elliptical, relatively delicate and nearly smooth, up to 1¾ in. long; length-breadth ratio about 1/0.6.

Spisula elliptica ELLIPTICAL TROUGH SHELL Plate xviii.

Shell more angular with prominent umbones, well-marked striations although smooth surface, broader than other species. Up to 1¼ in. long; length-breadth ratio about 1/1.4.

Spisula subtruncata CUT TROUGH SHELL Plate xviii.

Shell heavier, yellowish-white with concentric but smooth grooves, most equilateral of three species of *Spisula*. Up to 1¾ in. long, length-breadth ratio about 1/0.8.

Spisula solida THICK TROUGH SHELL Plate xviii.

Shell distinguished from those of closely related genus *Spisula* by presence of brownish rays running from umbo to margin, also internally by smooth surface of teeth and sockets, those in *Spisula* being vertically striated or milled. Shell solid and up to 2 in. long.

Mactra corallina (stultorum) RAYED TROUGH SHELL Plate xviii.

Family CARDIIDAE

Cockles; somewhat globular shells with over-arching umbones and conspicuous external ligament between. Conspicuous ribs. Clearly not adapted for rapid movement through sand, etc. in which they burrow superficially, the siphons, terminally separate and without horny sheath, are very short. Foot exceptionally large and bent at acute angle when withdrawn; in some cases permit animals to " leap " on surface. There are a number of species, most of them living offshore, but the common cockle is a true shore animal.

Shell with 24-28 conspicuous ribs, also well-marked concentric lines, somewhat rhomboidal in shape, up to 2½ in. long. On sand or sandy mud on middle and lower shore; where conditions favourable (ample plankton in water) in immense numbers forming dense cockle beds. Collected for human food. Widely distributed, common.   *Cardium edule* COMMON COCKLE Plate xviii.

Shell solid, 18-19 conspicuous ribs tending to disappear towards umbones and covered with short, backwardly curved spines. Much same size as *C. edule*, also in sand but less common on shore. Widely distributed.

Cardium echinatum PRICKLY COCKLE Plate xviii

Other large species include *Cardium aculeatum*, Spiny Cockle or Red Nose—a name associated with the bright red foot. About 20 ribs deeply ridged round the edge and bearing stout spines with backwardly directed points. Up to 3 in. long. A southern species living offshore in sand. *Cardium tuberculatum* grows almost as big but has heavier, more globular shell and 21-22 ribs with rounded tubercles has a similar distribution. *Laevicardium crassum* (*Cardium norvegicum*) living in greater depths in shell gravel has an almost smooth shell although some 40 very low ribs can be counted around the margin. Also widely distributed.

Shell dull, not more than ½-in. long, some 20 flattened ribs, often brownish. Usually below shore in sandy mud but occasionally found on lower shore. Widely distributed, common.

Cardium exiguum LITTLE COCKLE Plate xviii.

Other small species occur offshore.

Families LUCINIDAE and UNGULINIDAE

Species of both these families have characteristically rounded shells with umbones facing forwards. The valves are compressed with well-marked concentric ridges, hinge dentition of two cardinals and two plate-like laterals on each valve. Siphons are absent but the foot is exceptionally long and pointed and serves to make openings to the surface, then lined with slime, for intake and expulsion of water. In muddy sand or gravel about or below lowest tidal levels.

Chalky white shell with concentric striations; a little longer than broad, greatest diameter some 1½ in. Widely distributed, often in beds of eel-grass (p. 254); never common.

Lucinoma (Lucina) borealis NORTHERN LUCINA Plate xix.

A smaller species, not more than ¾ in. diameter, with the same general characters but with ridges overlapping so that they give a spiny appearance to the upper margin; not uncommon.

Myrtea (Lucina) spinifera

Shell somewhat glossy with concentric ridges less regular, slightly broader than long with greatest diameter about 1 in. On muddy sand or gravel offshore in shallow depths. South and locally in west, not common.

Diplodonta rotundata ROUND DOUBLE-TOOTH Plate xix.

Family *VENERIDAE*

This is one of the major families of bivalves; species of three genera are common between tide marks and in shallow water. All have solid shells, rounded or oval and with the umbones characteristically inturned and facing the anterior end. The dentition consists of some three or four cardinal teeth in each valve. Siphons occur but are only of moderate length without horny sheath and united except at the tip. The foot is large and active.

Smooth rounded shells with heart-shaped *lunule* (fig. 95) in front of hinge; internal margin of valves smooth. *Dosinia*

Shell more triangular, with lunule (fig. 95), internal margin of valves serrated. *Venus*

Shell rhomboidal, without lunule, umbones nearer anterior end, wedge-shaped posterior end, internal margin smooth.

Venerupis (Tapes or *Paphia)*

 Fig. 95. *Venus*, viewed from above showing lunule in front of ligament

Shell round with smooth concentric ridges, 2 in. diameter, pale with faint rays from umbones to margin. Easily identified. In sandy bays on lower shore and below. Widely distributed, common.

Dosinia exoleta RAYED ARTEMIS Plate xix.

Very similar to above but smoother and not exceeding 1½ in. diameter. Siphons longer and almost qualifies as a deep burrower. In sand around low water mark of springs. Widely distributed, common. *Dosinia lupinus* SMOOTH ARTEMIS Plate xix.

Shell covered with overlapping concentric ridges, pale with three reddish-brown rays, up to 1¼ in. long. In sand on lower shore and below. Widely distributed, common.
Venus striatula (gallina) STRIPED VENUS Plate xix.

Larger species up to 1½ in. long, very solid shell, concentric ridges forming tubercles especially on hinder half. Inhabits shell gravel in moderate depths but shells may be washed up. Widely distributed. *Venus verrucosa* WARTY VENUS Plate xix.

Shell equilateral forming regular triangular oval, yellow tinged with pink or red, up to ¾-in. long, with 40-50 radiating ribs giving a superficial resemblance to the cockles. In sand, about low water level and below. Widely distributed, common.
Venus ovata OVAL VENUS Plate xix.

Shell roundish triangle, very solid with pronounced concentric ridges. Most variable in colour—yellow, pink, red, brown—with darker rays. In gravel and sand, middle shore and below. Widely distributed, very common.
Venus fasciata BANDED VENUS Plate xix.

Shell pale with zigzag purplish markings on flattened concentric ridges. Essentially offshore species living in shell gravel, valves frequently washed up. Widely distributed, common.
Venerupis rhomboides (Tapes or *Paphia virginea)*
BANDED CARPET SHELL Plate xix.

Massive shell, up to 2 in. long, characteristic sculpturing due to numerous prominent concentric ridges crossed and broken by radiating ribs. Yellowish with purple markings. In muddy gravel and sand on lower shore. South coast, often common.
Venerupis (Tapes or *Paphia) decussata*
CROSS-CUT CARPET SHELL Plate xix.

About same size and general appearance as above but sculpturing less pronounced. Variable in colour, suggestive of plumage of hen, hence name Pullet given locally. In muddy gravel, at base of rocks, in dead shells, etc. sometimes attached by few byssus threads. Lower shore and below. Widely distributed, very common. *Venerupis (Tapes* or *Paphia) pullastra*
PULLET CARPET SHELL Plate xix.

Smaller species, sometimes irregular in shape, occurs in rock crevices and holes made by rock borers, often attached by byssus threads. South coast, locally common.

Venerupis saxatilis (*Tapes* or *Paphia perforans*)
BANDED CARPET SHELL Plate xix.

Families DONACIDAE and ASAPHIDAE

Closely related families with elongate compressed shells and relatively short but completely divided siphons; large foot and active burrowers.

Shell very characteristic, highly polished with fine radiating grooves, bright and variously coloured, yellow, brown, olive, violet, inner surface usually blotched with violet. Inequilateral, *anterior* region the larger, margins serrated internally, 1¼ in. long, half as broad. Inhabitant of *exposed* sandy shores from middle shore down. Widely distributed and very common where conditions suitable.

Donax vittatus BANDED WEDGE SHELL Plate 23.

Shell nearly equilateral, oblong, truncated posteriorly with a slight gape, up to 1¾ in. long, half as broad, surface opaque with fine concentric ridges, posterior ribs keeled. Pink with darker radiating rays, inner surface polished and purple. In sand on lower shore and below. Commonest in north.

Gari (*Psammobia*) *fervensis* FAROE SUNSET SHELL Plate 23.

Shell oval, solid and broad, little sculpturing, yellowish with purplish-brown or lilac rays. Seldom on shore except at very low tides. South and west, locally common.

Gari depressa (*Psammobia vespertina*)
LARGE SUNSET SHELL Plate 23.

2. *Deep Burrowers.* All have either long siphons or else, in the case of the Razor Shells, the capacity to move vertically in sand at speed when disturbed.

Families TELLINIDAE and SEMELIDAE

Very similar in appearance and habits, major differences being the large external ligament in the *Tellinidae* with internal ligament and reduction of hinge teeth on the *Semelidae*. Shell rounded, oval or elongate, always very flattened permitting rapid movement through sand or mud. Siphons always *very long* (fig. 96a), may be several times length of shell, always separate from one another. Inhalant siphon the longer and gropes on surface of bottom drawing in organic deposits, i.e. these animals *not* suspension feeders as are most other bivalves. At base of siphons a characteristic crossed-over, or cruciform, muscle.

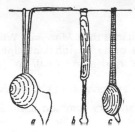

Fig. 96. Types of burrowing bivalves; a. Tellinid (separate very long siphons, large foot); b. Razor Shell (short fused siphons, very large foot); c. Gaper (long fused siphons, very small foot)

Shell very flattened, up to ¾-in. long, glossy and beautifully coloured —rose-pink, long, glossy or white—same colour within. Force of ligament such that united empty valves extended flat like butterfly wings and so often found on sand. In clean sand from top of middle shore to depths of up to four fathoms, greatest densities (up to 3000 per square yard) about bottom of lower shore. Widely distributed, very common. *Tellina tenuis* THIN TELLIN Plate xvii.

Very similar in both size and appearance to *T. tenuis*, but shell somewhat more angular behind while right valve (only) with diagonal striations visible through lens. Same localities but from low water level to some 20 fathoms, i.e. only slightly overlapping *T. tenuis*. Widely distributed, common.   *Tellina fabula*

Shell larger, up to 2¼ in. long, solid with concentric ridges, yellowish white with faint pink rays. Left valve more flattened than right (i.e. somewhat inequivalve, a not uncommon feature in this family) although shell as a whole less flattened than in two preceding species. In moderate depths in coarse sand and shell gravel. Widely distributed, common.

Tellina crassa BLUNT TELLIN Plate xvii.

Shell somewhat resembling that of *Donax* owing to angular, oblong shape but with obvious pink rays and different habitat— in shell gravel at moderate depths. Widely distributed but not very common.   *Tellina donacina*

Shell more globular and rounded in outline, dull with fine concentric but rather irregular striations, up to 1 in. long. Less active than the previous species, occurs in muddy gravel often in estuaries. Its tolerance of low salinities explains its presence in the Baltic and so its specific name. Widely distributed, very common.

Macoma (Tellina) balthica BALTIC TELLIN Plate xvii.

Shell rounded, breadth some ¾ of length which reaches 2 in., very compressed, dull grey or yellowish external ligament. Very long siphons (fig. 96), burrows to depths of 2-8 in. in mud or muddy sand, intertidal and often higher in estuaries than *Macoma*. When tide out presence revealed by marks made by inhalant siphon radiating out from position where emerged above mud. Widely distributed, very common locally.

> *Scrobicularia plana* PEPPERY FURROW SHELL Plate xvii.

Various species of *Abra* (*Syndosmya*) are very common in muddy bottoms at moderate depths. They are closely allied to *Scrobicularia* but usually under ½-in. long.

RAZOR SHELLS—This aptly descriptive name embraces one species which should be associated with the *Tellinidae* while the remainder are included in the *Solenidae*. Only in the former are the hinge and ligament in the *middle* of the upper surface.

Shell reaching a length of 4 in. with hinge in the centre and siphons moderately long and *separate*. Shell pod-shaped, slightly iridescent and yellowish. Occurs in muddy sand apparently in a restricted zone around extreme low water mark, difficult to obtain intact either by digging or dredging. Widely distributed but local; hard to say how common. *Pharus* (*Solen*) *legumen Plate* xvii.

Family SOLENIDAE

Highly characteristic shell up to eight times as long as broad, and tubular, i.e. gaping at both ends. Short siphons, separated only terminally, project at hind end, powerful foot from front (lower) end (fig. 96b). Move rapidly vertically through sand.

Noting that the hinge and ligament are *anterior* the three genera of the Solenidae may be distinguished:

Shell straight or curved, solid, no constriction near front end. *Ensis*

Shell curved, about 1 in. long, translucent, not living on shore.
> *Phaxas* (*Cultellus*)

Shell straight, truncated at margins, constriction near front end.
> *Solen*

Shell straight, up to 8 in. long, anterior end truncated, posterior not tapering; foot cream-white. Largest British species; in lower stretches of clean sandy shore. Widely distributed, common.
> *Ensis siliqua* POD RAZOR Plate 23.

Shell slightly curved, up to 6 in. long, anterior end truncated, posterior slightly tapering, foot cream-white. Sandy shores. Widely distributed, common. *Ensis arcuatus* Plate 23.

Shell more curved than in *E. arcuatus*, usually not over 4 in. long, anterior end rounded, posterior markedly tapering, foot pale reddish-brown. Sandy shores. Widely distributed, common.

Ensis ensis Plate 23.

Shell straight, but more cylindrical than in *E. siliqua*, with deep constriction round anterior end; foot dullish red. Sandy mud usually, burrowing to depths of 18 in. South and west, locally distributed.

Solen marginatus (vagina) GROOVED RAZOR Plate 23.

Thin translucent shell seldom over 1 in. long. Offshore on muddy gravel bottom where often extremely common. Widely distributed.

Phaxas (Cultellus) pellucidus Plate 23.

Families *LUTRARIDAE* and *MYIDAE*—" Gapers "

Here are included four species, two of *Lutraria* and two of *Mya* with the same type of very large oval shells which gape widely behind and have massive siphons (fig. 96c), fused throughout, covered with a thick horny sheath, and extending to lengths double that of the shell. When fully grown they live at depths of a foot or more, and do not move about but penetrate deeper as they grow. In contrast with the razor shells, these gapers are largely immobile but their siphons can be withdrawn.

The *Lutraridae* are related to the *Mactridae* and have the same type of hinge with a spoon-shaped process (apophysis) in each valve where the partially external ligament is attached. In the *Myidae* the left valve only has a conspicuous projecting apophysis (see fig. 98, p. 165), the ligament being internal. The two are compared in fig. 97.

Fig. 97. Gapers, contrast between arrangement of ligament in a. *Lutraria*, and b. *Mya*

Shell elliptical, relatively thin and usually glossy, yellowish-white, up to 6 in. long. Siphons more than twice as long, with purplish-brown patches and streaks with *transparent* sheath. In sand and sandy mud on lower levels of shore. Widely distributed, common.

Lutraria lutraria (elliptica) COMMON OTTER SHELL Plate xviii.

Shell smaller and more slender, up to 4 in. long, turned up some-

L. magna)

Shell more elongate with umbo well forward and posterior margin upcurved (fig. 97c), moderately thick and somewhat irregular surface, periostracum dark brown, up to 4 in. long. Especially in estuarine mud, confined to south and west. *Lutraria magna*.

Shell solid and opaque, irregular concentric grooves, characteristically·truncated posteriorly. In muddy gravel and sand from lower shore to moderate depths. Widely distributed, common.

Mya truncata BLUNT GAPER Plate 23.

Shell oval and larger than *M. truncata*, up to 5 in. long, grey or brownish. In sand or sandy mud, often extending into estuaries, a true shore species much commoner there than *M. truncata*. An edible species, the American "Soft Shelled Clam". Widely distributed, very common. *Mya arenaria* SAND GAPER Plate 23.

See also under Rock Borers, some of which burrow in stiff clay.

ii. Two valves clearly dissimilar (inequivalve)

Although certain species already mentioned, notably in the Tellinidae, are inequivalve, this feature is only immediately obvious in:
Shell up to ½-in long, white tinged with yellow, pink or brown; marginal areas of left valve uncalcified, i.e. of horny layer only, so that it fits within right valve like an operculum. Same hinge characters as other Myidae; short siphons with horny sheath. From extreme low water to some depth on muddy gravel. Widely distributed, not common on shore. *Corbula gibba* COMMON BASKET SHELL Plate 23.

Shell rough elongated oval, up to 1 in. long, posterior end extended and somewhat upturned, left valve convex, right valve flat. Siphons very short. Lives on *surface* of sand (cf. free species of *Pecten* and *Chlamys*) usually with convex valve underneath. Shore species but confined to very sheltered bays. S. only, near Weymouth, Channel Isles, etc. *Pandora albida* (*inaequivalvis*) PANDORA SHELL Plate xviii.

D. BORING IN ROCK OR WOOD.

The animals here considered have the same habit of life, boring instead of burrowing and essentially for protection although certain wood borers also obtain food. The majority of the rock borers belong to the one family, the *Pholadidae*, to which the wood borers are closely allied.

i. Rock Borers.

Family PHOLADIDAE

The piddocks, all of which bore into rock or stiff clay. The shell is cut away anteriorly where there is a perpetual gape through which the rounded foot projects; this acts as a sucker gripping the head of the boring. The ligament is either completely or almost completely lost but the two valves articulate both in the hinge region above and in the marginal region below, and as there is also a posterior gape the valves are rocked by the alternate contraction of the two adductor muscles which are situated one in front and the other behind the two areas of articulation. Accessory shell-plates between the valves on upper surface. The surface of the shell is typically ridged in connection with boring, while internally a long blade-like *apophysis* (fig. 98A) is attached to the hinge region of each valve. To these the muscles of the foot are attached. The siphons are long and united, they are covered for half their length by a horny sheath.

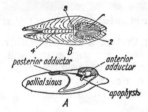

Fig. 98. Piddock (*Pholas dactylus*); A. interior of left valve, B. shell viewed from above, 1-4, four accessory shell plates

Shell elongate, white and rather delicate with up to 50 longitudinal rows of spines where ribs and concentric ridges cross. Four accessory plates (fig. 98B), three anterior and one posterior. Largest British species, up to 3 in. long. On lower regions of shore, usually in shale, chalk or red sandstone, but also in submerged wood or peat. South-west only, where locally common.

Pholas dactylus COMMON PIDDOCK Plate xx.

Shell oval, solid and coarse with furrow dividing valves into anterior and posterior regions former, with some 20 rows of spines. Small accessory shell plate. About 2 in. long. Long siphons, bores usually into shale, oolite or clay. Widely distributed but very local.

Zirphaea crispata (L.) OVAL PIDDOCK Plate xx..

Shell solid, somewhat oblong, markedly cut away in front, covered with complex scale-like ridges especially anteriorly; white but often stained red from boring. Under 2 in. long. A single accessory shell-plate. South-west only, locally distributed.

Barnea parva LITTLE PIDDOCK Plate xx.

Shell elongate oval, thin and rounded, up to 30 longitudinal rows of spines, white, one accessory shell-plate, smaller anterior gape. Up to 3 in. long. South-west, locally distributed.

Barnea candida WHITE PIDDOCK Plate xx.

Shell very rounded in transverse section, furrow diagonally from umbones to margin, upper surface especially very ridged. Two accessory shell-plates, may be united. Base of siphons protected with characteristic *membranous cup*. Anterior gape closes and foot atrophies when animal adult and ceases to bore. In sandstone, clay, peat, etc. Extreme south-west, locally distributed.

Pholadidea loscombiana PAPER PIDDOCK Plate xx.

Other Rock Borers:

Shell resembling that of a piddock with wide oval gape anteriorly on under side but shell smoother; *no* accessory plates. Siphons united without horny sheath. From low water to some depth, boring in limestones, shells, red sandstone, etc. Unlike piddocks forms limy tubes around siphons. South and south-west, locally distributed, not common.

Gastrochaena dubia FLASK SHELL Plate xx.

Shell also superficially resembling that of a piddock with ridges and spines but with hinge teeth, no accessory plates and with siphons separate. About 2 in. long. Introduced, probably with relaid oysters, from North America. Bores into limestone and stiff mud often on shore. Around mouth of Thames and north along coast of Essex where locally common.

Petricola pholadiformis Lamarck AMERICAN PIDDOCK Plate xx.

Shell roughly oblong and frequently most irregular, attached by byssus and found boring deeply into limestone, chalk or fine-grained sandstone. On lower shore and below. Widely distributed, very common. (Details on p. 151).

Hiatella (Saxicava) arctica and *H. (S.) striata (gallicana)* Plate xx.

ii. Wood Borers

Family TEREDINIDAE

These are the Shipworms in which the shell is reduced to a small but highly specialised boring instrument at the end of a long naked body like that of a worm. They live exclusively within timber in sea water, heavy infection causing complete destruction (see Plate xxv). Details of valve with apophysis shown in fig. 99a, b. Base of siphons attached to boring, the small opening being closed by a pair of limy *pallets* after the siphons, which are separate, have been withdrawn. Foot acts as a sucker holding cutting valves against head of boring. Some food obtained from the wood, fragments of which pass through the gut. Three species occur in British seas:

Largest and commonest species, up to 1 ft. long, pallets racket-

Fig. 99. Shipworms; a, b, outer and inner views of shell of *Teredo norvegica*, blade-like apophysis shown in b; c, d, e, pallets of *Teredo norvegica*, *T. megotara* and *T. navalis* respectively

shaped (fig. 99c). In pier piles, wooden boats, etc. May be a serious pest in regions where timber has not been suitably protected.

Teredo norvegica Plate xx.

About half-size of *T. norvegica*, pallets notched at tips (fig. 99e). Similar distribution. *Teredo navalis*

Less common, probably confined to floating timber (where other two species may also occur). Characterised by large size of posterior region of shell or auricle, pallets (fig. 99d) more blunt-ended than in *T. norvegica*. *Teredo megotara*

Family *XYLOPHAGINIDAE*

Shell very similar to that of the *Teredinidae* but surrounds all of body, only siphon projects behind (fig. 100). Not attached to boring and without pallets. Excavate shallow, rounded borings in floating timber; wood *not* digested. One species only:

Xylophaga dorsalis WOOD PIDDOCK Plate xx.

Fig. 100. Wood piddock (*Xylophaga dorsalis*) appearance in life; no pallets

E. SMALL SURFACE-LIVING BIVALVES, free and commensal

Members of three families of bivalves are here included, all are small and all have the ingoing (inhalant) siphon at the *anterior* end; for this reason they cannot burrow. Some are free-living, others are attached to, without being truly parasitic upon, other and larger animals. This condition where two animals may be said to share the same food is known as commensalism. All of these bivalves are attached by a few byssus threads.

Family *ERYCINIDAE*

Free-living with thin shell and internal ligament.

Shell globular, about $\frac{2}{8}$-in. long and broad, white and shiny, easily identified. Usually within dead shells or under stones, solitary and attached by few byssus threads. Occasionally on lower shore, commoner offshore. Widely distributed, never common.   *Kellia suborbicularis*

Very small, about $\frac{1}{20}$-in. long but often in very great numbers especially among tufts of shore lichen, *Lichina pygmaea* (p. 255) and roots of corallines on middle shore, also in crevices and in empty barnacle shells with small gastropods (fig. 87, p. 136). Oval shell, white with reddish tinge. Widely distributed, very common.

Lasaea rubra

Families *LEPTONIDAE* and *MONTACUTIDAE*

Commensals and to be recognised by the company they keep.

Fig. 101. *Lepton squamosum;* appearance in life with tentacles extending around margin of shell and large foot on which it crawls

Lives around mouths of burrows occupied by burrowing shrimp, *Upogebia* (p. 121). Shell translucent and very flat, some $\frac{3}{5}$-in. long and $\frac{2}{5}$-in. broad; mantle fringed with long white tentacles (fig. 101). Beautiful but rare bivalve. South coast, local.

Lepton squamosum COIN SHELL

Commensal with sea cucumber, *Leptosynapta inhaerens* (p. 184), attached to body about $\frac{1}{3}$ of length from mouth. Extremely flat foot while mantle also extends beyond shell margins (fig. 101). Shell about $\frac{1}{3}$-in. long. Appears to be confined to *Leptosynapta* from south coast.

Devonia perrieri

Commensal with burrowing brittle star, *Acronida brachiata* (p. 181), attached by byssus to burrow. Shell yellow to brown, oblong about $\frac{1}{3}$-in. long. Common offshore and occasionally at low water springs. Widely distributed, common.   *Mysella (Montacuta) bidentata.*

Commensal with burrowing sea urchin, *Spatangus purpureus* (p. 182), where attached by byssus to spines near anus. Yellowish-white shell, about $\frac{1}{8}$ in. long. Widely distributed although rare between tide marks.   *Montacuta substriata*

Commensal with burrowing sea urchin, *Echinocardium cordatum* (p. 183), attached to wall of burrow opposite anal siphon. Shell glossy but stained reddish, oblong some $\frac{1}{3}$-in. long. Widely distributed, common.   *Montacuta ferruginosa*

CEPHALOPODA

Cuttlefish, Squids and Octopuses

By far the most complex of the molluscs (fig. 102), more elaborate in structure and much more active, all being predacious carnivores feeding on living prey. The shell (with one tropical exception) is internal, in the octopuses being reduced to the merest vestige. The respiratory chamber with its pair of feathery gills persists but the water current is created by muscular means and is expelled with great force through a *funnel* formed from the modified molluscan foot. This provides a means of jet propulsion which enables the animals to dart very rapidly through the water. The most obvious features are the tentacles, formed from and surrounding the head. There are four or five pairs with suckers used for seizing the prey. The mouth is armed with powerful jaws like a parrot's beak turned upside down; there is also a radula. As indispensable aids to rapid movements, capturing prey or escaping enemies, these cephalopods have eyes as elaborate and efficient as those of vertebrates. They have remarkable powers of instantaneous colour change and may also discharge *sepium*, a black substance formed in the ink-sac near the anus.

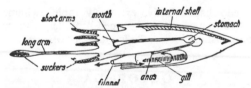

Fig. 102. Ten-armed Cephalopod (cuttlefish or squid) diagrammatic longitudinal section to shown major features. Arrows show circulation of water in respiratory chamber and discharge through funnel (=foot) in jet propulsion movements

Although cephalopods are not often members of the shore fauna, octopuses can be taken from time to time in pools or under stones at low water of springs, while cuttlefish occur on sandy bottoms, often among eel-grass (p. 254), in very shallow water; their " bones " (see Plate xxv) are often cast up on the shore. Squids are only likely to be seen alive if brought in by fishermen, but their dead bodies may be cast ashore especially on the east coast when they come into shallow water for spawning.

DECAPODA

Five pairs of tentacles, one pair longer than others and having suckers restricted to broad terminal region. These tentacles are used for capturing prey and are usually retracted.

Broad body with lateral fins, up to 1 ft. long, cavity with conspicuous funnel on under surface as animal swims. Back striped black and white, zebra fashion, but much colour change in life. Broad internal " bone " often washed ashore (Plate xxv). Comes close inshore, usually in sheltered bays or estuaries, often among eel-grass, spawning midsummer. Widely distributed but much commoner along south coast.

Sepia officinalis COMMON CUTTLEFISH Plate xxi.

Smaller species, about 5 in. long and relatively narrower in body. Southern and western coasts, not uncommon.   *Sepia elegans*

Smallest and commonest of British cephalopods, 1-2 in. long with rounded body and lobe-like lateral fins. Occurs over sand into which burrows and may be taken in shrimping nets just below low-tide mark in summer. Widely distributed, often common.

Sepiola atlantica LITTLE CUTTLE Plate xxi.

Somewhat larger, up to 3 in. long, also comes close inshore. Commoner in north.   *Sepietta oweniana*

Larger still, 5 or more in. long, but same general form; mantle free all around head. Common only on north and west of Scotland.

Rossia macrosoma

Typical torpedo-shaped body, extremely rapid swimmer, triangular lateral fins. Skeleton a long horny " pen." Widely distributed although never common inshore.   *Loligo forbesi* COMMON SQUID Plate xxi.

OCTOPODA

Four pairs of tentacles, all same length. Body bag-like and less adapted for swimming; lives in crevices among rocks, pouncing on prey. Moves about on bottom using tentacles but swims when alarmed. Shell reduced to pair of minute stylets.

Tentacles with *double row* of suckers. In Laminarian zone, sometimes in pools on shore or under rocks. Southern species found only in English Channel; after mild winters may be so common as to constitute a plague.   *Octopus vulgaris* COMMON OCTOPUS Plate xxi.

Tentacles with *single row* of suckers. Widely distributed around British Isles but commonest in the north, rarest in southern North Sea. May be captured on the shore, especially in summer.

Eledone cirrhosa CURLED OCTOPUS Plate xxi.

BRYOZOA (Polyzoa)
Sea-Mats

MOST OF these animals found between tide marks are encrusting layers on stones or seaweeds or else may resemble palmate seaweeds growing independently; others form little bushy growths often puzzling to place. But in various ways all are made up of many small compartments, like the cells of a honeycomb, an individual animal occupying each one. This is most easily observed in the encrusting types. Thus a small area contains many individuals (hence Polyzoa=many animals) while from each a horseshoe of delicate tentacles extends for feeding, so that the surface may be covered with a soft and moss-like haze (hence Bryozoa=moss animals). Although the expanded animals resemble superficially the polyps of hydroids, they are more complicated in structure and lead a more truly individual life. Each has a U-shaped gut, the mouth lying within the circle of tentacles and the anus opening outside it (except in group E, see below). Unlike the hydroids the tentacles are covered with minute vibratile hairs or cilia, the beating of which creates a current of water from which the animal obtains oxygen and also sieves out fine particles which are passed to the mouth. Thus it has essentially the same mode of feeding as sponges, some worms, bivalve molluscs and sea quirts.

A smaller, less conspicuous group of superficially similar animals has the anus opening within the ring of tentacles. On the beach this group (see E below) is represented by open-mouthed bells which bob erratically on contractile stalks. These are not now regarded as Bryozoa but are conveniently considered with these animals.

A
Closely encrusting patches, usually on seaweeds, very irregular in shape and size, but typically covering perhaps from 4 to 20 sq. in.

B
Much branched tufts, up to 3 in. long, sandy or white.

C
Flattened, round-ended " fronds," usually cast ashore.

D
Sponge-like masses, 4-12 in. long, irregularly lobed and fingered into blunt-ended shapes.

E
Minute stalked open-mouthed bells, up to $\frac{1}{5}$ in. tall, see fig. 108, p. 174.

171

A. CLOSELY ENCRUSTING PATCHES, usually on seaweeds, very irregular in shape and size, but typically covering perhaps 4-20 sq. in.

Closely encrusting, white patches with wavy edges of denser texture, on *Laminaria* (p. 225 and pl. xxxi) and *Fucus* (p. 226 and pl. xxxii); may cover considerable areas; delicate rectangular tracery of individual compartments each of which has a blunt spine at each angle of one end; and from some of the compartments rise blunt, round " towers," fig. 103 *a* and *b*. Middle and lower shore. Widely distributed. Abundant. *Membranipora membranacea* pl. iii.

Rather coarse grey-brown encrusting patches, on bottom 6 in. of *Ascophyllum* (p. 227 and pl. xxxii) and *Fucus* (p. 226 and pl. xxxii), or *abundantly* round base of *Gigartina stellata* (p. 248 and pl. xxxix) many reddish-brown spines, individual compartments embedded in rough texture of encrustation, see fig. 103c. Tentacles of individuals large and when many expanded give delicacy to rather dull-looking patches. Middle and lower shore. Widely distributed. Abundant. *Flustrella hispida* pl. iii

Patches rose-red, fairly smooth, up to 2 in. across, thin, brittle; among holdfasts of *Laminaria* (p. 225 and pl. xxxi), and on stones. Individual compartments oval, rising from edges to central mound or boss from which lines radiate; and just to one side of which is almost circular opening to compartment, see fig. 103d. Widely distributed. Probably not uncommon. *Umbonula verrucosa*

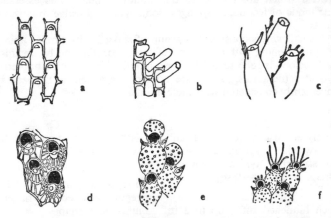

Fig. 103. "Individual compartments" of a. *Membranipora membranacea*, without towers; b. *M. membranacea*, with towers; c. *Flustrella hispida;* d. *Umbonula verrucosa;* e. and f. *Mucronella coccinea.* All x c 15

Patches orange-red, otherwise much as *U. verrucosa*. Individual compartments round-oval, rough, often spiny. On either side small almost circular opening large oval-triangular pointed process, see fig. 103*e* and *f*. Widely distributed. Probably not uncommon.

Mucronella coccinea

B. MUCH BRANCHED TUFTS, up to 3 in. long, sandy colour or white.

Tufts 1-2 in. long, pale sandy colour with orange tints; feel rather hard and scratchy. Hang in great quantities on rock overhangs, middle and lower shore, among purse sponges and red seaweed, particularly *Plumaria elegans* (p. 241 and pl. 1 and 38). When teased or floated out branches seen to be arranged spirally. Individual compartments boat-shaped, almost too small to see even through a lens, see fig. 104. Widely distributed. Abundant.   *Bugula* [*turbinata*] pl. iii.

Much branched bushy tufts, 1-3 in. long, sandy-grey; on stem and branches dense clusters of elongated-oval individual compartments, clusters sometimes running into each other, of which walls transparent, see fig. 105. Widely distributed, particularly on *Corallina* (p. 250 and pl. 35), *Fucus* (p. 226 and pl. xxxii) and on other Polyzoa. Common.

Bowerbankia imbricata fig. 105.

Fig. 104. *Left:* "Individual compartments" of *Bugula turbinata*, x *c* 15
Fig. 105. *Centre: Bowerbankia imbricata*, x 1
Fig. 106. *Right: Crisia* sp., x *c* 20

Individual compartments tubular, one leading from half-way down next below in series of bent joints to stems which together form white tufts about ½ in. tall; mouths of tubes circular with long spine growing behind each, see fig. 106. Widely distributed. On shells, rocks and red seaweeds. Low on middle shore and lower. Common. *Crisia* spp.

C. FLATTENED, ROUND-ENDED "FRONDS," usually cast ashore.

Flattened fronds dividing, often dichotomously, and sub-dividing into broad, blunt, rounded ends. 4-6 in. tall. Compartments rectangular, on both sides of fronds, and in alternate rows, fig. 107a. Brown when fresh. Not truly on the shore, but constantly cast ashore where it becomes brittle and pale straw-sand colour. Widely distributed. Common. *Flustra foliacea* HORNWRACK pl. iii and xxv.

As *F. foliacea* but narrow segments of frond not more than ¼ in. across, individual compartments square-ended, fig. 107b. N. of a line from Flamborough to Liverpool. Common in Scotland.

Flustra securifrons pl. iii.

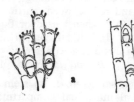

Fig. 107. "Individual compartments" of a. *Flustra foliacea;* b. *Flustra securifrons.* Both x 10-15

D. SPONGE-LIKE MASSES, 4-12 in. long, irregularly lobed and fingered into blunt-ended shapes.

Gelatinous masses lobed and fingered into a great variety of shapes, 4-12 in. long. May be growing independently or on seaweeds or hydroids; greenish-yellow, ginger-khaki or grey. Mass of colony covered with tiny raised rough spots which are the individual compartments. Lower shore and downwards. Widely distributed. Common. Often cast ashore; when dry acquires almost velvety texture.

Alcyonidium spp. pl. iii.

E. MINUTE STALKED OPEN-MOUTHED BELLS, to 1/5 in. tall.

From creeping "rootlets" on shells, hydroids and seaweeds rise tiny "stalks," which may or may not be spiny, topped by open-mouthed bells which may be 1/5 in. tall, and which flex and bob jerkily. See fig. 108. Lower shore. Widely distributed. Common. Family *Pedicellinidae*

Fig. 108

Beware of the tunicate *Perophora listeri*, see p. 189 and fig. 140.

PHORONIDEA

THIS IS a very small group of animals most of which belong to a single genus *Phoronis*, of which only one species occurs in Britain. *Phoronis hippocrepia* makes membranous tubes in limestone, shells, etc. about ½ in. deep. From an open end of the tube emerges a horseshoe-shaped pattern of tentacles (pl. ii), which retreat at the slightest disturbance by vibration or shadow. Large numbers live together. Widely distributed but nowhere common.

CHAETOGNATHA

Arrow Worms

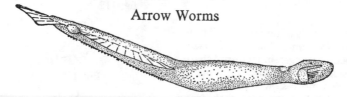

Fig. 109. *Spadella cephaloptera*, x 10

THIS IS a group of worm-like animals with a type of structure all their own. They are almost transparent and are carnivorous, capturing their prey—small crustaceans or even fishes—by sudden darting movements. They are armed with spines and teeth. British species are not more than about ½ in. long and for this reason and their transparency are not easy to see (when preserved they turn opaque and are then easily distinguished). They are contained in two genera, *Sagitta* and *Spadella*. Species of the former (pl. ii) are members of the surface-dwelling plankton of all seas. They may occasionally be found in pools low on the shore. But the other genus, represented by *Spadella cephaloptera* (fig. 109) is a typical inhabitant of rock pools at least along the south and west coasts. Unlike *Sagitta* it lives on the bottom, fixing itself there by means of an adhesive papilla (shown in the figure) on the underside of the body. It would appear to make occasional rapid movements from one point of attachment to another. It lives attached in this way either to weeds or mud in rock pools. But it needs exceptionally careful search.

ECHINODERMATA

Spiny-skinned Animals; Starfish, Sea-Urchins, etc.

A HIGHLY charácteristic group of purely marine animals, largely with radial symmetry and with a remarkable "water vascular system" which communicates with the surrounding sea water and operates, by means of hydrostatic pressure, rows of radially arranged suckers, the so-called "tube-feet."

A

Body consists of inconspicuous disc with five pairs of feathery arms.
CRINOIDEA Feather-stars pl. 26

B

Body consists of disc with radiating arms, sometimes blunt and short, sometimes longer, but without sharp division between disc and arms. Animals move slowly by means of rows of tube-feet under each arm.
ASTEROIDEA Starfish pl. 24 and 25.

　i. More than 5 arms, fig. 110.

Fig. 110

　ii. Typical starfish with 5 arms, fig. 111.

Fig. 111

iii. Cushion-stars, having flat discs coming to points representing very short arms; fig. 112.

Fig. 112

C

More or less clear demarcation between disc (usually not more than 1 in. in diameter) and long, thin arms. Animals move by means of arms which are usually jerked forward in pairs; fig. 113.

OPHIUROIDEA Brittle-Stars pl. 26.

Fig. 113

　i. Length of arms up to five times diameter of disc.
　ii. Length of arms about 15 times diameter of disc.

D

Spiny, globular animals, round, oval, or heart-shaped with a brittle limy skeleton or test covered with spines each articulating with a small tubercle. Bared test perforated with lines running in meridians from centre, or petal-like patterns of holes through which tube-feet project in life. ECHINOIDEA Sea-Urchins pl. 27.

i. Spherical viewed from above, more or less flattened at poles. Strong spines. The typical, regular shaped urchins.

ii. Oval, much depressed. Very short, close spines.

iii. Heart-shaped urchins. Weak spines largely directed backwards following shape of body. Burrowing urchins which move in a definite direction (by means of spines) and are not radially symmetrical.

E

Usually leathery, gherkin-shaped animals, mouth at one end surrounded by circle of retractile tentacles; fig. 114. HOLOTHUROIDEA Sea-Cucumbers pl. 28.

Fig. 114

i. With five rows of suckers (tube-feet), of which some may be reduced. Not adhesive.

ii. Without suckers. Skin adhesive when touched. More elongated.

A. BODY AN INCONSPICUOUS DISC WITH FIVE PAIRS OF FEATHERY ARMS   CRINOIDEA FEATHER-STARS.

Beneath concave disc short processes for temporary attachment. Five pairs of feathery arms, usually 3-6 in. long, wave sinuously in water; shades of red, pink, orange, yellow, mauve. Lower shore. On sides of and under stones. Only occur above lowest tides in S.W.

Antedon bifida FEATHER STAR pl. 26.

B. BODY CONSISTS OF DISC WITH RADIATING ARMS sometimes longer; but *without sharp division between disc and arms.* Animals move forward slowly by means of rows of tube-feet under each arm. When describing the relative length of the arm of a starfish in relation to that of the radius of the disc the following formula is used : R=4r means that the total distance from centre of disc to tip of arm (R) equals four times the radius of the disc (r).

ASTEROIDEA Star-fish pl. 24 and 25.

i. More than five arms, fig. 115.

Fig. 115

Usually 6-10 in. across, may be 16 in. R=2.5r. Usually 9-10 stiff arms; may have 7-13. Upper surface rough, hard texture; violet or yellowish-red, cream below, Lower shore. All coasts except S. and S.E. Uncommon. *Solaster endeca* (Linn.) PURPLE SUNSTAR pl. 24

Usually 4-8 in. across, may be 14 in. R=2r. Usually 10-12 arms, may have 8-13. Upper surface very rough, with spines in regular rows. Variable colours; disc normally red or purplish-red; may be yellow; arms pale, particularly towards tips, and banded; whitish below. Lower shore. Widely distributed. Not uncommon.

Solaster papposus COMMON SUNSTAR pl. 24.

ii. Typical starfish with five arms, fig. 116.

Fig. 116

Total diameter up to 20 in., but those found on shore usually 2-4 in. R usually=4-5r, but may be 3.5-7. Arms, very occasionally four or six, rather rounded and tapered, rough, with well-marked line of spines down middle. Yellow-brown, red-brown with paler markings; reddish-yellow, or even violet. Lower shore. Widely distributed. Very common.

Asterias rubens COMMON STARFISH pl. 24.

Total diameter up to 28 in., but usually 9-12 in. R=about 5-9r. Body rather soft, covered with knobs and spines, so that it is very rough. Readily throws off arms when handled. Rather pale, often ice-greenish, yellowish, reddish. Lower shore. W. and S. coasts. Not uncommon. *Marthasterias glacialis* SPINY STARFISH pl. 24.

Total diameter up to 10 in., but usually about 5 in. R=4-5r. Rays stiff, rounded, tapering. Usually dark red above, or orange or purple; pale sandy below. Widely distributed. Not uncommon.

Henricia sanguinolenta pl. 24.

Total diameter 3-5 in., may be 8 in. R=3.5r to 4.5. Very regular shape; flat, with ridged lateral margins fringed with spines. Centre of disc prominent. Variable colour, brick-red, light pink, reddish-violet, yellow; may have purple tips to arms. Widely distributed. Lives *in sand*, usually below low water of extreme spring tides, but is cast ashore. *Astropecten irregularis* pl. 25.

iii. Cushion-stars, having flat discs coming to points representing very short arms; fig. 117.

Fig 117

Up to 4 in. across, but usually about 1 in. R=1.5r. Rays often turn up at ends when out of water. Stiff, rough. Rather yellowish-flat, green, with red, purer green and cream tints. Lower shore. Under stones and overhangs. S. and W. coasts only. Common.

Asterina gibbosa CUSHION STAR pl. 25.

To 8 in. across; usually 4-6 in. Almost a pentagon with concave edges. Thin, leathery. Red above (when dead, red persists round central disc and five radiating lines); yellow below with red edge. All coasts except Dover-Hartlepool. Lives below tide marks but may be cast ashore. Rare on shore. *Palmipes membranaceus* pl. 25.

Up to 4 in. across, usually to 2 in. Thick; very short arms rise to central disc. Flat below. Smooth; greasy to touch. Scarlet, perhaps with white markings, or yellowish-white above; white below. All coasts except Dover-Aberdeen. Lives below tide marks but may be cast ashore. Rare on shore. *Porania pulvillus* pl. 25.

C. MORE OR LESS CLEAR DEMARCATION BETWEEN DISC AND LONG THIN ARMS.

Fig. 118

Disc usually not more than 1 in. in diameter. Animals move by means of arms which are usually jerked forward in pairs; fig. 118.

These animals are difficult to identify in the field (in the laboratory too, for that matter). Listed below are only certain of the common species which have fairly distinctive characters. Most of them have related species which look very similar. Few identifications based on these descriptions will be absolutely certain. OPHIUROIDEA Brittle-Stars

i. Length of arms up to about five times diameter of disc

Diameter of disc about $\frac{1}{2}$-1 in. Arms emerge from top, not edge, of disc; lying inwards across root of arm are four plates, *outer pair of which have comb edge*, fig. 119a. Between arms on lower (mouth) side are large characteristically shaped mouth-shield plates, fig. 119b. Disc scaly above and below. Arms with small spines that lie along arm rather than stand off stiffly. Reddish-brown, often spotted above; yellowish or white, particularly the mouth-shield plates, below. Widely distributed. In sand. May be cast ashore. Common. *Ophiura* spp. pl. 26.

Disc diameter $\frac{1}{8}$ in., arms four times as long. Disc evenly scaly except at base of arms where are a much larger pair of scales in contact throughout their length, fig. 119c. Greyish-white, or bluish-grey; may be phosphorescent. Lower shore. Under stones; in pools, particularly among *Corallina* (p. 250 and pl. 35); on sand and gravel. Widely distributed. Common.

Amphipholis squamata pl. 26.

Disc diameter to 1 in., arms about five times as long. Disc so finely granulated as to feel smooth. No large scales by base of arms. Arms thinly tapering, with many long, erect, glassy, hollow spines. Black or brown to grey or even pink. S. and W. coasts common; probably rare Dover-Durham. *Ophiocomina nigra* pl. 26.

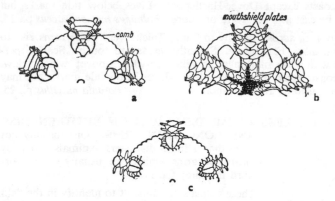

Fig. 119. Discs of a. *Ophiura* spp., from above; b. *Ophiura* spp., from below; c. *Amphipholis squamata*, from above;

Disc usually about $\frac{2}{5}$ in. diameter, but may be $\frac{4}{5}$ in.; arms about five times as long. *Disc patterned by five rays of spines converging on spiny centre;* in the sections are five pairs of triangular plates with a small line of division between each pair that marks the line of the arms, fig. 119d. Thin, slender, tapering arms, with overlapping scales; on each joint in arm seven long, glassy spines armed with teeth. Colour extremely variable, often violet, purple, or red, sometimes pale grey or yellow; may be spotted with red; arms often white or grey, banded pink. Extremely fragile, to point of throwing off all arms in pieces. Lower shore. Widely distributed. Abundant. *Ophiothrix fragilis* pl. 26.

Disc $\frac{2}{5}$-$\frac{4}{5}$ in. diameter; arms 3-4 times as long. Disc *almost five-pointed rather than round*, with points bulging out between arms;

very granular, hardly spiny, above (fig. 119e) with usually ten radiating rows of round plates showing through granules. Arms rather thick, with short, thick, porcelain-like spines. Disc usually red, radiating rows being paler; may be bluish; arms often banded darker. Lower shore. In crevices; under stones. Widely distributed. Rare in S., commoner in N. *Ophiopholis aculeata* pl. 26.

Fig. 119. d. *Ophiothrix fragilis*, from above; e. *Ophiopholis aculeata*. All x *c* 2

ii. Length of arms about 15 times diameter of disc

Disc $\frac{1}{2}$ in. diameter, arms about 15 times as long. Grey-sandy colour. Lives in sand. Middle and lower shore. S. and W. coasts. Locally common. Commensal bivalve, p. 168. *Acronida brachiata* pl. 26.

D. SPINY, GLOBULAR ANIMALS, round, oval or heart-shaped with a brittle, limy skeleton or test covered with spines each articulating with a small tubercle. Bared test perforated with lines running in meridians from centre, or petal-like patterns of holes through which tube-feet project in life. ECHINOIDEA Sea-Urchins pl. 27.

i. Spherical viewed from above, more or less flattened at poles. Strong spines. The typical regular-shaped urchins.

Up to 2 in. horizontal diameter; strong, short spines (fig. 120a). Pale green, with violet tips to spines. May cover itself with bits of seaweed. Lower shore. Under stones and overhangs. Widely distributed. Common. *Psammechinus miliaris* pl. 27.

Usually 3-4 in. horizontal diameter, may be 6 in. Nearly spherical, but flattened at both poles. Test deep red, with white tubercles; spines blunt-ended, fig. 120b, reddish, may be white, usually with purplish tips. Lower shore. Widely distributed. Common, particularly in spring. *Echinus esculentus* COMMON SEA-URCHIN pl. 27.

Among the spines may be found the scale-worm *Scalisetosus assimilis*, see p. 68.

Up to 2 in. horizontal diameter; considerably flattened. Long, tapering, sharply pointed spines (fig. 120c). Test greenish. Spines violet, shining purple; sometimes brownish or olive-greenish. Bores holes in rocks. Often many together. Among *Zostera* (p. 254 and pl. 40). Lower shore. Ireland, not uncommon; Devon, Cornwall, Hebrides rare. *Paracentrotus lividus* pl. 27.

Up to 3 in. horizontal diameter. Considerably flattened. Short, round-ended, longitudinally striated spines, fig. 120d. Test greenish-brown. Spines greenish or reddish, sometimes violet with white points. May bore holes in rocks. Only E. coast.
Strongylocentrotus drobachiensis (Muller) pl. 27.

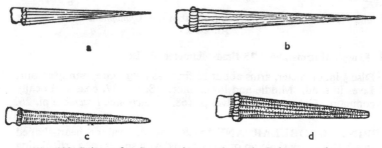

Fig. 120. Spines of a. *Psammechinus miliaris;* b. *Echinus esculentus;* c. *Paracentrotus lividus;* d. *Strongylocentrotus drobrachiensis.* All x c 5

ii. Oval; much depressed. Very short, close spines.

Body about ½ in. long. Very short, close spines. Greyish or bright green; turns greener if damaged, and dirty white when dead. On coarse sand or gravel. Lower shore. Widely distributed. Probably common. *Echinocyamus pusillus* GREEN SEA URCHIN

iii. Heart-shaped urchins. Weak spines largely directed backwards following shape of body. Burrowing urchins which move in a definite direction (by means of spines) and are not radially sym-metrical.

Body 4 in. long by 3½ in. broad, or larger. Violet with pale spines, especially those long and curved on back. Lies buried in coarse sand and gravel. Lower shore and below. Irregularly distributed, but locally common. *Spatangus purpureus* PURPLE HEART-URCHIN pl. 27.

Careful lifting will often reveal the tiny bivalve mollusc *Montacuta substriata* (p. 168) lying near the anus on the posterior side.

Body usually about 1¾ in. long by 1½ in. broad, may be smaller or much bigger, to 3½ in. long. Slopes upwards from front. Obvious furrows in rather soft, brittle, easily-rubbed-off spines. Sandy coloured. Near-white, fragile test often cast ashore. In fairly clean sand, burrows 3 in. deep; usually many together. Middle and lower shore. Widely distributed. Very common.

Echinocardium cordatum SEA POTATO pl. 27.

Careful lifting will often reveal the tiny bivalve mollusc *Montacuta ferruginosa* (p. 168) lying near the anus.

E. USUALLY LEATHERY, GHERKIN-SHAPED ANIMALS,
mouth at one end and surrounded by circle of retractile tentacles, fig. 121.
HOLOTHUROIDEA Sea-Cucumbers pl. 28.

i. With five rows of suckers (tube-feet), of which some may be reduced. *Not adhesive.*

Usually 3-5 in. long, may be 8 in. Skin soft, thick, coarse texture; dark brown above, perhaps pale spotted; much lighter below. *Under surface*

Fig. 121

with three rows of strong suckers; above are two furrows marking lines of much reduced suckers. *Twenty yellow,* short, bunched, retractile tentacles. Near anus are cotton glands through which white, sticky threads can be ejected to confuse or entangle aggressors. Lower shore and below. On rocks. S.W. only. Uncommon.

Holothuria forskali NIGGER OR COTTON SPINNER pl. 28.

Body usually 2-4 in. long, may be 6 in. Almost cylindrical. *Thin, smooth skin.* Five distinct rows of suckers, double below; rather zigzag above and reduced in size. White, with ten dark branched tentacles. Lower shore. Among rocks; in crevices; under stones. S. and W. coasts; not Scotland.

Cucumaria saxicola SEA GHERKIN pl. xxviii.

As *C. saxicola* but skin tough, leathery, wrinkled; dirty brownish-white, becoming black when exposed to light. *Tube-feet in double rows.* S. coasts. Locally not uncommon. *Cucumaria normani* pl. 28.

Usually ¾ in. long, may be 1½ in.; cylindrical. Skin very thick, leathery and smooth. Few strong suckers, only about nine in a line. Ten white, branched tentacles. Body pinkish-brown or whitish.

Lower shore. On stony or shelly bottom; on seaweeds and hydroids. All coasts except Dover to Tees. Locally common.

Cucumaria lactea pl. 28.

ii. Without suckers. *Skin adhesive when touched.* More elongated.

Usually 4-6 in. long, may be 12 in. Thin, semi-transparent skin; pale pink or greyish. Twelve tentacles, *much branched*, outer branches longest, fig. 122. Burrows in sand and mud. Lower shore. S.W., W., N.E. coasts. Commensal bivalve, p. 168. *Leptosynapta inhaerens*

Fig. 122. Tentacle of *Lepto-synapta inhaerens*, x 5

Fig. 123. Tentacle of *Labido-plax digitata*, x 5

Usually 6-8 in. long, may be 12 in. Red or brownish, paler below. Twelve tentacles that have but *four fingers each*, fig. 123. Lower shore. Burrows in sand or mud. S.W. and W. coasts. Uncommon.

Labidoplax digitata fig. 124.

Fig. 124. *Labidoplax digitata*, x 1-⅓

CHORDATA

TUNICATA
Tunicates, Ascidians or Sea-Squirts

THE CHORDATES include the vertebrates, animals with backbones ranging from fish through amphibians and reptiles to birds and mammals. They also include some animals without backbones, notably the tunicates or sea squirts. Although these have no resemblance to a vertebrate, they pass through a " tadpole " stage in development, which is not unlike the early stages of some vertebrates. But the adult sea squirt is little more than a stout bag with two openings or siphons. Through one of these water containing oxygen and food enters to be strained through a fine meshwork which occupies much of the space within the enclosing tunic. Food is passed to the gut while the water with waste products, etc., leaves by the second, or anal, siphon. Although so simple, sea squirts are highly successful and are amongst the commonest animals on the sea shore.

A

Long, rounded objects, some jelly-like and semi-transparent, others stiff and leathery; the two siphons usually made obvious if squeezed, when water squirts out.

   i. Living separately and singly; certainly not fused with neighbours. Terminal siphon with eight lobes, lateral (anal) siphon with six, between each of which a red spot; fig. 125 and 126.

   ii. Living separately and singly; rather hard, round or nearly so. Siphons six- and four-lobed. Most of them embedded in or covered with mud; fig. 138, p. 189.

   iii. Living singly but connected by loose network of creeping " rootlets "; fig. 140, p. 189.

   iv. Individuals often living in numbers together, sometimes with bases and perhaps also lower parts of individuals fused; fig. 127.

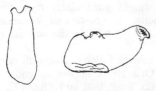

Fig. 125   Fig. 126

Fig. 127

185

B

Colonial (or compound) tunicates fused in groups throughout length of individuals, whose identity is lost in the characteristics of the group.

i. Colonies more or less stalked bunches; fig. 128.

ii. Colonies flat jelly-like layers, marked with patterns of stars or wavy lines; fig. 129.

iii. Colonies flat, thin, adhering commonly to *Laminaria* (p. 225 and pl. xxxi), without patterning; may feel gritty and porous. Easily confused with sponges, common exhalant siphon may resemble sponge osculum (see p. 41). Overall stippling indicates contained individuals.

iv. Colonies little-finger-thick lobes patterned with star shapes. In quiet water.

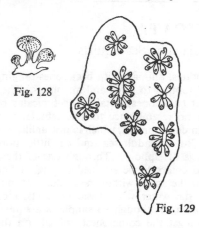

Fig. 128

Fig. 129

A. LONG, ROUNDED OBJECTS, some jelly-like and semi-transparent, others stiff and leathery; *the two siphons usually made obvious if squeezed, when water squirts out.* Fig. 130.

i. Living separately and singly; certainly not fused with neighbours. Terminal siphon with eight lobes, the lateral siphon with six lobes, in between each of which is a red spot.

Fig. 130

Body 2-6 in. long, round-oval or perhaps pear-shaped. Attached by only part of one side, with short siphon at unattached end and other about half-way along; fig. 131. Both colour and shape variable. Body rather rough texture, greenish or pale cream, translucent, showing from inside brown-red tinges particularly near siphons. Lower shore. On rocks and shells. S. coasts and W. except in Scotland; absent E. coast. *Ascidia mentula* pl. 29.

Body 1-2 in. long, flattened-oval, attached along almost all one side, with small roughnesses on it. One short siphon at end; other (longer) siphon about 2/3 way back from that end; fig. 132. Skin thin, translucent; with green blood vessels and contrasting bright

186

pink eggs showing through. Lower shore. On stones and shells. Widely distributed. Common. *Ascidia conchilega*

Body 2-5 in. long, oval; usually attached by base. Body rough, rather stiff, with small irregular projections; dark grey or brown. One siphon at end, other 1/3 body length away; fig. 133. Lower shore. On stones; on harbour works; particularly in estuaries. S. and W. coasts only. Probably common; locally abundant.
Ascidiella aspersa pl. 29.

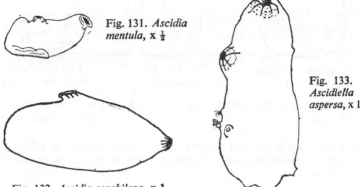

Fig. 131. *Ascidia mentula*, x ½

Fig. 133. *Ascidiella aspersa*, x 1

Fig. 132. *Ascidia conchilega*, x 1

Body ¾-2 in. long, flat-oval; attached along most of one side, rather stiff, with roughnesses round base of siphons, one of which is at end, other only ¼ body length away, both rather prominent; fig. 134. Nearly transparent with red tints showing through towards siphons. Lower shore. On rocks and shells. Widely distributed. Common.
Ascidiella scabra pl. 29.

Body 3-5 in. long, elongated cylindrical; contracts readily. Attached more or less at base. Very soft and thinly transparent, yellowish or pale green, five longitudinal muscle bands visible. Siphons prominent, somewhat tubular, one at end, other close to it. Pale green, grey, yellow, prominent red spots on siphon lobes; fig. 135. Lower shore. Particularly on harbour works, piles, buoys, etc. Widely distributed. Common. *Ciona intestinalis* pl. 29.

Body 1-2 in. high, square-oval, attached by part of base. Smooth, rather stiff, completely transparent, with crimson, yellow and white flecks visible inside. Larger but not prominent siphon at end; small, more tubular, one to one side; fig. 136. Lower shore and below. On stones and shells; amongst *Laminaria* (p. 225 and pl. xxxi) hold-

| Fig. 134. *Ascidiella scabra*, x 1 | Fig. 135. *Ciona intestinalis*, x 1 | Fig. 136. *Corella parallelogramma*, x 1 |

fasts. Widely distributed. Rather rare S. and E.; not uncommon
W. and N.   *Corella parallelogramma*

ii. Living separately and singly; rather hard, round or nearly so.
Siphon six- and four-lobed. Most of them embedded in or covered
with mud.

Fig. 137. *Molgula citrina*, x 1

Individuals ⅕-¾ in. tall, very round, hard, not quite smooth. May
be in groups. Short prominent siphons at angle 45°; fig. 137. Translucent greenish-yellow. Not covered by sand, but in it or in mud.
Lower shore. On stones, harbour works, etc. S.W., W. and N.
coasts. Not uncommon.   *Molgula citrina*

Individuals ½-1¼ in. long, oval-globular, rather hard, covered with
sand grains or mud particles *including area of siphons;* fig. 138.
Lower shore. In sand or mud. E., S. and W. coasts. Locally not
uncommon.   *Molgula occulta*

Individual 2-3 in. tall, oval-globular, completely covered with sand
except for clearly marked area round two siphons and space in between;
fig. 139. Siphons short and wide. Lower shore. In sand and mud;
with *M. occulta.* S.W. coasts. Not common.   *Molgula oculata*

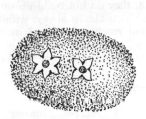

Fig. 138. *Molgula occulta,* x 1

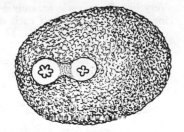

Fig. 139. *Molgula oculata,* x 1

iii. Living singly but connected by loose network of creeping " rootlets "

Body ¼-½ in. tall, flat-topped-globular with siphons at summit and side of top; colourless; fig. 140. Lower shore. On stones and seaweeds. All coasts except Scotland. Probably common. (Beware confusion with *Pedicellinidae,* p. 174 and fig. 108). *Perophora listeri*

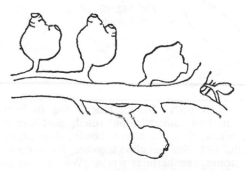

Fig. 140. *Perophora listeri,* x 2

iv. Individuals often living in numbers together, sometimes with bases and perhaps also lower parts of individuals fused

Individual body ¼-½ in. high, rounded, stiff, rather wrinkled, with two stiff red siphons protruding. Usually deep cherry-red but may be brownish lower down, or dirty yellow. Great numbers of individuals may live side by side and become fused into common base. Small ones may be attached to sides of larger ones, giving overall texture of bed of rounded knobs. Lower shore. On rather exposed coasts, under deep rock overhangs; on oyster beds; on *Laminaria* (p. 225 and pl. xxxi) stalks. Solitary ones occasional all round Britain. Fused masses S. and W. coasts very commonly.

Dendrodoa (Styelopsis) grossularia pl. 29.

Very like *D. grossularia*, only ¼ in. high, rather rounded. Although individuals fused to half their depth, they do not build up on each other to knobby lumps; fig. 141. Siphons almost always withdrawn when tide is out leaving only round marks. Brick-red or brick-brown. Lower shore. On stones; on *Laminaria* (p. 225 and pl. xxxi) holdfasts and stalks. Probably only S.W. and W. coasts. Locally abundant.   *Distomus variolosus*

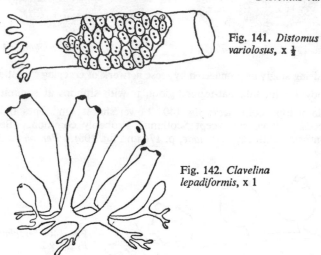

Fig. 141. *Distomus variolosus*, x ½

Fig. 142. *Clavelina lepadiformis*, x 1

Individual rather stalked body, 1-2 in. long, rising in compact clusters from common base, otherwise not fused; soft and transparent, with white, yellow, pink, and brown showing through, darker pigments in lines; fig. 142. Siphons close together, the larger at tip. Lower shore. On stones; on harbour works. Widely distributed. Common.   *Clavelina lepadiformis* pl. 29.

B. COLONIAL (or compound) TUNICATES FUSED IN GROUPS THROUGHOUT LENGTH OF INDIVIDUALS, whose identity is lost in the characteristics of the group.

    i. Colonies more or less stalked bunches, fig. 143.

Fig. 143. [*Morchellium argus*], x ½

Colony usually about ½ in. long, may be 1½ in., rather club-shaped, attached by narrowing stalk. Usually 40-50 individuals in colony. Lower shore. Under rocks; on overhangs; among *Laminaria* (p. 225 and pl. xxxi) holdfasts.
                                    [*Aplidium (Amaroucium)* spp.]

Yellow or off-white, with some red spots. S.W. coasts.
Aplidium punctum

Perhaps several colonies branching from one thick base stalk; fig. 144. Fleshy, yellow, grey or orange. W. coasts. Common.
Aplidium proliferum (Milne-Edwards).

Colony usually 1½ in. long, on thick, strong, brilliant red stalk; yellowish with red spots; fig. 143. Lower shore. Under rather exposed rocks. S. and W. coasts. Locally abundant.
[*Morchellium argus*]

Morchellium and *Aplidium* cannot be certainly distinguished on these characters alone.

Colonies only ¼ in. tall, singly or in groups, flat-topped, connected by creeping "rootlets," but without stalks; fig. 145. Yellow-orange, off-white; perhaps red spots. Lower shore. On stones and seaweeds. All except E. coasts. Common. *Sidnyum turbinatum* pl. 29.

Fig. 144. *Aplidium proliferum,* x 1

Fig. 145. *Sidnyum turbinatum,* x 1

Colonies ¼-½ in. tall, ¼-1 in. across, usually in groups, flat-topped, narrow base, almost no stalk. Some large communal exhalant siphons; fig. 146. Yellow or yellow-brown. Lower shore. Under stones; on seaweeds; in cracks. S. and W. coasts. Probably common. *Polyclinum aurantium*

Fig. 146. *Polyclinum aurantium,* x 1

ii. Colonies flat jelly-layers with patterns of stars or wavy lines. Figs. 147-148.

Thin encrustations on rocks, seaweeds, etc., have typical star-shaped pattern with 3-12 " petals " round larger central opening of common exhalant siphon; fig. 147. Beautiful variety of colours, sometimes alongside each other; delicate orange, blues, yellows, etc. Patches may be from ¼ in. to 6 in. or more across. Same organism in quiet water develops lobes as thick as little finger, similarly patterned. Lower shore. Widely distributed. Abundant, particularly in August.

Botryllus schlosseri STAR ASCIDIAN, STAR SEA SQUIRT pl. 29.

As *B. schlosseri* but patterns are in lines, sometimes branched; sometimes pattern may to some extent lose its coherence; fig. 148. Colours variable, mostly grey, orange or yellow. *Botrylloides leachi* pl. 29.

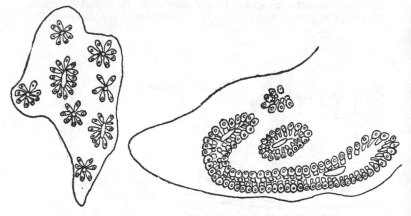

Fig. 147. *Botryllus schlosseri*, x 1

Fig. 148. *Botrylloides leachi*, x 1

Encrustations ¼-½ in. thick, usually 2-4 in. across, rose-pink, paling to yellow lower. Regular systems, often star-shaped, grouped round communal larger exhalant siphon; fig. 149. Lower shore. On stones in fairly sheltered water. S.W. coasts. Not uncommon.

Aplidium (Amaroucium) nordmanni

iii. Colonies flat, thin, adhering commonly to *Laminaria* (p. 225 and pl. xxxi), *without patterning; may feel gritty and porous*. Easily confused with sponges, common exhalant siphon may resemble sponge osculum (see p. 41).

About six species are common but not describable within the limits

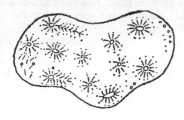

Fig. 149. *Aplidium nordmanni*, x 1

here set, except perhaps *Didemnum maculosum*, pl. 29, because of its colour, grey-bluish or violet with branched purple lines over surface; all coasts except Scotland.

iv. **Colonies little-finger-thick lobes** patterned with star shapes; in quiet water. *Botryllus schlosseri* pl. 29. See **ii.** above

ENTEROPNEUSTA

A group of worm-like animals known as the Hemichordata although their relationship to the true chordates is dubious. The body, a few inches long, is exceptionally soft, so that the animals frequently break up while being collected, but with care a reasonably intact specimen can be obtained and seen to be unsegmented and to consist of three very distinct regions; see pl. 28. An anterior pointed proboscis is separated by a round collar from a long and very soft trunk. The branchial region of this which adjoins the collar is perforated by pairs of gill openings, while the hinder region may show, through the soft skin, groups of hepatic (" liver ") pouches opening out of the gut. All burrow, usually where there is organic debris, etc.

Hepatic pouches present, proboscis acorn-shaped or conical. In muddy sand and shell gravel, on lower shore and off-shore. S. coast and W. and N.E. coasts of Ireland. *Glossobalanus sarnienis*

No hepatic pouches; proboscis spatulate, honey-coloured, branchial region greenish. In silty sand with gravel substrata; bottom of middle and upper region of lower shore, or offshore. Isle of Man, Anglesey.

Protoglossus koehleri

No hepatic pouches; proboscis very elongate, deep pink to salmon. In fairly clean sand and shell gravel with gravel substrate; middle of lower shore. Along W. coasts Wales, Scotland, Ireland.

Saccoglossus cambrensis pl. 28.

No hepatic pouches; proboscis cream or pale pink, 100-140 pairs of gills compared with 80-90 in *S. cambrensis*. In glutinous grey mud to coarse sandy gravel, middle shore. S. and S.E. coasts, Solent to Whitstable.

Saccoglossus horsti

PISCES
Fish

Fish are familiar animals to us all. Those that live on the shore tend to be of unusual shape, such as the narrow-bodied almost snake-like pipe-fish and the flattened sucker-fishes. But all are members of the great group of the Teleosts or Bony Fishes. With few exceptions the body is covered with scales; there are two sets of paired fins, pectorals in front and pelvics behind, and also unpaired fins along the back and the belly (see fig. 152). The mouth lies at the point of the head (unlike the dog-fishes and skates and other cartilaginous fishes where it is on the under side of the head). At the back of the head are the gills, not opening separately as in the cartilaginous fishes, but covered over by an opercular flap which is attached in front and allows water to leave the gills behind. The internal anatomy is that of a vertebrate animal, with a backbone composed of many articulated vertebrae and through which runs the spinal column which swells out within the cavity of the cranium forming the complicated brain. The anus opens on the underside of the body some distance in front of the tail; with it are the openings of the kidneys and of the reproductive system. Typically many eggs are discharged but the shore fishes are somewhat exceptional in that many of them lay a smaller number of largish eggs and then the male usually guards these until they hatch.

A
No pelvic fins. Elongated fish; figs. 150-151.

i. Dorsal, caudal (tail) and anal fins all run into each other without any break. Long, round, slippery bodies. *Anguillidae* Eels pl. xxii.

ii. Very small fins. Short separate dorsal fin. Tail may be absent. More or less rounded body tapers markedly towards tail; fig. 150. Feels stiffly pliant. Poor swimmers. Lower shore. *Syngnathidae* Pipe-fish pl. xxii.

iii. One long regular dorsal fin separate from tail, as is the anal fin. Body compressed. Big, rather shovel-shaped lower jaw; fig. 151. *Ammodytidae* Sand Eels pl. xxiii.

N.B.—Vestigial pelvic fins. Body compressed. Row of 10-18 dark spots along back. See *Centronotus gunnellus*, the Butter-fish, p. 213 and pl. 31.

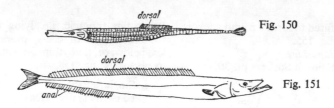

Fig. 150

Fig. 151

B

Pelvic fins very small, abdominal, i.e. placed in middle of belly between pectorals and anal. Anterior dorsal spiny; fig. 152.
Gasterosteidae Sticklebacks pl. 31.

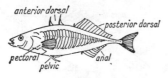

Fig. 152

i. 3-4 spines on anterior dorsal.
ii. 15 spines on anterior dorsal.

C

Pelvic fins modified to form a sucker; figs. 153-156

i. Body scaly. Two dorsal fins, anterior having flexible spines. Markedly goggle-eyed. Two small pelvics united to form oval sucker which hangs just clear of belly line; fig. 153.
Gobiidae Gobies pl. 32

Fig. 153

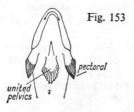

(*a*) First dorsal with seven spines, the posterior of which is separated from the anterior bunched group of six.

(*b*) First dorsal with six spines.

ii. Body without scales. Thick-set and rounded, with rows of tubercles on skin. Anterior dorsal fin represented by row of sharp lumps. Rather complicated sucker is quite obvious and may be extraordinarily effective; fig. 154.
Cyclopteridae Lumpsuckers pl. 30.

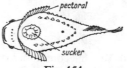

Fig. 154

iii. Body without scales or tubercles. Heavy bellied; smooth-headed. Single dorsal fin starts by tail and extends forward undivided more than half total length of fish. Anal fin also starts by tail but is shorter than dorsal. Pelvics

fused to form a round sucker;
fig. 155.

Liparidae
Smooth Suckers pl. 30.

Fig. 155

iv. Body without scales or tubercles or spines. Small dorsal
fin and smaller anal fin
always in posterior half of
body. Large sucker occupying up to 1/3 length of fish
is partly fused pelvics and
partly modified bone; fig.
156.

Gobiesocidae
Suckers pl. xxxiii.

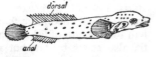

Fig. 156

(a) Tail fin continuous with
dorsal and anal fins.
(b) Tail fin separate from
dorsal and anal fins; fig.
157.

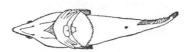

Fig. 157

D

Pelvic fins thoracic, i.e. lying forward in region of chest, more or
less below, or, if anything, posterior
to pectorals; fig. 158.

i. Single dorsal fin; long, may
be partly spiny. Heavily built
fish with particularly thick
lips that fold up inside mouth
which has strong teeth in
jaws; fig. 158. Some brilliantly coloured.

Labridae Wrasses pl. 30.

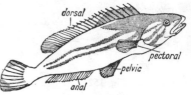

Fig. 158

(a) Three anterior rays of
anal fin spiny; fourth
may sometimes be doubt-
ful.
(b) Five anterior rays of
anal fin spiny.

ii. Two dorsal fins, first with
rather weak spines. No scales.
Each ray in tail divides into
two. Solid little fish with
spiny gill covers. Broad,
rather flattened heads.

Cottidae Sea Scorpions pl. 32.

(a) 13-14 rays in posterior
dorsal. Four spines on
gill cover.
(b) 11-12 rays in posterior
dorsal.

E

Pelvic fins jugular, i.e. lying in front of pectorals in region of throat; figs. 159-162.

i. A " flatfish "; fig. 159.

(a) Lying on left side, i.e. when held vertically so that pelvics are below head and mouth opens sensibly upwards, the pale side (underside) becomes the left side; fig. 159. *Pleuronectidae* Plaice, Dabs, etc. pl. xxiv. and *Soleidae* Soles pl. xxiv.

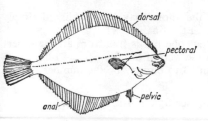

Fig. 159

(h) Lying on right side. Dorsal fin reaches forward of eye (this is also true of *Soleidae*). Rounded oval body. *Bothidae* Topknots pl. xxiv.

ii. Not a " flatfish."

(a) Anterior dorsal black or nearly so. Spines on gillcovers, anterior dorsal and pelvis fins which inject poison and cause painful swellings. Line of lips points very much upwards; fig. 160. On or in sand where shrimps abound.

Trachinidae Weevers pl. xxiii.

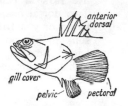

Fig. 160

(b) Spiny plates on flat head. Coarsely scaly body, fining away rapidly to stalky tail. Lower jaw bearded. *Agonidae* Armed Bullheads pl. xxiii.

(c) No spines on gill-covers. Less than five rays in pelvic fins, which may be rudimentary. Dorsal fin long, but may be in 2-3 connected parts and occupies nearly whole length of body. Pectoral fins large and rounded. Heavy head and large eyes; fig. 161. *Blenniidae* Blennies, Butterfish pl. 31.

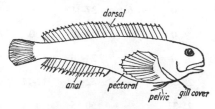

Fig. 161

197

(d) No spines on gill-covers or elsewhere. More than five rays in pelvic fins. Two dorsal fins, the anterior only a fringe and sunk in a groove along back. Smooth, shapely, rather elongated fish. Barbels and tentacles present above and below mouth; fig. 162.

Gadidae Rocklings pl. xxiii.

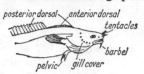

Fig. 162

FIN-RAY COUNTS OF INTERTIDAL FISH

A Simple Key to Identification

The identity of all fish found on the shore may be established simply by counting the number of rays in all the fins.

A figure such as 1/3-4 means that one ray is free from all the others and is followed by either 3 or 4 in the web of the fin.

73-86 means that anything from 73 to 86 may be the number of rays in the fin.

A. No Pelvic Fins. Elongated fish; see figs. 150-151, p. 195.

Number of rays in

ANAL	TAIL	DORSAL	PECTORAL	PELVIC	
	480-500		17-18	0	*A. anguilla* COMMON EEL pl. xxii
	525-546		16-19	0	*C. conger* CONGER pl. xxii
4	9-10	38-46	15	0	*Syngnathus typhle* BROAD-NOSED PIPE-FISH
3	3-10	40-44	13	0	*Syngnathus acus* GREATER PIPE-FISH pl. xxii
0	6	37-44	0	0	*Entelurus aequoreus* SNAKE PIPE-FISH pl. xxii
0	0	34-38	0	0	*Nerophis ophidion* STRAIGHT-NOSED PIPE-FISH
0	0	24-26	0	0	*Nerophis lumbriciformis* WORM PIPE-FISH pl. xxii
28-33		52-61	12-14	0	*Ammodytes lanceolatus* GREATER SAND-EEL fig. 164
25-31		50-56	10-14	0	*Ammodytes lancea* LESSER SAND-EEL pl. xxiii
26-35		55-67	12-15	0	*Ammodytes dubius* LESSER SAND-EEL

B. Pelvic Fins very small, abdominal; i.e. placed in middle of belly between pectorals and anal. Anterior dorsal fin spiny. Fig. 152, p. 195.

Number of rays in

ANAL	TAIL	DORSALS		PECTORAL	PELVIC	
		Ant.	*Post.*			
1/8-9	12	2-3	1/10-12	10	1/1	*Gasterosteus aculeatus* THREE-SPINED STICKLEBACK pl. 31, fig. 165
6-7	12-14	15	6-7	9-10	1/1	*Spinachia vulgaris* FIFTEEN - SPINED STICKLE-BACK pl. 31

C. Pelvic Fins modified to form a sucker; see fig. 153-156, p. 195.

Number of rays in

ANAL	TAIL	DORSALS		PECTORAL	PELVIC	
		Ant.	*Post.*			
10-12	15	7	10-12	19	1/5	*Gobius ruthensparri* SPOTTED GOBY pl. 32
10-12	13	6	12-13	18	1/5	*Gobius niger* BLACK GOBY pl. 32
12-14	13	6	14-16	20	1/5	*Gobius paganellus* ROCK GOBY pl. 32
9	13	6	10	20	1/5	*Gobius pictus* PAINTED GOBY pl. 32
10-12	11	6	10-12	21	6	*Gobius minutus* COMMON GOBY fig. 166
9-10	10-11	10-11		20-21	1/5	*Cyclopterus lumpus* LUMPSUCKER pl. 30
27-28	12-14	34-36		28	1/5	*Liparis liparis* COMMON SEA-SNAIL
24	14	26-30		30	6	*Liparis montagui* MONTAGU'S SEA-SNAIL p l.30
——	44-50	——		20-25	1/4	*Lepadogaster gouanii* CORNISH SUCKER pl. xxiii
8-11	18	14-16		25	1/4	*Lepadogaster candollii* CONNEMARA SUCKER fig. 169
4-6	12	5-7		17	5	*Lepadogaster bimaculatus* TWO-SPOTTED SUCKER pl. xxiii

D. Pelvic Fins thoracic; i.e. lying forward in the region of the ' chest,' more or less below, or, if anything, posterior to the pelvics.

Fig. 158, p. 196.

Number of rays in

ANAL	TAIL	DORSALS		PECTORAL	PELVIC	
		Ant.	*Post.*			
3/8-10	14	20-21	9-11	14-15	1/5	*Labrus bergylta* BALLAN WRASSE pl. 30
3/10-12	13-15	16-18	(11)12-14	17	1/5	*Labrus mixtus* CUCKOO, STRIPED OR RED WRASSE fig. 171
3/9-10	14	14-17	8-9	14	1/5	*Crenilabrus melops* CORKWING pl. 30
3/8	15	16-18	8-10	14	1/5	*Ctenolabrus rupestris* GOLDSINNY WRASSE pl. 30
5/7-8	15	18-20	6	14	1/5	*Centrolabrus exoletus* ROCK COCK pl. 30
9-13⁻	11	9-10	13-14	16-17	2-3	*Cottus scorpius* FATHER LASHER
9	10	8	11-12	16	1/3	*Cottus bubalis* LONG-SPINED SEA-SCORPION pl. 32

NOTE: The wrasses do not, in fact, have two dorsals but rather, one fin in two distinct parts.

E. Pelvic Fins jugular, i.e. lying in front of the pectorals in the region of the throat. Fig. 159-162, p. 197.

Number of rays in

ANAL	TAIL	DORSALS	PECTORAL	PELVIC	
		Ant. *Post.*			
45-56		61-72			*Rhombus maximus* TURBOT pl. xxiv
53-65		76-85			*Rhombus laevis* BRILL
69-80	14-16	87-101	10	6	*Zeugopterus punctatus* COMMON TOPKNOT pl. xxiv
50-57	17-18	66-77	10-11	6	*Pleuronectes platessa* PLAICE pl. xxiv
50-62	14	65-78	10-11	6	*Pleuronectes limanda* DAB pl. xxiv
39-45	14	60-62	10	6	*Pleuronectes flesus* FLOUNDER pl. xxiv

ANAL	TAIL	DORSALS		PECTORAL	PELVIC	
		Ant.	Post.			
61-73	16	73-86		7	5-6	*Solea solea* SOLE
50-56	19	65-72		R.5. L.3	5	*Microchirus boscanion* SOLENETTE pl. xxiv
31	12	5-6	29-31	16	1/5	*Trachinus draco* GREATER WEEVER fig. 173
25-26	12	6	21-24	14	1/5	*Trachinus vipera* LESSER WEEVER pl. xxiii
36-40	17	50-52		14	1/3	*Chirolophis galerita* YARRELL'S BLENNY fig. 175
84-89	0	76-80/10/20-25		19	3	*Zoarces viviparus* VIVIPAROUS BLENNY pl. 31
39-45	15	75-82		11-12	1/1-2	*Centronotus gunnellus* BUTTERFISH pl. 31
18-20	13	11-13	18-20	13	2	*Blennius pholis* BLENNY OR SHANNY pl. 31
16-18	11	11-12	14-16	12	2	*Blennius ocellaris* BUTTERFLY BLENNY fig. 176
17-18	11	12-13	15-17	12	2	*Blennius montagui* MONTAGU'S BLENNY pl. 31
21-22	12-13	12-14	19-20	14	1/2-3	*Blennius gattorugine* TOMPOT pl. 31
40-46	20-21	47-55		15	7-8	*Onos mustelus* FIVE-BEARDED ROCKLING
48-50	21	55-57		16-18	6-7	*Onos mediterraneus* THREE-BEARDED ROCKLING pl. xxiii, Fig. 177

A. NO PELVIC FINS. Elongated fish. Figs. 163, 164, p. 202-3.

i. **Dorsal, tail and anal fins all run into each other** without any break. Long round slippery bodies. *Anguillidae* EELS pl. xxii.

Females to 3 ft. long; males to 18 in. Small scales embedded in skin. *Dorsal fin ending well behind pectoral fin.* Great variation in colour. Most of year females olive-green above shading to yellow below; males rather bronzy on back. In late summer those that are going to migrate to breed lose yellow colour and become silvery and finer-headed. In spring three-year elvers arrive at mouths of streams and rivers, 3-6 in. long, eel-shaped and shiny-bright. All three stages common in sea and are widely distributed.

Anguilla anguilla COMMON EEL pl. xxii.

As found near shore, usually 1-2 ft. long; grey above, paling to near white below. No scales. *Dorsal fin comes forward as far as pectorals.* Eyes large. Gill-slits prominent, extending to low on body. Lower shore. Under stones in muddy areas. Widely distributed. Common in S. and W. Uncommon in E. *Conger conger* CONGER EEL pl. xxii.

ii. Very small fins. *Short separate dorsal fin.* *Tail may be absent.* More or less rounded body tapers markedly towards tail, fig. 163. Feels stiffly pliant. Poor swimmers. *Syngnathidae* PIPE-FISH pl. xxii.

dorsal

Fig. 163. *Syngnathus acus*, x c 1/6

(*a*) *Body with ridges running lengthwise. Having pectoral and tail fins*

To 10-12 in. long; dark brown with light spots below. Tapers off fairly regularly from maximum girth which is just behind the gills. Large and heavy snout with but little shallowing at half-way line between eyes and large mouth. Widely distributed. Not common.

Syngnathus typhle BROAD-NOSED PIPE-FISH

To 10-15 in. long; brown above, paler below; banded. Maximum girth half-way between gills and dorsal fin, giving a paunchy effect, and then sudden tapering below dorsal fin. Snout not heavy and with marked shallowing at point half-way between eye and mouth, fig. 163. Widely distributed. Not uncommon.

Syngnathus acus GREATER PIPE-FISH pl. xxii.

(*b*) *Body round, smooth and thin. No pectoral fins*

Typically about 15 in. long but may be 30 in. Olive-green with thin bluish stripes on sides to about hinder edge of dorsal fin, which has yellow rays; purple stripe leads forward along snout from each eye. *Tail with six rays*, except in very large specimens when it may be absent. *About* 40 *rays in dorsal fin.* Off all coasts but not truly intertidal. Clings by tail to ropes, moorings and flotsam. *Entelurus aequoreus* SNAKE PIPE-FISH pl. xxii.

10-12 in. long; greenish with very pale, small, irregular markings below. *No tail fin.* Dorsal with more than 30 *rays* and set about half-way along body. Widely distributed. Not common.

Nerophis ophidion STRAIGHT-NOSED PIPE-FISH

Typically 4-6 in. long, may be 9 in.; olive-brown with small pale dots and lines underneath. Short-nosed head. *No tail fin. Dorsal with less than* 30 *rays* and set noticeably forward of half-way along body. Off all coasts. Common, particularly in W.

Nerophis lumbriciformis WORM PIPE-FISH pl. xxii.

iii. **One long regular dorsal fins eparate from tail, as' is the anal fin.** Body compressed. *Big, rather shovel-shaped lower jaw,* fig. 164. In spring and summer come inshore and at low tide may be found buried in sand in bays. *Ammodytidae* SAND-EELS pl. xxiii.

Up to 12 in. long. Bluish- or greenish-yellow above; silvery-white below. Dark mark stretches from before eye on to upper jaw. Lower jaw shovel-shaped and much longer than upper. *Dorsal fin does not reach forward further than hinder tip of pectoral,* fig. 164. 165-195 *scales on lateral line.* Widely distributed. Not uncommon.

Ammodytes lanceolatus GREATER SAND-EEL

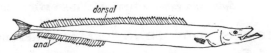

Fig. 164. *Ammodytes lanceolatus*, x c ¼

Up to 8 in. long. Greenish-blue or greenish-yellow above. Silvery sides and below. Lower jaw very protractile. *Dorsal fin reaches forward half-way along pectoral.* 120-138 *scales along lateral line.* Widely distributed. Common.

Ammodytes lancea Yarrell LESSER SAND-EEL pl. xxiii.

As *A. lancea* but *dorsal fin reaches forward only just beyond posterior tip of pectoral.* 135-155 *scales on lateral line.* N. coasts only.

Ammodytes dubius Reinhardt or *Ammodytes marinus* Raitt
The difference between these two is internal.

B. **PELVIC FINS VERY SMALL, ABDOMINAL,** i.e. placed in middle of belly between pectoral and anal fins. *Anterior dorsal fin spiny;* fig. 165. *Gasterosteidae* STICKLEBACKS pl. 31.

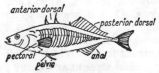

Fig. 165. *Gasterosteus aculeatus*, x ½

i. 3-4 spines on anterior dorsal

2-3 in. long; shining grey with green reflections from back and bronzy from sides; may be suffused pink below; fins possibly yellowish. Rather plump body narrowing abruptly to provide " stalk " for tail, fig. 165. Widely distributed. Not common in sea, but common in brackish and estuarine waters.

Gasterosteus aculeatus THREE-SPINED STICKLEBACK pl. 31.

ii. 15 spines on anterior dorsal

To 6 in. long. Colours variable; olive-green above, becoming silvery on flanks; clear silver line runs forward from below eyes, with dark line above it that leads through eye to dark line on gill-covers; below yellow, as far back as anal fin, marked dark lines. Along sides of body raised ridge of about 40 keeled plates. Body tapers to long slender " stalk " for fan-shaped tail. Occasionally spineless, but with line of tubercles instead. Widely distributed. Common, perhaps particularly E. coast.

Spinachia vulgaris FIFTEEN-SPINED STICKLEBACK pl. 31.

C. PELVIC FINS MODIFIED TO FORM A SUCKER, figs. 166-169.

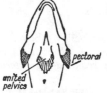

i. **Body scaly.** Two dorsal fins, anterior having flexible spines. Markedly goggle-eyed. Two small pelvics united to form oval sucker which hangs just clear of belly line, fig. 166.
Gobiidae GOBIES pl. 32.

Fig. 166. *Gobius minutus*, x 1

(a) *First dorsal with seven spines*, posterior of which is separated from anterior bunched group of six.

2½-4 in. long; yellowish-brown, paling irregularly below; *dark spot on body by pectorals and another by base of tail;* pale fins, dorsal perhaps yellowish with two lines of spots across it; tail palely blended. Often in shoals. Widely distributed. Common, locally abundant.

Gobius ruthensparri Euph. SPOTTED GOBY pl. 32.

(b) *First dorsal fin with six spines*

3-5 in. long, may be 9 in.; variable dull colours, browns and dark greys, with shadings and blotchings. Dark upper edge to anterior dorsal and in this fin fourth and fifth spines longest and all are markedly bent backwards. Up to 42 scales along lateral line. Eyes are set high in head and sockets almost touch. Widely distributed. Not uncommon. *Gobius niger* BLACK GOBY pl. 32.

About 4 in. long; rather uniformly dull and dark coloured; *very pale band on top of anterior dorsal,* first three spines of which are almost the same length and longer than the progressively shorter posterior three. At least 50 scales along lateral line. Eyes set high in head and sockets almost touch. Widespread. Rare in Scotland; not uncommon elsewhere.

Gobius paganellus ROCK GOBY pl. 32.

About 2 in. long; light brown or grey with regular markings; two dark bands radiating downwards from below eye. Pale fins, dorsals with 2-4 rows of spots divided by reddish bands. Dorsals very nearly meet on back. Anterior spine of posterior dorsal 9/10 length of second spine. In shoals. Widely distributed, particularly on S. and W. coasts. Not uncommon.

Gobius pictus PAINTED GOBY pl. 32.

Usually 2 in. long, but up to 3½ in. Variable colours, females lighter than males; usually dark sandy to grey above, with 6-12 blotches, sometimes ill-defined, along sides, the most definite being at base of tail. Single dark spot at posterior end of anterior dorsal. Dingier specimens perhaps E. coast. Two dorsal fins well separated. Anterior spine of posterior dorsal 3/5 length of second spine. In shoals. Widely distributed. Estuarine. Very common.   *Gobius minutus* COMMON GOBY. Fig. 166.

ii. **Body without scales.** Thick-set and rounded with rows of tubercles on skin. Anterior dorsal fin represented by row of short lumps. Rather complicated sucker is quite obvious and may be extraordinarily effective, fig. 167.   *Cyclopteridae* LUMPSUCKERS pl. 30.

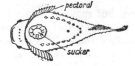

Fig. 167. *Cyclopterus lumpus,* x 1/6-1/10

Usually 5-8 in. long, but may be up to 24 in. Has deep belly and heavy rounded head. Males reddish, particularly on sides and below; females dark blue to nearly black, shading to perhaps pale yellowish below. *Four rows of large tubercles along each side;* whole texture of body surface is sticky and rough. *Anterior dorsal represented by line of tubercles;* posterior dorsal and anal fins balance each other in shape above and below tail. (Very small specimens may have an anterior dorsal and almost no tubercles). Widely distributed. Uncommon in S.; not uncommon in N.

Cyclopterus lumpus LUMPSUCKER pl. 30.

iii. Body without scales or tubercles. Heavy-bellied, smooth-headed.

Single dorsal fin starts by tail and extends forward undivided for more than half total length of fish. Anal fin also starts by tail but is shorter than dorsal. Pelvics are fused to form a round sucker, fig. 168.

Liparidae SMOOTH SUCKERS or SEA-SNAILS pl. 30

Fig. 168. *Liparis montagui*, x ½

2-4 in. long. Purplish or yellowish brown, with *dark spots peppered all over body.* Fins yellow dotted with black; *dorsal with up to 30 rays.* Pectoral fin continues under chin, fig. 168; lowest six rays giving it an irregular shape. No scales; smooth skin. Round, blunt head; heavy-bellied. Occurs in estuaries. Widely distributed. Common.

Liparis montagui MONTAGU'S SEA-SNAIL pl. 30.

Up to 6 in. long. Variable colours; pale grey or brown, with *darker, horizontal, rather wavy lines on head*, back and flanks. Pectoral fin and tail yellowish, banded darker. *Dorsal fin with over 30 rays.* Otherwise as *L. montagui.* Widely distributed. Not uncommon, perhaps particularly in N. *Liparis liparis* COMMON SEA-SNAIL

Body without scales or tubercles or spines. Small dorsal fin and

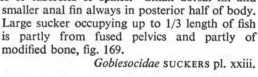

smaller anal fin always in posterior half of body. Large sucker occupying up to 1/3 length of fish is partly from fused pelvics and partly of modified bone, fig. 169.

Gobiesocidae SUCKERS pl. xxiii.

(a) Tail fin continuous with dorsal and anal fins

Typically 2 in. long, but may be 4 in. Red or purplish, paler below; sometimes brown or green. 2-3 dark-edged yellow lines between eyes. *Two near-black round marks, ringed near-white, on shoulders.* Flattened snout. Rare in Scotland; scarce in E., common in W.

Fig. 169. *Lepadogaster gouani*, x ½

Lepadogaster gouani CORNISH SUCKER pl. xxiii.

(b) Tail fin separate from dorsal and anal fins

1-2½ in. long. Body red, with contrasting red fins, all rather indistinctly spotted paler. May have dark round spot behind eye. *Dorsal fin has more than 10 rays*, only just separated from tail. *Anal with more than eight rays.* S.W. coasts only. Not common.

Lepadogaster candollii CONNEMARA SUCKER fig. 170.

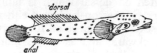

Fig. 170. *Lepadogaster candollii*, x 1

Up to 2 in. long. Orange-red; reddish V-shaped lines pointing backwards from eye. *Dark eye-spot, ringed very pale, on body by end of pectorals. Dorsal fin with less than 10 rays;* well separated from tail. *Anal with six or fewer rays.* Widely distributed. Common.

 Lepadogaster bimaculatus TWO-SPOTTED SUCKER pl. xxiii.

D. PELVIC FINS THORACIC, i.e. lying forward in region of 'chest,' more or less below, or, if anything, behind pectorals, fig. 171.

 i. Single dorsal fin is long and may be partly spiny. Heavily built fish with particularly *thick lips that fold up inside mouth which has strong teeth in jaws;* fig. 171. Some brilliantly coloured.

           Labridae WRASSES pl. xxx.

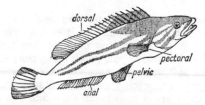

Fig. 171. Male *Labrus mixtus*, x c 1/5

 (*a*) *Three anterior rays of anal fin spiny;* fourth may also sometimes be so.

Usually 7-10 in. long, but may be 16 in. Very varied and gay colours; reds, greens, blues, etc.; each scale with a white centre. Unpaired (vertical) fins with orange or yellow rings. Thick lips and strong, sharp, single row of teeth in both jaws. Spines on anterior part of dorsal stiff and straight, and this part twice as long as spineless posterior part and, in adults, not so tall. In young spinous and soft parts of dorsal may be equal in height. 41-47 scales along lateral line. Widely distributed. Common.

 Labrus bergylta (=*L. maculatus*) BALLAN WRASSE pl. 30.

Usually about 6-10 in. long, but may be 13 in. Colours differ greatly between sexes, which are themselves variable. Males generally orange or yellow, paler below; 5-6 blue bands radiating backwards from eye. Dark patch on dorsal reaching back to about tenth or twelfth ray. Top of head and shoulders blue.

Females generally reddish; no blue bands behind eye. Fins yellow-orange; sometimes dark patch on dorsal which is faint and covers only 3-4 spines. 2-3 dark patches on body, on either side of hinder end of dorsal. Both sexes have spines on fore part of dorsal rather soft and sloping backwards and as tall as hind part of dorsal. 50-60 scales along lateral line. Single row of teeth in each jaw. Widely distributed. Not uncommon.

Labrus mixtus CUCKOO WRASSE fig. 171.

Usually 2-4 in. long, may be 9 in. Many colour varieties; generally reddish-brown on back, greenish-yellow on sides and pale below. May have about eight dark bands round body but these bands are often broken up into blotches; 3-4 yellow, red or green bands cross face. Vertical (unpaired) fins variously marked; some body bands may continue into dorsal and anal fins. Pale rings on hind part of dorsal and tail. Dark spots on anal fin. *Single dark spot very close to lateral line near junction with tail.* 32-35 scales on lateral line. Single row of teeth in each jaw. Widely distributed. Not common in N.; very common in S.

Crenilabrus melops CORKWING pl. 30.

3-6 in. long. Usually pinkish or golden, darker on back. Fins reddish; lower half of first about five spines of dorsal covered by dark patch. Dark spot often at junction of back and tail. May have broad, vertical bands, or long pale patch on upper part of body. Three anal spines soft and not sharply pointed (often seems to have two small points to each spine). 16-18 spines of front part of dorsal have extra spine in between each and are a little shorter than the soft rays of hind part. 38-40 scales along lateral line. Teeth in several rows, with outermost strongest and most pointed. Probably all coasts. Not uncommon. S. and E.

Ctenolabrus rupestris GOLDSINNY pl. 30.

(b) *Five anterior rays of anal fin spiny*

2-3 in. long, may be 5 in. Clear brown on back shading to yellowish on sides; thin yellow lines run along scales. Dark spot over eye. Dull blue blotch on gill covers. Fins silvery with yellow tints; single line of dark marks on 18-20 sharply spined rays of anterior part of dorsal; these spines reach to same height as six soft rays of posterior part which are crossed by two lines of dark marks. First anal spine easily shortest. Single row of not very prominent teeth in small mouth. 32-35 scales along lateral line. Probably all coasts. Uncommon.

Centrolabrus exoletus ROCK COCK pl. 30.

ii. **Two dorsal fins,** first with rather weak spines. No scales. Each ray in tail divides into two. Solid little fish with spiny gill-covers. Broad, rather flattened heads.

Cottidae BULLHEADS or SEA-SCORPIONS pl. 32.

(*a*) 13-14 *rays in posterior dorsal.* Four spines on gill-covers.

Usually 5-7 in long, but may be 15 in. Brown-grey above, mottled and banded darker; shading to pale white-grey below, with yellow tints. Lateral line appears paler than background. Fins brownish-yellow, sometimes banded or spotted reddish. No spine on ridge of back forward of front end of anterior dorsal. All coasts. Common, particularly in N.   *Cottus scorpius* FATHER-LASHER

(*b*) 11-12 *rays in posterior dorsal.* Five spines on gill-covers, of which one is much larger than others.

Usually 4-6 in. long, but may be 12 in. Colour often as *C. scorpius*, sometimes much brighter, with reds, greens or yellows. Ridge of back has small hollow in front of anterior dorsal; on head side of hollow a single spine. All coasts. Common, particularly in N. and W.   *Cottus bubalis* LONG-SPINED SEA-SCORPION pl. 32.

E. PELVIC FINS JUGULAR, i.e. lying in front of pectorals, in region of throat, figs. 172-177.

i. A " flatfish," fig. 172.

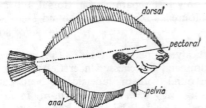

Fig. 172. *Pleuronectes platessa*, x ½-⅒

(*a*) *Lying on left side,* i.e. when held vertically so that pelvics are below head and mouth opens sensibly upwards, pale underside becomes left side; fig. 172.

Pleuronectidae PLAICE, DABS, etc. pl. xxiv.
and *Soleidae* SOLES pl. xxiv.

At edge of sea usually only 3-5 in. long, but may be 14-18 in. or longer. Round-oval body; browny-green on right side, with large orange spots, darker, almost blood-red, in larger specimens. On left (under) side pale watery-grey. *Lateral line almost straight, only a slight upward curve just behind gill-covers, fig. 172. Tail has* 17-18 *rays.* Bony knobs between eyes. Teeth better developed on blind side. Widely distributed. Very common.

Pleuronectes platessa PLAICE pl. xxiv.

At edge of sea usually 3-5 in. long, but may be 9-10 in. Round-oval body. Brown with green tints on right side, sometimes with dull, rather vague spots; on left (under) side pale watery-brown-grey. *Lateral line smooth, with semi-circular bend by pectoral fin.* No bony knobs between eyes or along base of dorsal and ventral fins. *Tail has 14 rays.* Teeth better developed on blind side. Widely distributed. Common, particularly over sand and in late summer. *Pleuronectes limanda* DAB pl. xxiv.

At edge of sea usually 3-6 in. long, but may be 9 in. Round-oval body; right (upper) side olive-brown to dark green-black, with irregular blotches; left (under) side pale watery-white. *Lateral line marked all along with bony knobs and has a small upward curve by pectoral fin. Bony knobs mark base of rays in dorsal and ventral fins. Tail has 14 rays.* Teeth better developed on blind side. In muddy/sandy bays; in estuaries; and sometimes in fresh water. All coasts. Common. *Pleuronectes flesus* FLOUNDER pl. xxiv.

Usually 4-8 in. long, but may be 14-18 in. Long-oval body; brown-grey-green on upper (right) side, blotched darker, may have pale ill-defined spots; on under (left) side watery-white. Pectoral fin usually with dark blotch at outer end. Feels rough if rubbed from tail to head. Tail only just separate from dorsal and anal fins which are evenly coloured. Teeth only on blind side. All coasts. Common. *Solea solea* SOLE

2-4 in. long. Long-oval body; upper (right) side sandy-grey with darker, more or less prominent, blotches. Under (left) side pale grey with brown tints. Round front of underside of head patch of dark " scribble " marks. *Every sixth or seventh fin-ray in dorsal and ventral fins is very dark (black).* Pelvic and pectoral fins tiny. Probably all coasts. Not very common.

Microchirus boscanion (=*Solea lutea*) SOLENETTE pl. xxiv.

(*b*) *Lying on right side,* i.e. when held up vertically so that pelvics are below head and mouth opens sensibly upwards, pale underside becomes right side. Dorsal fin reaches forward of eye (also true of *Soleidae*). Rounded-oval body.

2-4 in. long, may be 6-7 in. Upper (left) side rough, each scale with spine; dark brown relieved only by few darker spots. From either eye a dark band backwards to side of head. Under (right) side watery-white. *Dorsal and anal fins unite below tail* on underside. Probably all coasts. Not common except perhaps S.W.

Zeugopterus punctatus COMMON TOPKNOT pl. xxiv.

Upper (left) side dull brownish-grey, perhaps rather blotchy. White below. Rather diamond-shaped body. No scales. *On upper side blunt bony knobs. 61-72 rays in dorsal fin.* Widely distributed. Specimens 2-3 in. long may be found at extreme edge of sea (in shrimp nets) not uncommonly in S., less commonly in N. *Rhombus maximus* TURBOT pl. xxiv.

Upper (left) side brownish-greenish-grey with blotchings and, when alive, pale specklings. Underside white. Oval shape. *Smooth. 76-85 rays in dorsal.* Widely distributed. Specimens 2-3 in. long may be found in extreme edge of sea (in shrimp nets) not uncommonly in S., less commonly in N. *Rhombus laevis* BRILL

ii. Not a " flatfish "

(a) *Anterior dorsal black or nearly so.* Spines on gill-covers, anterior dorsal and pelvic fins which inject poison and cause painful swellings. Line of lips points very much upward, fig. 173. On or in sand and where shrimps abound. *Trachinidae* WEEVERS pl. xxiii.

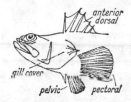

Fig. 173. *Trachinus draco*, x c 1/5

Up to 6-10 in. long, but may be 16 in. Grey or yellowish, darkest along back, sometimes patterned with thin lines of bright brown running vertically and paling as they descend: head may be fine marked brown or grey. *Anterior dorsal nearly black. 29 or more spines in posterior dorsal.* Sixth and seventh rays (from top edge) of pectorals the longest. *Two small spines above and before each eye.* All coasts. Scarce in N.; not uncommon elsewhere, particularly in early summer. *Trachinus draco* GREATER WEEVER fig. 173

Up to 4-5 in. long. Grey-sandy above, with perhaps faint lengthwise lines, shading paler below with yellow tints. *Anterior dorsal black. 24 or fewer spines on posterior dorsal.* Second and third rays (from top edge) of pectorals longest. *No spines above eyes.* All coasts. Scarce in N., common in S.W.

Trachinus vipera LESSER WEEVER or STING-FISH pl. xxiii.

(*b*) *Spiny plates on flat head.* Coarsely scaly body, fining away rapidly to stalky tail. Lower jaw bearded.

Agonidae ARMED BULLHEADS pl. xxiii.

Usually 3-5 in. long; grey with yellow tints, spotted, body banded darker. Fins tend to be more yellow. Upturned snout armed with spines. By harbours and river mouths; not much on rocky coasts. N.E.; occasional S.E.; rare elsewhere.

Agonus cataphractus ARMED BULLHEAD or POGGE pl. xxiii.

(*c*) *No spines on gill-covers.* Pelvic fins with less than five rays and may be rudimentary. *Dorsal fin long, but may be in two or three connected parts, and occupies nearly whole length of body. Pectoral fins large and rounded. Heavy head and large eyes;* fig. 174. *Blenniidae* BLENNIES and BUTTERFISH pl. 31.

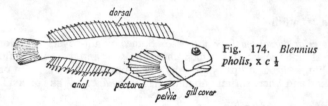

Fig. 174. *Blennius pholis*, x c ½

4-5 in. long, may be 7 in. Reddish-brown above, shading paler below, usually with about 10 long-oval pale patches up and down on flanks, but may be mottled. Dorsal and anal fins paler with darker central band. *Dorsal fin forming long unbroken line with at least* 50 *rays all spined.* Obviously scaly. *Large erect tentacles above eyes*, with smaller pair just in front. Scarce N. coasts; very rare S. coasts.

Chirolophis galerita (Linn.) YARRELL'S BLENNY fig. 175.

Fig. 175. *Chirolophis galerita*, x c 1/3

Usually 5-8 in. long, but may be 16-20 in. Olive with paler patches on upper part of body and on dorsal fin. *Dorsal and anal fins continuous.* No tail fin, except in fish up to about 4 in. No spines on dorsal except *about* 10 *rays sunk in notch towards tail.* No tentacles. Body tapers to sharp point. Only N. and E. coasts. Common.

Zoarces viviparus VIVIPAROUS BLENNY or EEL-POUT pl. 31.

Usually 3-5 in. long, may be 11 in. Bronzy-grey colour that loses yellow tints at death. 10-13 *white ringed dark spots overlapping from base of dorsal on to back*. *Dorsal fin forming unbroken piece of 75 or more rays*, all slightly spined. Pelvic fins minute (one spine and one ray). Body flattened sideways and tapers gently towards rounded tail. Slippery. All coasts. Very common.

Centronotus gunnellus BUTTERFISH or GUNNEL pl. 31.

Typically 3-5 in. long, often only 1 in., at which size characters are hard to see. Variable colours; often olive or darker green, blotched with black; but may be yellowish. No tentacles above eye (but a pair of inconspicuous small tentacles on " cheek bones "). Dorsal fin continuous, with anterior two-fifths not so tall as rest. All coasts very common; commonest by far of the blennies.

Blennius pholis COMMON BLENNY or SHANNY pl. 31 and fig. 174.

Usually 3-5 in. long, but may be up to 7 in. Grey, with about six paler vertical bands on body. *Large round white-ringed black spot on anterior half of dorsal* which is much taller than posterior part. Pair of inconspicuous tentacles above eyes. Heavy, short, blunt head. Rare S. and W. coasts; not uncommon in extreme S.W.

Blennius ocellaris BUTTERFLY BLENNY fig. 176.

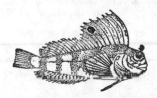

Fig. 176. *Blennius ocellaris*, x c 1/3

2-3 in. long. Pale brownish- or yellowish-grey, with 6-9 vertical bands down to about level with *line of white marks running from lower edge of pectoral fin to tail*. Body spotted all over bluish-white. *Pair of conspicuous tentacles* rather behind eye. Dorsal sharply divided into two parts by abrupt shortening of web between about 12th and 13th rays. Dark band at base of pectorals which has 12 rays of which seventh, eighth and ninth from top are much the longest. Probably on S. and W. coasts. Rare.

Blennius montagui (= *B. galerita*) MONTAGU'S BLENNY pl. 31.

Usually 4-7 in. long, may be 9 in. Dull colour; olive or brown-grey without much paling beneath and faint uncertain vertical banding. *Lateral line curves upwards to sweep round above pectoral fin*. Dorsal not sharply divided into two parts, but about 12th or 13th spines mark lowest point in the depression. Posterior web of dorsal runs without break into tail. Rounded pectoral reaches greatest length at ninth ray from top. *Pair of conspicuous tentacles on edge of eye socket.* Uncommon S. and W. coasts; rare elsewhere. *Blennius gattorugine* TOMPOT or GATTORUGINE pl. 31.

(*d*) *No spines on gill-covers or elsewhere.* Pelvic fins with more than five rays. Two dorsal fins, the anterior only a fringe and sunk in groove along back. Smooth, shapely, rather elongated fish. Barbels and tentacles present, above and below mouth; fig. 177.

Gadidae ROCKLINGS pl. xxiii.

Fig. 177. *Onos* [*mediterraneus*], x c ⅓

Typically 3-6 in. long, but may be 12 in. or even 18 in. Reddish-grey, shading to near-white below; larger ones may be marked irregularly with dark spots. *Two barbels on upper lip and one on chin.* Common in S. and S.W.; rather rare elsewhere, particularly in far N.

Onos [*mediterraneus*] (Linn.) THREE-BEARDED ROCKLING pl. xxiii. and fig. 177.

Typically 3-6 in. long, but up to 12 in. or more. Olive- or reddish-grey on back, shading paler below; fins darker and some have orange tints near base. *Four barbels on upper lip and one on chin.* All coasts. Common. *Onos mustelus* FIVE-BEARDED ROCKLING

THE STRANDLINE

ALL MANNER OF THINGS may be found cast ashore along the strandline. They have been more or less broken up, either by long soaking or by being pounded by other hard jetsam and stones, or by wave action directly. But some remain recognisable, for instance:

A
Wood with holes bored in it.

B
A bean.

C
" Bones."

D
" Mermaids' Purses."

E
Bits of " sponge."

F
Dried " leaves " of sandy-coloured " plants."

G
Curled ribbon of honeycombed patterned sand.

H
Inflated thin skin sack.

I
" Stone bullets."

A. WOOD WITH HOLES BORED IN IT

Holes—tunnels—about $\frac{1}{4}$ in. diameter, often lined with hard white " cement," have been bored by *Teredo* spp. SHIPWORMS pl. xxv. These are not worms but bivalve molluscs (see p. 166 and pl. xx). By their boring activities wooden ships and wooden pier piles unless suitably protected have been completely destroyed.

Many minute holes about $\frac{1}{8}$ in. diameter connecting like a series of small man-holes, with long galleries running in the superficial areas of the wood, have been bored by the crustacean isopod *Limnoria lignorum* THE GRIBBLE p. 99 and pl. viii.

The animal itself may be found at the end of the boring, usually this is the female.

Associated with the gribble, although not itself apparently boring, is the somewhat larger amphipod, *Chelura terebrans* p. 109 and pl. viii.

B. A BEAN. On extreme S.W. coasts (and perhaps elsewhere on W. coasts) a brown bean, 1-2 in. wide, may be found.

Broad-bean-shaped; hard shiny skin; uniform colour.

Entada gigas (L.) pl. xxv.

This species drifts to us from the West Indies. In Pembrokeshire parents give them to babies to cut teeth on.

Disc-shaped; all except 7/8 of the rim dark purple-brown, but 7/8 of the rim black with creamy-brown border.

Mucuna urens (L.) fig. 178.

Fig. 178. *Mucuna urens*, x c ½

This species probably comes to us from tropical America.

C. "BONES"

Flat, white, oval "bones," about 4-6 in. long and up to ½ in. thick in centre, may have an oval pattern of lines. These are the remains of the internal shell of *Sepia officinalis* CUTTLEFISH pl. xxv. (see also p. 170 and pl. xxi)

Pieces of bone, perhaps 3 in. long, curved, on which are hard, white, very shortly stalked knobs, each $\frac{1}{10}$ in. across and $\frac{1}{10}$ in. tall, in close pattern of rows. Sometimes these knobs will have sharp points on one side and the rows may overlap each other, strongly suggesting modified fish scales which is what they are. Arranged in this way they come from the jawbone of a ray, pl. xxv.

Delicately thin, rounded, hollow, empty, "skulls" marked with five rows of holes are the tests of sea-urchins, usually of *Echinocardium cordatum*, the sea-potato (see p. 183 and pl. 27).

D. "MERMAIDS' PURSES."

Flat, horny, roughly quadrilateral, dark-coloured "mermaids' purses" are the, usually empty, egg cases of dogfish or rays. From each corner more or less stiff processes, the pair at one end unlike the pair at the other end. Various kinds may be found all round the coasts:

i. With long tendrils from all four corners.

About 2 in. long, excluding tendrils,
Scyliorhinus caniculus LESSER SPOTTED DOGFISH pl. xxv.

About 4 in. long, excluding tendrils,
Scyliorhinus stellaris GREATER SPOTTED DOGFISH

ii. With points instead of tendrils; when fresh having sticky hairs which may have been rubbed off those cast ashore.

About 2 in. long excluding points, one pair of which are 3-4 times length of second pair and curl across each other.

Raja naevus CUCKOO RAY

About 2½ in. long excluding points, one pair of which is about twice as long as the other pair but are widely separate at the tips. Each point has slit along outer edge near tip.

Raja montagui SPOTTED RAY

About 6 in. long excluding points, wider at one end than at other. Four more or less equal horns, each pair hooking inwards. Sticky hairs, if present, may be as long as the " purse," the longest emerging in a bunch on either side towards one end.

Raja batis COMMON SKATE pl. xxv.

About 3 in. long excluding points, all four of which are more or less equal. " Purse " much more convex on one side than the other. If fresh will be covered with mat of short hairs.

Raja clavata THORNBACK RAY

About 5 in. long excluding points which are more or less equal and slightly inward hooking. *Raja oxyrhynchus* LONG-NOSED RAY

E. BITS OF " SPONGE "

Rounded lumps resembling coarse bathroom sponge, pale sandy-coloured, 1-5 in. in diameter, made up of many hollow, empty receptacles each about ¼ in. wide, with tough membranous skin becoming brittle when dry.
Empty egg cases of *Buccinum undatum* COMMON WHELK pl. xxv and see p. 104 and pl. xvi.

Perhaps rather angular lumps, 2-3 in. across, dark sandy colour, with soft texture of felt when quite dry, in midst of which are stiff stalks which may stick out 2-3 in. at one end. Found particularly on E. coasts, this comes from deeper water with a sandy bottom and is the basal mass of the hydroid *Antennularia antennina* pl. xxv.

Usually 3-6 in. long, sandy-coloured, oval or rounded, divided and subdivided, blunt-ended, texture of felt, may be the remains of the sea-mat *Alcyonidium* spp. p. 174 and pl. iii.

F. DRIED " LEAVES " of sandy-coloured " plants."

Flat, brittle, broadly or narrowly palmate, with pattern of minute honeycombing on either side. Common everywhere particularly on E. coasts. *Flustra* spp. HORNWRACK p. 174 and pl. iii and xxv.

G. CURLED RIBBON of honeycomb-patterned sand.

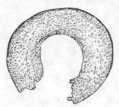

Fig. 179. Egg-mass
of Necklace-shell,
x c ½

Ribbons of sand, 1 in. or more wide, and 2-4 in. long, curled, sometimes into necklace shape. Honeycomb patterning. Each "cell" is an egg-capsule and the whole is the egg-mass of *Natica* sp. NECKLACE-SHELL p. 137, pl. xv, fig. 179

H. INFLATED THIN SKIN SACK

To 6 in. long, with crenellated crest and perhaps an unidentifiable something dried up at one end, is the sail of *Physalia physalia* PORTUGUESE MAN-O'-WAR p. 54 and pl. 3.

I. " STONE BULLETS "

Looking like stone bullets, tapering towards one end, may have hollow centre. Translucent yellow-brown. These are fossil remains of a relation to the squids and cuttlefish, namely   BELEMNITES pl. xxv.

Also often cast ashore are Ship's Barnacles (see p. 92 and pl. vi), shells of crabs, particularly of the Shore-crab (p. 117 and pl. 15), Starfish (pp. 178 and pls. 24-25), worm tubes on stones (pp. 76 and pl. iv).

Bars of gold are seldom found and should be pocketed promptly. Together with amber and messages in bottles they are, alas! outside the scope of this book.

ALGAE
Seaweeds

BOTANISTS divide seaweeds into Chlorophyceae (Greens), Phaeophyceae (Browns) and Rhodophyceae (Reds). This division by colour is a good guide to the groups described in the following pages. All the same a warning is necessary that some Reds may look more brown than red and many Browns are olive-green and some, particularly in the early stages of decomposition, may look green. The colour drains from many seaweeds when they have been torn away by storms. Off-white fragments, slimy and rather smelly, are commonly cast ashore or are found floating at the edge of the flooding tide. No matter what colour they may be when alive all dead seaweeds bleach white after a while.

Most seaweeds grow on rocks or shells or on other seaweeds. Usually no large ones are found on shingle or sandy beaches, where wave action moves the particles and so prevents the spores or sporelings of the larger seaweeds from developing. As already noted (p. 15) there is a zonation on rocky shores due to the degree of wave action or exposure. Different kinds of rock and their slope, the salinity of the water and its temperature also influence the distribution of seaweeds.

About 700 species of seaweeds have been recognised round the coasts of Britain. Identification of the majority depends on microscopic examination beyond the scope of this book. Some algologists think that the division of some genera has been carried too far. The specific limits of a number of species are uncertain because the same species may exist in several different forms at different stages of its life history, or when growing under different conditions. Different views may be held amongst systematists on what are and what are not good algal species. Nevertheless seaweeds as a whole are not such a difficult group that many of the common species which make up the bulk of the plant cover on a rocky shore cannot be recognised in the field.

An attempt has been made below to describe species from characters that can mostly be seen with the naked eye; occasionally recourse has been made to details that cannot be made out without a hand-lens magnifying 10 times. Identifications derived from the list should not be thought scientifically valid until a more elaborate technique has been used. Particularly is this true of filamentous, hair-thin algae and of membranous Reds. Many are superficially so like each other that these lists are no better than indications of probabilities. In some cases genera and groups of related genera are omitted or only briefly summarised, as the characters are not recognisable even with a hand-lens.

Where a specific name has been put in square brackets the inference is that the identification based on the characters here given is particularly uncertain.

Roughly speaking, the larger the plant the greater the chance that the identification derived from these descriptions and drawings will prove to be correct. For plants less than 3 in. long probabilities degenerate perhaps into possibilities. Seaweeds are certainly not easy to identify but in nuance of colour and rhythm of pattern they are beautiful plants and worth closer study than they usually receive.

CHLOROPHYCEAE

Green Seaweeds

A
Membranous or tubular fronds; figs. *a*, *b*.

B
Plant of threads.
  i. Branched threads; figs. *c*1, *c*2.
  ii. Unbranched threads; fig. *d*.

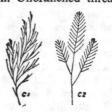

C
Plant of definite shape, but neither membranous nor of threads.

N.B. Beware of *Zostera* spp., eel-grass or sea-grass, which are flowering plants, not seaweeds (see p. 254 and pl. 40).

A. MEMBRANOUS OR TUBULAR FRONDS, figs. *a*, *b*.

Pale, watery-green when small, becomes brighter and harder in colour and darkens with age to very dark green. The margins of older fronds may appear white (after release of spores). When tide is out patches of *broad-leaved and translucent* " sea-lettuce " which open out into flat membrane of irregular shape, growing in bunches, usually 4-8 in., but may be up to 18 in. long. All except upper levels of beach and in pools. Particularly abundant July and August, and where fresh (and sewage-tainted) water occurs. Always has a small and solid stalk. Common on most rocky shores.   *Ulva lactuca* SEA-LETTUCE pl. xxvi.

The genus *Ulva* has fronds two cells thick. The genus *Monostroma* has fronds only one cell thick and can look exactly like *Ulva*. Only the most delicate and practised sense of feel can perhaps detect the difference.

Inflated long pods of frond which *never branches* but is usually *constricted at irregular intervals*. Attached by disc to rocks, quite small stones and shells. Has a small stalk. As plants become older they may break away and float freely in the water. Pieces a foot long may often be found. At most levels on the shore but mostly where fresh water present. May be abundant in estuaries and high level pools, sometimes covering the whole surface. Period of rapid growth in the late winter and early spring which makes it very noticeable in March and April. Probably a number of different generations succeed each other throughout the spring and early summer. By August much of it is white and dead on the shores. *Enteromorpha* [*intestinalis*] pl. xxvi.

There are five more common species, none of them branched; all might be mistaken for *E. intestinalis*, the differences between them being based on microscopic characters.

Inflated or compressed green fronds, branched (at least once); sometime branches bear branchlets. Branches somewhat compressed, become wider towards ends and usually only slightly constricted. *Where they meet main frond, branches narrow but their tips are blunt.* All levels between tide marks; on stones. Widely distributed. Common, especially in brackish water where it may form a carpet.

Enteromorpha [*compressa*] pl. xxvi.

Again there are several species so like *E. compressa* that this specific name cannot be given for certain to a specimen answering the description above.

Bright green, long, narrow frond, not inflated, often spirally twisted. Up to 20 in. long. Attached by small disc. Has small *hollow stalk*. Under water holds itself a little stiffly. All levels of beach. Common in pools and where fresh water runs. May grow on other seaweeds, particularly perhaps *Corallina* (p. 250 and pl. 35). Widely distributed. Can be confused with narrow *Ulva* among which it is often found.

Enteromorpha linza (= *Ulva linza*) pl. 33.

Very small, dark green plant, usually less than 1 in. tall, *half total length is stalk* from which frond expands into rather oblong shapes with curled edges. On rocks high on middle shore, sometimes in neighbourhood of sea-bird colonies. Widely distributed. Probably common. *Prasiola stipitata* pl. xxvi.

B. PLANT OF THREADS

i. Branched threads; figs. *c*1, *c*2.

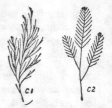

If branched threads are as much as 3 in. long plant is almost certainly a species of *Cladophora.*

Dark green dense tufts, which look and feel rather coarse and wiry. Branches either opposite or in threes or fours. Growing on rocks in damp places, particularly underneath large brown seaweeds (*Ascophyllum nodosum* p. 227 and pl. xxxii). Middle shore. Widely distributed. Common. Particularly well developed and conspicuous in summer. Dies back in winter. *Cladophora rupestris* pl. xxvi.

Characteristic middle green, slender densely tufted filaments which feel soft. Branchlets nearly all occur on one side of branch. Lower and middle shores, particularly perhaps in shady pools. Widely distributed. Not very common. *Cladophora [glaucescens]* pl. 33.

Other species, particularly *C. flexuosa*, are so similar that identity of *C. glaucescens* cannot be certain on the above characters.

Plant slightly branched, each branch bearing numerous branchlets, giving feather-like appearance. Branches decrease in length towards top and are *arranged in two vertical rows* on either side of branch, lower half or third of which is usually bare. Plant limp, rather shiny; appearance of flat, green fan. To 4 in. high. On rocks, particularly steep-sided small pools. Middle shore. Widely distributed. Common. *Bryopsis plumosa* pl. 33.

Plant much branched, with *branchlets on all sides* and perhaps further divided. General appearance of a rather sharply pointed green tuft. To 4 in. high. Middle shore. Deep shaded pools; on rocks and other seaweeds. Extreme W. peninsula and Ireland not uncommon. but scarce elsewhere. *Bryopsis hypnoides* pl. 33.

Note *Rhizoclonium* below.

ii. Unbranched threads; fig. *d.*

With no obvious holdfast, tangle of bright green unbranched threads round other seaweeds or in brackish pools at high water. Several inches, up to 1 ft. long. Particularly noticeable in summer. *Chaetomorpha* spp. pl. 33.

With definite holdfast from which grey-green threads rise in long, rather stiff tufts. *Cells so large as to be easily seen by naked eye* (which

222

distinguishes this from all other species). Lower shore, in pools, particularly in summer. Widely distributed. Not common.

Chaetomorpha melagonium

If there is only slight branching, particularly if the colour is yellowish and the habitat is a muddy shore or sand, a tangle of threads is more likely to be a species of *Rhizoclonium*

C. PLANT OF DEFINITE SHAPE, not filamentous or membranous.

Dark green frond, texture of felt, much dichotomous branching, branches circular in section, to 1 ft. long, longest in winter. Holdfast so closely woven as to look all of a piece. Middle shore. In deep pools. Widely distributed. Probably common.

Codium [*tomentosum*] pl. 33.

PHAEOPHYCEAE

Brown Seaweeds

A

Very large plants, low water level and below, usually 3 ft. long or more. Brown frond an expanded lamina, usually tough and massive. " Stalk " or stipe usually well developed and attached to rocks by bunch of ramifying strong root-like processes forming a holdfast.

Kelps, Tangles or Oar-weeds

i. More or less digitate frond, usually 3 ft. and may be 6 ft.; fig. *e*.

B

Large, tough, leathery plants—the typical seaweeds of rocky shores—with strap-like fronds that arise from a disc holdfast. Most of them 2 ft. or more long; but those growing nearer the high tide level are shorter. Wracks.

i. Olive-brown, becoming green black when dry. Dichotomously branched; fig. *g*.

(*a*) Frond inrolled and channelled on one side.

(*b*) Frond nearly or entirely flat.

ii. Long undivided frond. Yellow-sandy colour. Round, smooth " stalk "; fig. *f*.

ii. Olive-green, becoming green-black when dry. Irregularly branched; fig. *h*.

C

Frond a smooth, round "boot-lace."

D

Long, leathery, branched straps arising from olive-brown, stalked, button-like structure, reminiscent of a toadstool; fig. *i*.

E

Other large plants.

F

Medium-sized plants, about 1 ft. long.

i. Much branched, leathery, stiff, "twiggy" plants; fig. *j*.
ii. Flat, dichotomous frond, fig. *k*.

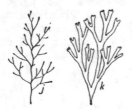

iii. Flat, thin frond, irregularly branched or lobed; figs. *l, m*.

iv. Flat, membrane, not branch-ed; fig. *n*.
v. Thin, hollow membrane, not branched; fig. *o*.
vi. Frond of limp, branched threads.

G

Small plants, about 6 in. long.

i. Frond gelatinous.
ii. Frond of branched threads.
  (*a*) Rather stiff plants.
  (*b*) Limp plants.
iii. Frond of unbranched threads.
iv. Frond of tough, leathery in-rolled straps.

A. VERY LARGE PLANTS of low water level and below, usually 3 ft. long or more. Brown frond an expanded lamina, usually tough and massive. "Stalk" or stipe usually well developed and *attached to rocks by bunch of ramifying strong root-like processes forming a holdfast.*   KELPS, TANGLES, OAR WEEDS

i. More or less digitate frond, usually 3 ft. and may be 6 ft.; fig. *e.*

Intertwined " rootlets " short and thick and bent downwards on to rock rather than spread out flat. *Stalk rough, stiff, hard, round in cross section.* On rocks on lower shore and downwards. At low tide fronds form brown belt at edge of sea. In pools. Widely distributed. Common.

Laminaria hyperborea (= L. cloustoni)

Intertwined " rootlets " not thick and tend to spread out flat so extending area of holdfast. *Stalk flexible and oval in cross-section.* On rocks on lower shore as *L. hyperborea*. Widely distributed. Very common. *Laminaria digitata* pl. xxxi.

Both species when young may have a frond less than 1 ft. long that shows little or no division into fingers. But beware *Petalonia fascia* p. 231 and pl. xxix.

Holdfast a large hollow stiff rounded markedly knobby structure from which flattened stalk emerges, twisted and having *broad wavy frills* along lower edges. Frond may be truly massive, commonly 6 ft. tall, and is annual, being removed during winter gales. Plant is therefore an extremely fast grower. Lower shore. Isolated plants. Widely distributed. Common.

Saccorhiza polyschides (=*S. bulbosa*) pl. xxxi.

ii. Long, undivided frond. Yellow-sandy colour. Round, smooth " stalk "; fig. *f.*

Flat frond, without midrib, from 8 in. to 8 ft. long, and up to 1 ft. wide, undivided with *wavy edges, and crinkly undulations throughout its length.* Frond renewed each year by growth from top of stalk. Middle shore and downwards. Attached to small stones and rocks; in pools; on muddy/sandy flats. Widely distributed. Abundant.

Laminaria saccharina pl. xxxi.

Frond with midrib, thin and easily torn. Slightly wavy edges. At base of stalk lateral bunches of stalked, flattened, round-ended fruiting segments. Yellowish midrib contrasts with yellow-brown frond. Only really common on very *exposed shores* where it replaces *L. digitata* on the lower shore. *Alaria esculenta* pl. 34.

B. LARGE, TOUGH, LEATHERY PLANTS—the typical seaweeds of rocky shores—with strap-like fronds that *arise from a disc holdfast.* Most of them 2 ft. or more long; but those growing nearer the high tide level are shorter.   THE WRACKS

i. **Olive-brown,** becoming green-black when dry.   Dichotomously branched; fig. *g.*

(*a*) *Frond inrolled and channelled on one side*

Tufted bunches up to 6 in. long, frond about $\frac{1}{3}$ in. across, *inrolled* to form a channel along length of frond, ending in divided tips that are often swollen and granular. Hangs downwards with channelled side inwards towards rocks. In belt about 2-4 ft. deep from mean high water of springs, but may extend higher on the splash zone. In quiet weather becoming dried up, brittle and almost black. Widespread, common, often abundant.

Pelvetia canaliculata CHANNEL WRACK pl. xxxiii.

(*b*) *Frond nearly or entirely flat*

Frond broad with smooth edge, 5-8 in. long, may be 15 in. No bladders. When plant held up appears somewhat spirally twisted although rarely making a complete turn. Tips often with heavy, swollen, granular, fruiting bodies, in which, if held up to the light, *granules do not anywhere extend to extreme rim* (i.e. sterile margin). Occupying zone about 3 ft. deep at mean high water of neap tides, immediately below *P. canaliculata*, on all except very exposed rocky shores.   *Fucus spiralis* FLAT WRACK pl. xxxii.

Frond with edges that may be wavy and, in larger pieces, often irregularly torn. Prominent midrib on either side of which may be *air-bladders, commonly in pairs.* Tips of lateral branches bear swollen, granular, fruiting bodies which do not leave a translucent rim (cf. *F. spiralis*). In brackish water these fruiting bodies may be much enlarged and themselves have two points. Plants grow through two dichotomies each year. Pieces up to 3 ft. long may have frond worn away lower down, leaving only tough cord of midrib. Longer plants tend to have more and rather smaller bladders in each group of pairs. Middle shore, on rocks. Very widely distributed. Abundant.

Fucus vesiculosus BLADDER WRACK pl. xxxii.

Frond with *serrated edges*, no bladders. Not regularly branched. Tips carry in autumn and winter flattened and pointed fruiting

226

bodies (or fruiting areas) that have also serrated edges and may be 2 in. long. Infertile ends often have soft silken hairs scattered thinly on them. Low on middle shore. On all except extremely exposed rocky coasts. Widely distributed. Very common.

Fucus serratus SAW or SERRATED WRACK pl. xxxii.

Often on the fronds of *F. serratus* are small white tubes of the worm *Spirorbis*, see p. 76 and pl. iv.

Frond *thin and with very well marked midrib*, with unbroken edges, up to 3 ft. long, dichotomously branched, no bladders, with tips forked and often carrying lateral fans of fruiting bodies. In *brackish water*, particularly estuaries, and mouths of streams; growing on stones. Middle shore. Widely distributed. Common.

Fucus ceranoides pl. xxxii.

F. spiralis and *F. vesiculosus* may also grow in mouths of streams in atypical shapes. They may cross with each other and they may perhaps also cross with *F. ceranoides* to produce plants showing some characteristics of both parents.

In many ways like a *Fucus* is *Dictyopteris membranacea*, p. 230, and pl. 34 or even *Desmarestia ligulata* p. 228, and pl. xxix.

ii. **Olive-green,** becoming green-black when dry. Irregularly branched, fig. *h*.

No midrib. *Single egg-shaped bladders at intervals in middle of frond.* Fruiting bodies like stalked yellow-green raisins grow in spring and early summer from sides of frond, to some extent opposite each other in pairs. Middle shore. On sheltered rocky beaches may develop so luxuriantly that it blankets whole beach. Extends well up estuaries on rocks. Where exposure to wave action begins to increase plants are at once less luxuriant. In moderate exposure the only trace may be broken remnant of straps a few inches long. Widely distributed. Abundant.

Ascophyllum nodosum EGG or KNOTTED WRACK pl. xxxii

Unattached masses usually at heads of W. coast lochs
A. nodosum var. *Mackaii.*

Where fruiting bodies have dropped away, the filamentous red seaweed, *Polysiphonia lanosa* (=*P. fastigiata*), may attain lodgment and develop into dark red tufts, at its most luxuriant considerably modifying the appearance of *Ascophyllum* (see pl. xxxii). *Ascophyllum* may have also wart-like branches, see *Tylenchus*, p. 87.

Oppositely branched, flat but not tough, strap-like fronds arising from disc holdfast. *Desmarestia ligulata* see below and pl. xxix.

C. FROND A LONG, SMOOTH, ROUND " BOOTLACE "

Round in section, slippery, unbranched " bootlace," 6-20 ft. long, reaching greatest length in summer. Quantities may be left rolled together in heavy bundles at low tide. Attached by disc to small stones and rocks. Lower shore and downwards. Widely distributed. Abundant. In summer becomes slimy with covering of *Litosiphon pusillus* (see p. 234). *Desmotrichum* (p. 231) grows on it.

Chorda filum pl. xxxi.

D. LONG, LEATHERY, BRANCHED STRAP coming from olive-brown, stalked, button-like structure, reminiscent of a toadstool; fig. *i*.

Olive-brown button frond, developing into stalked " toadstool " about 1½ in. high. From centre of concave top arise strap-shaped, dichotomously branched, spotty reproductive parts, normally up to 4 ft. long, but may be 8 ft. Lower shore. Exposed rocky coasts. Widely distributed. Locally abundant.

Himanthalia elongata (=*H. lorea*) THONG-WEED
pl. xxxiii.

E. OTHER LARGE PLANTS

Plant dichotomously branching, round in section, smooth and shiny, olive-coloured but much darker and brittle when dry. Few small bladders in branches, at divided ends of which long, oval-in-section, pointed, rather fat fruiting bodies, all of which reach to about the same height, usually 1 ft. but may be 2 ft. In large pools on middle shore; on rocks. Probably mostly on exposed beaches. Probably not uncommon S. and S.W. coasts; absent in N.

Bifurcaria rotunda (=*B. tuberculata*) pl. xxxiii.

From disc holdfast and cylindrical stalk long, thin, flattened frond, *opposite branches* which carry *opposite branchlets on which are sharp points*. Olive-brown, quickly going green out of water. 2-6 ft. long. Lower shore. Spring and summer only. On rocks and in pools. S. and W. coasts. Not uncommon. *Desmarestia ligulata* pl. xxix.

From disc holdfast strong, main stem *alternately branched*, with *alternate thorn-like branchlets* which remain bare in winter. In summer plants clothed with fine little stiff tufts. Green when small, becoming brown. 1-6 ft. long. Lower shore. On rocks. Probably fairly widely distributed. Not very common. *Desmarastia aculeata* pl. xxix.

Much as *D. aculeata* but *branches and branchlets opposite*. Lower shore. Spring and summer only. Probably widespread. Not very common. *Desmarestia viridis*

F. MEDIUM-SIZED PLANTS, about 1 ft. long.

i. Much branched, leathery, stiff, " twiggy " plants; fig. *i*.

Frond rather flattened, with alternate branches, some small, some large. Branches with alternate branchlets, on end of which may be long oval-chambered air bladders, the larger having a sharp point. Usually 8-16 in. long, may be more than 3 ft. Ginger-brown. Lower shore, but on rocky shores and perhaps in more sheltered place may be on middle shore. Widely distributed. Not very common. *Halidrys siliquosa* pl. xxxiii.

Whole plant seems crowded together and has short spines on it. Circular stem, irregularly branched, branches subdivided irregularly with small air-bladders towards ends. At tips are spiny, scaly, long-oval fruiting bodies. Yellow-olive colour, going much darker when dry. Iridescent under water. Usually 1 ft. long, in clumps; may be over 2 ft. Lower shore. In pools. Rocky shore and gravelly flats. Not in N. Becoming commoner in S. and W.

Cystoseira [tamariscifolia] (=C. ericoides) pl. xxxiii.

ii. Flat, dichotomous frond; fig. *k*.

Arising from disc holdfast frond *heavily spotted all over*, very long and narrow, particularly near junction with holdfast and in terminal divisions which are less than $\frac{1}{1\frac{1}{2}}$ in. across. Yellow-brown colour, thin, limp. Lower shore. On rocks. Widely distributed. Rare. Almost entirely sub-littoral but commonly thrown up on to beach.

Cutleria multifida pl. xxix.

Coming from disc holdfast, frond is thin, limp, slightly spotted and has fine lines along it. *Final division is blunt*. Olive-brown, becoming lighter towards tips. Middle shore. On rocks and small stones. Not common in N. and E., becoming abundant in S. and W.

Dictyota dichotoma pl. 34.

An easily recognisable variety (var. *intricata* (=*implexa*)) is very much more divided into thin branches which often tangle together into a loose bunch.

From not well-defined disc holdfast, frond resembling flat fine *Fucus*; prominent *midrib throughout*, from lower part of which edges are straight but often torn down to midrib. Tips bluntly rounded. Small shoots may arise from the midrib. Rather green, even yellowish if small. S. and W. coasts. Local and rare.

Dictyopteris membranacea pl. 34.

iii. Flat, thin frond, irregularly branched or lobed; figs. *l, m*.

Frond divided into *long triangular sections, spotted, translucent*. Olive-brown at base, becoming paler upwards with wavy dark bands running across irregularly. Ends of sections split, sometimes deeply, and divide again irregularly. Lower shore. Very rare in N.; locally abundant in S. and E. *Taonia atomaria* pl. 34.

Rounded fan-shaped thin sections of frond, dividing irregularly, arising from stalk, narrowing all the way down to holdfast. 2-6 in. high. Upper surface yellowish-green, becoming darker lower down; under surface more ginger, particularly lower down, with silvery concentric markings. Lower shore. Only S. coasts. Locally common. *Padina pavonia* pl. 34.

iv. Flat membrane, not branched; fig. *n*.

Frond a rather *thin membrane, dotted all over with oval spots or hairs*, growing as open tuft on very small bristly stalk, from small disc holdfast. May be long and narrow or up to 2 in. wide, coming to a distinct point, with wavy edges. Olive. Middle and lower shore. Very small in January, often on limpets. Maximum in summer on rocks or on other seaweeds. In pools. Dies back by mid-August. Widely distributed. Common. *Punctaria plantaginea* pl. xxx.

Very like *P. plantaginea*, but frond to 3 in. wide with round spots. Rather high on middle shore. In shallow pools. *Punctaria latifolia*.

As *P. plantaginea* but frond less than ½ in. wide, very thin. Middle shore. On seaweeds, particularly *Chorda filum* (p. 228 and pl. xxxi). Widely distributed. *Desmotrichum undulatum* (=*Punctaria tenuissima*)

Frond a *smooth, unspotted* membrane, rather tough, from disc hold-fast, on inconspicuous stalk that quickly broadens into base of frond, edge of which may be slightly wavy. Greenish-brown. Middle shore downwards. On rocks, in pools with plenty of sand. Appears in November, maximum in mid-winter, disappears by April. Widely distributed. Locally probably common.

Petalonia fascia (=*Phyllitis fascia*) pl. xxix.

Distinguish from minute *Laminaria* by holdfast and small stalk (see p. 225 and pl. xxxi.).

v. Thin hollow membrane, not branched; fig. *o*.

Disc holdfast from which each individual from a crowded group rises as if on a small *stalk that quickly swells into frond*. Olive-brown. Rather *slimy, shiny*, more or less divided by a series of *deeply nipped constrictions*. Middle shore. On rocks, in pools; on limpets and *Zostera* (p. 254 and pl. 40). Widely distributed. Common. *Scytosiphon lomentaria* pl. xxx.

From small disc holdfast frond, green when small, becoming olive-brown, soft membrane, *widens gradually upwards to less than ½ in. diameter*, tapers at end to blunt point. Slight narrowing by *shallow constrictions*. Stippled all over with small spots. Middle shore. On stones; in pools. Widely distributed. Common, particularly in summer.

Asperococcus fistulosus pl. xxix.

As *A. fistulosus* but so thin as to be translucent, frond *suddenly widens from stalk*, may be more than ½ in. across. Middle and lower shore. On stones, large seaweeds and *Zostera* (p. 254 and pl. 40), particularly in quiet water. Summer only. Widely distributed. Locally abundant. *Asperococcus bullosus*

vi. Frond of limp branched threads

Main thread irregularly branched, bearing irregular branchlets. Whole plant *covered with small spots*. Part of plant may be hollow. Usually about 8 in. long, but may be over 2 ft. Only in summer. On rocks and seaweeds, especially where stream runs into sea. Rare in N.; not common in S. *Stilophora rhizodes* pl. xxviii.

Well-marked central thread, usually about 8 in. long but may be 18 in., fine branches, bearing alternate branchlets, on end of which minute tuft of hairs. Lower shore. Summer only. On rocks. Rare in N., less so in S. *Sporochnus pedunculatus* pl. xxviii.

G. SMALL PLANTS, about 6 in. long.

i. Frond gelatinous

Frond olive-brown, rounded, lobed, lump up to 1½ in. across base and perhaps as thick. Small ones solid, larger ones become hollow. Middle and lower shore. On rocks and seaweeds. Appears in March, abundant by July, washed away by end of September. Widely distributed. Very common. *Leathesia difformis* pl. xxvii.

Frond yellow-brown, smudgy, slimy, solid, to 3 in. tall, irregularly branched, and branches carrying branchlets, all *thicknesses continually varying*. Middle and lower shore. On rocks and stones; in deep pools of more sheltered shores. Widely distributed. Abundant in N.E., common elsewhere. *Mesogloia vermiculata* pl. xxviii.

Frond olive, limp and slimy, typically 4-8 in. but can be much larger. Irregular branches, sometimes partly hollow, *covered with fine hairs*. Low on middle shore. In pools. Widely distributed. Very common. *Sauvageaugloia griffithsiana* (=*Mesogloia griffithsiana*)

Frond yellow or olive-brown, limp, may be long threads, typically 6 in. but up to 2 ft., more or less alternately branched, and with irregular short blunt branchlets. Low on middle shore. On sand-covered rocks and in pools. In summer. Widely distributed. Becoming abundant in S. *Eudesme virescens* (=*Castagnea virescens*)

Frond dark brown, *smooth, stiff strings of jelly*, about ⅛ in. across, central stalk bearing long branches with *few branchlets*. Middle shore. On rocks; in pools. Appears July, gone by end of November. Widely distributed. Common. *Chordaria flagelliformis* pl. xxviii.

Very much as *C. flagelliformis*, but branches bunched, may be *hollow towards ends* and bearing *many branchlets*. Summer only. Very rare. *Sphaerotrichia divaricata* (=*Chordaria divaricata*)

Olive-brown stiff button, developing into hollow-topped " toadstool " about 1½ in. high. Middle shore. Exposed coasts.
Himanthalia elongata (=*H. lorea*) p. 228 and pl. xxxiii and fig. *i*.

ii. Frond of branched threads

(a) Rather stiff plants

Main stem stiff, dark greenish-brown, *irregular branches*, bearing branchlets. Whole plant carrying whorls of stiff hooks, *not so close together that each whorl cannot be distinguished*. Usually about 6 in. long. Middle shore. On rocks and seaweeds. Widely distributed. Common. *Cladostephus verticillatus* pl. xxx.

As *C. verticillatus* but whorls so close together that they can be distinguished only by close inspection. Usually about 3 in. long. Middle shore. On rocks, particularly perhaps those covered in sand held on by *Rhodochorton* (p. 250 and pl. 38). Widely distributed. Common. *Cladostephus spongiosus*

Small, dense, brown tufts, about 1 in. tall, of *stiff* threads, which, if teased out, are seen to be branched, with *branches bearing regular opposite branchlets*. Middle shore. Growing on other seaweeds. Widely distributed. Very common.
Sphacelaria [*cirrhosa*] pl. xxvii.

There are several other species of *Sphacelaria*, mostly rather rare, which do not have branchlets sub-divided in this way, and two others which do, of which both are rare, one on mud under *Zostera* (p. 254 and pl. 40), the other in sandy pools.

Central thread rises stiff and bare from holdfast. Then closely branched, with branchlets closely sub-divided, with minute further sub-divisions, to give feathery effect. 2-4 in. long. Greenish-brown. Lower shore. On rocks among other seaweeds. Rare, least so in S.W. *Halopteris filicina* pl. xxx.

Stiff threads divided and sub-divided several times. Bunched into cones from which successive cones arise. In summer these are shaggy " shaving brushes " but in winter they are worn down into thin straggly remnants. Lower shore. On rocks. Rare in N., becoming fairly common in S.
Halopteris scoparia (=*Stypocaulon scoparium*) pl. xxx.

(b) Plant limp

Check for small pieces of *Stilophora rhizodes* (p. 231 and pl. xxviii) or *Sporochnus pedunculatus* (p. 232 and pl. xxviii).

Plant so fine that it sways in the water or hangs as wet matted hair. Each thread is divided and sub-divided. Olive-brown or yellow-brown. Some too minute to see details, 1-10 in. long. All levels of beach. Most frequently growing on other seaweeds but also on rocks, etc. Abundant. There are at least 20 species of the genus *Ectocarpus* (pl. xxvii) and more than 20 others in related genera which may be separated only after much careful work with a microscope.

iii. Frond of unbranched threads

Simple threads that radiate about 1 in. up from a " pin-cushion," rather stiff, greenish-brown. Like series of miniature shaving brushes. On other seaweeds.

On *Fucus serratus* and *Fucus vesiculosus* (p. 226 and pl. xxxii), may be widespread and abundant.   *Elachista fucicola* pl. xxvii.
On *Cystoseira* and *Halidrys* (p. 229 and pl. xxxiii), not uncommon.
                                        Elachista flaccida

Other species of *Elachista* and several other genera can easily be confused.

Tufts 2-4 in. long, yellow-brown soft threads with cells visible through lens. Slimy. Summer only. On *Chorda filum* (p. 228 and pl. xxxi). Widespread. Abundant.   *Litosiphon pusillus*

iv. Frond of narrow, leathery, inrolled straps

See *Pelvetia canaliculata* CHANNEL WRACK p. 226 and pl. xxxiii.

RHODOPHYCEAE

Red Seaweeds

A

Plant consisting of stem and branches from which develop " leaves " that may have a midrib and *lateral veins*; fig. *p*.

B

Plant consisting of a ribbon frond through which runs a midrib that divides to carry " leaves " which also have a midrib but *no lateral veins;* figs. *q* and *r*.

C

Plant tough, thick, flat, leathery, bladed or shaped like a palm and fingers (palmate), the fingers being open or closed; figs. *aa* and *s*.

D

Plant a thin membrane.

    i. Lobed and divided; fig. *t*.

    ii. Brownish-purple and shapeless.

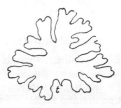

E

Rather small plants, about 6 in. long, with main axis or obvious main branches altogether thicker than rest of plant, *flat, not regularly dichotomous* but repeatedly divided and subdivided.

    i. Very fine feathery subdivisions, final divisions too small to see easily.

    ii. Well-developed main branches from which subdivisions not too small to see easily.

    v. Rather stiff plants, dichotomous branches, attaining uniform height for each plant and so giving somewhat level look to top line of plant. Small plants, about 6 in. long; fig. *ff*.

    vi. Stem and branches covered with whorls of little hooks. About 6 in. long; fig. *u*.

G

Stem and branches a flat membrane. Dichotomous. About 6 in. long; fig. *v*.

F

Stem and main branches cylindrical but not hair-thread thin.

    i. Plants about 1 ft. long, irregularly branched.

    ii. Round, worm-like, gelatinous texture. Slimy plants. About 6 in. long.

    iii. Generally opposite branches and branchlets; fig. *bb*.

    iv. Alternate branches. About 6-12 in. long; fig. *cc*.

H

Small plants constricted into small sections articulated together, giving effect of closely strung long-oval or disc beads; fig. *w*.

i. About 6 in long. Constrictions quite obvious.

ii. About ½ in. long. Constrictions masked at first sight by moss-like impression.

I

Plant pinkish-purple, with a hard skeleton (coat), of a rough abrasive texture, of calcium. After death skeleton turns white.

i. Thin and closely encrusting, feeling like surface of rock.

ii. Stiff, upright, branched, articulated plants.

J

Smooth, structureless crimson patches.

i. Shiny, sharply outlined, hard.

ii. Velvet-dull carpet pile mixed with sand.

K

Rather small plants, about 6-12 in. long, of branched threads.

i. Dichotomous threads with simple ends; fig. *x*.

ii. Dichotomous threads with tips divided into two inward-hooking points (forcipate); fig. *y*.

iii. Irregularly branched and entangled; fig. *z*.

iv. Others.

A. PLANT CONSISTING OF STEM AND BRANCHES from which develop "leaves" that may have a midrib and *lateral veins;* fig. *p.*

Stiff, strong stalk bearing large leaves which are *deeply indented* and resemble oak leaves, sometimes so much pointed at margins to be more like holly leaves. Plant may be 10 in. tall, rather brown-crimson. Lower shore. Usually on *Laminaria* stalks (p. 225 and pl. xxxi). In pools. Often cast up. Widely distributed. Common.

Phycodrys rubens pl. 37.

Rather short, much branched stem bearing large leaves with *wavy, undivided edges.* Deep pink. In rather large, deep, shadowy pools, growing as rather isolated plants. At its best in summer. Lower shore. Widely distributed. Common. *Delesseria sanguinea* pl. 36.

B. PLANT CONSISTING OF A RIBBON FROND through which runs a midrib that divides to carry " leaves " which also have a midrib but *no lateral veins*; figs. *q* and *r*.

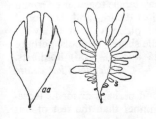

Whole plant 4-8 in. long in *flat pieces*, irregularly dichotomous, narrow branches bearing branchlets. Pinkish-crimson or blood-red. Middle and lower shore. On shady rocks, among other seaweeds. On *Laminaria* (p. 225 and pl. xxxi) stalks, in pools. Widely distributed. Very common. *Membranoptera alata* pl. 36.

Plant 2-8 in. long, *branches and branchlets arising from the midrib* and at right angles to it, each *leaf sharply pointed*. Red, tinged pink. Middle and lower shore. On rocks; on *Laminaria* (p. 225 and pl. xxxi) stalks; in pools. Widely distributed. Common, especially in S.
Hypoglossum woodwardii pl. 36.

Plant 2-4 in. long, branched as in *H. woodwardii*, each *leaf rounded* and with wavy edges. In summer has spot on midrib. Plant tears easily. Middle and lower shore. On rocks; in pools. Widely distributed. Not common. *Apoglossum ruscifolium* pl. 36.

C. PLANT TOUGH, THICK, FLAT, leathery, bladed or shaped like a palm and fingers (palmate), the fingers being open or closed; figs. *aa* and *s*.

Extremely tough, 4-12 in., completely opaque, rounded pieces that may be deeply cut by wave action, suddenly narrows below to join round stalk. Dark red in colour. Crisp to bite. Middle and lower shore. On rocks; on small stones on sandy flats. Widely distributed. Common. (In older records this plant was confused with *Rhodymenia palmata*, see below.)
Dilsea carnosa (= *D. edulis*) pl. xxxvi.

Tough, not quite opaque frond. Variable in size and shape, *arising directly from disc holdfast*. 4-12 in. May be a single broad or narrow blade, or palmate. May have small pieces growing out from main edges. In small pieces or in bunches. Dark red, with purple reflections. Middle and lower shore. On rocks; on *Fucus* (p. 226 and pl. xxxii); quantities on *Laminaria* (p. 225 and pl. xxxi) stalks. Widely distributed. Abundant. This is the edible dulse.　　　　*Rhodymenia palmata* pl. 39.

Same tough opaque texture but not so dark red as *R. palmata*, and plant only 2-4 in., *with stalk*, and frond dichotomously branched into wedge-shaped sections and re-dividing to rounded tips. Frond shape variable, but *never with small pieces growing out of main edge*. Middle and lower shore. On stones; on *Laminaria* (p. 225 and pl. xxxi). Widely distributed. Not common.

Rhodymenia pseudopalmata (= *R. palmetta*)

From disc holdfast and small stalk develop a *bright red*, broadly palmate frond, or wedge-shaped sections, about 3 in. tall, divided irregularly and subdivided into blunt pointed tips. Some small proliferations from *edges, which in summer are finely wrinkled*. Middle and lower shore. On rocks; among *Laminaria* (p. 225 and pl. xxxi). Widely distributed. Not common.　　　　*Callophyllis laciniata* pl. xxxix.

Holdfast of branched " rootlets." Short, unbranched stalk opening to dark red spear-blade *from edge of which various sizes of smaller blades arise*. Main blade may be divided. 6-12 in. tall. Rarely on shore but often cast up, especially in spring after reaching maximum development in winter. Widely distributed. Rare in N.; common in S.

Calliblepharis ciliata pl. 39.
Easily muddled with *Rhodymenia*, but see holdfasts.

Holdfast of branched " rootlets." Short, *branched stalk* opening to long, narrow, pointed blades, 2-7 in. long, which develop in summer a *long fringe of tendrils* $\frac{1}{2}$-$1\frac{1}{2}$ in. long, that may tangle together or round other seaweeds. In winter plant is denuded of tendrils and then looks rather like *Gelidium latifolium* (p. 242 and pl. xxxv), but is always darker, larger and less pink in colour. Middle shore. In pools, perhaps rather sunny ones; on *Laminaria* (p. 225 and pl. xxxi) holdfasts. S. and W. coasts. Not common.　　　*Calliblepharis lanceolata*

Plant 4-12 in. long, wide straps, long-oval and perhaps divided. Rose-coloured and almost transparent. Much thinner than the rest of this group. Irregularly shaped proliferations at all angles from margin and from middle. Lower shore. Summer only. Not common in S., very rare in W. and absent N. and E.　　　　*Halarachnion ligulatum*

D. PLANT A THIN MEMBRANE

i. Lobed and divided, fig. *t*.

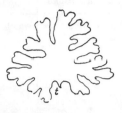

Four closely related genera of confusingly similar shapes. The real differences between them are in the structure of the fruiting bodies. Even now the latest list considers that the first two should be lumped into a single genus. The list of characteristics below is not likely to lead to more than suspicion falling on one genus rather than another. Plate 37 inevitably shows them as flat. When found, particularly if they have been cast ashore, they are often rolled into lumps or bunched. The shape of the frond may be distorted by tearing.

	Nitophyllum spp.		*Polyneura* spp.	*Cryptopleura ramosa*
	Nitophyllum punctatum	*Myriogramme bonnemaisonii*		
STALK	none or very short	½ in.; round	½ in. or less; round.	none, or very short and pliable.
FROND SHAPE	broad, round sections, regularly dichotomous; or simply in few main undivided sections	tends to be wider than long; perhaps short fingers or deep divisions nearly to stalk, each subdivided more or less dichotomously; rounded.	roundish fan-shapes, cut variously into segments, dichotomously or in fingers or jagged. Only this genus ever has pointed segments.	same width as height, many times divided, usually dichotomously but may also be quite irregular.

239

	Nitophyllum spp.		Polyneura spp.	Crytopleura ramosa
	Nitophyllum punctatum	*Myriogramme bodnemaisonii*		
MARGIN	may be repeatedly furnished with overlapping dichotomous divisions, to give total effect of bunching.	may have proliferations	wavy	wavy, and sometimes with proliferations
TEXTURE	very thin and delicate	thin	becomes thinner and thinner towards the top	very thin but yet not delicate
VEINS	none	near stalk	radiating from top of stalk	in lower part only; branching
COLOUR	pinkish-red, sometimes and at some angles there may be an almost iridescent blue reflect as from the tips	pinkish-red	crimson	purplish- or brownish-red
HEIGHT	4-20 in.	2-4 in.	to 3 in.	4-8 in.
LEVEL ON BEACH	middle and lower shore	lower shore	middle and lower shore	middle and lower shore
HABITAT	on seaweeds in pools	on *Laminaria*, rocks and stone	on large seaweeds and stone	on *Laminaria* and stones
DISTRIBUTION	wide but local; not uncommon	wide; rare	S and W not uncommon; N rare	wide; common
PLATE	37	37	37	37

Elongated oval straps, really too long and thick to be called a membrane, see p. 238.   *Halarachnion ligulatum*

ii. Brownish-purple and shapeless

Frond an expanded, thin membrane, usually attached by some point. Irregular shape, divided into lobes. Pieces 5-10 in. long. Dark purplish-red; almost black and brittle when dry, becoming pale greenish-brown as it withers; on pressing between fingers colours brighten up and is more purple. On rocks and stones at most levels on exposed beaches, particularly where stones are liable to be covered with sand, so that it often appears to be growing in sand. Widely distributed; common.   *Porphyra* [*umbilicalis*] pl. xxxiv.

Two other species of *Porphyra* are not separable on these characters. (It is eaten fried with bacon or rolled in oatmeal and is called laverbread. Swansea and Llanelly count it as a delicacy.)

E. RATHER SMALL PLANTS, about 6 in. long, with main axis or obvious main branches altogether thicker than rest of plant; flat, not regularly dichotomous, but repeatedly divided and subdivided.

i. Very fine feathery subdivisions; final divisions too small to see easily.

Wide main branches, 4-8 in., flattened and not soft, irregularly branched. Branchlets and their sub-branchlets opposite. So close is subdivision that each section looks like rounded feather and quill. To be seen pattern must be teased out with needle. Dark red, almost crimson. Lower shore. Typically on *Laminaria* (p. 225 and pl. xxxi) stalks. N. coasts. Common.   *Ptilota plumosa* pl. 38.

Strong main axis but not conspicuous main branches, 2-4 in. long, *soft and limp*, irregularly branched. Branchlets and their subdivisions opposite. Dark crimson. Middle and lower shore. Hangs lankly from shady rock overhangs with no detail of structure visible until floated in water. Often has purse sponges (see p. 42 and pl. 1) attached to it. Widely distributed. Very common.

Plumaria elegans pl. 38 and pl. 1.

Main axis and branches *cylindrical*, regular opposite branches and branchlets, see p. 244.   *Lomentaria clavellosa* pl. xl.

ii. Well-developed main branches from which subdivisions not too small to be seen easily.

Number of branches about 3 in. long, with a rather distinctive stiff feel, carrying branchlets and subdivisions which establish a pattern difficult to describe but clear in plate xxxv. Very dark, dried-blood-red. Low on middle shore. Often in shallow pools, usually in quantities. Widely distributed. Not very common.

Gelidium corneum pl. xxxv.

Main branches are long narrow ribbons with contrasting extremely narrow thread branchlets. About 3 in. Lower shore. On rocks. Widely distributed; locally common. *Gelidium latifolium* pl. xxxv.

Gelidium is one of the genera which is being fundamentally revised. How many species we shall be left with is still uncertain, but several others have been described. The proportionate width of the parts varies greatly. The overall pattern is the important generic character.

Tufts 2-6 in. tall with well-marked main axes that tend not to branch for half the height of the plant. Then thin branches equal in length to half the height of the plant, which may be subdivided. Middle and lower shore. Shady places. Widely distributed. Rare.

Pterocladia pinnata (=*P. capillacea*) pl. xxxv.

From disc holdfast a tuft of main axes which are compressed rather than truly flat, 2-5 in. tall, dark violet or black-green. Long thin irregular lateral branches bearing even thinner branchlets, all drawn out to fine point. Middle shore, *where fresh water runs over rocks*. Not in N. and E. Very rare W. Not so rare S.

Grateloupia filicina pl. xxxv.

Rather solid flat lamina, 3-10 in. tall, with irregular branches and rather stubby branchlets, at end of which are several teeth. Little bunches of fruiting bodies between teeth in winter. Lower shore. In pools; on rocks. Frequently cast up by waves. N. England and Scotland. Common. *Odonthalia dentata* pl. xxxvii.

Strong, rather thick stalk and lower part of main branches, becoming thinner higher up and subdividing several times irregularly, becoming fan-shaped. *Edges of finer divisions fringed* with little pointed proliferations. 6-12 in.; scarlet-pink. S. and W. coasts. Locally not uncommon. *Sphaerococcus coronopifolius* pl. xxxiv.

Strongly developed main branching system, 3-8 in. long, which is rather bare in lower section but irregularly branched and several times subdivided; *last subdivisions all originate on the same side*. Lower shore. On rocks; in pools. Often cast up. Widely distributed. Common. *Plocamium coccineum* pl. 39.

Typically purplish-red, very low on the shore, with a strong main stalk, 3-4 in. tall, alternate branches divided and subdivided with progressively shorter branchlets, so that ends of each section often look as if narrowly spear-shaped frond was proliferating from edges.

But plant is variable. On steep, rather sunny rocks on the middle shore colour is yellow-green or whitish-green and growth is no more than dense turf on rocks. Widely distributed. Abundant.

Laurencia pinnatifida pl. xxxvii.

Flat pattern from plant round in cross section, see p. 246.

Gymnogongrus griffithsiae pl. xxxix.

F. STEM AND MAIN BRANCHES CYLINDRICAL but not hair thread thin.

i. Plants irregularly branched. About 1 ft. long.

From holdfast of branched " rootlets " arises a soft, bushy plant, 6-18 in. long, with *main stem altogether bigger than any of the irregular branches* which bear irregular branchlets and further subdivisions. *All branches and branchlets are smallest at point of origin and taper away again to terminal point* (cf. *Dumontia incrassata* p. 244 and pl. xxxv). Fruits appear in summer as swellings in branches. Dull purple-red in colour, or rather pinker in water. Middle and lower shore. Particularly in pools; on rocks. Dies back to mere vestiges in mid-winter. Widely distributed. Common.

Cystoclonium purpureum pl. xl.

From very small disc out of which creep " rootlets " grows plant of rather stringy texture, especially when dry. 4-18 in. long, particularly lengthy when growing through sand. Irregularly branched and re-branched without successive decrease in size and all pieces going to *smooth, slender points*. In summer *branches bear fruiting bodies as rough knobs*. Middle shore. Largely dies away in winter. Widely distributed. On rocks; gravelly flats. Locally common.

Gracilaria verrucosa (=*G. confervoides*) pl. xl.

Plant 4-12 in. long, with a rather tough, usually undivided main stem. Irregular branches tend to be longer lower down and carry short undivided branchlets much narrowed at point of origin, *but are blunt-ended*. Purplish-red. Lower shore. Summer only. In pools with mud or sand in them. Widely distributed. Common.

Chondria dasyphylla pl. xxxviii.

As *C. dasyphylla* but *ultimate branchlets are sharp pointed* as bristles. Lower shore. Summer only. In pools. Widely distributed. Rare.

Chondria tenuissima

From branching thread-" rootlets " arises firm main stem and branches, brownish-red, 2-8 in., almost bare, but at top bunches of hollow, smooth, elongated processes like red grains of wheat. Middle and lower shore. In pools; on rocks among other seaweeds. Widely distributed. Common.

Gastroclonium ovatum (=*Chylocladia ovatus*) pl. xl.

Holdfast of branching " rootlets." Tough main stem, 4-10 in. Dries rigid. Branches bear *branchlets all on one side* (comb pattern) and all curve upwards. Forms thick tufts. Lower shore. On rocks. Only S. coasts. Not uncommon. *Halopitys incurvus* pl. xxxvii.

ii. **Round, worm-like, gelatinous texture.** Slimy plants. About 6 in. long.

Distinct main axis, 6-8 in. long, with more or less alternate branches that become shorter and shorter towards top, bearing stubby branchlets. Pale red or red-brown. Angles of junctions more or less right angles. Lower shore. On stones and seaweeds. Summer only. Distribution irregular. May be locally common to abundant.

Helminthora divaricata pl. xxxiv.

Rather strong disc holdfast, *more or less dichotomous* branches with blunt ends. Brown or brownish-purple. 4-10 in. long. Middle shore. Summer only. In pools; on shells. Widely distributed. Varying in abundance from year to year. *Nemalion multifidum* pl. xxxiv.

As *N. multifidum* but quite unbranched, or with a single division near the holdfast. Widely distributed. Very local. *Nemalion elminthoides*

Disc holdfast. Plant 3-12 in. long, irregularly branched, with some branchlets. *Branches and branchlets smallest at point of origin,* but are blunt-ended (cf. *Cystoclonium purpureum* p. 243 and pl. xl). Shallow constrictions on all limbs as thickness of branches varies. Colour varies from pale yellow to purplish-red. Middle shore. On rocks; on small stones on flats. Widely distributed. Common.

Dumontia incrassata pl. xxxv.

Rather slimy. Dichotomously branched. See p. 246.

Scinaia furcellata pl. xxxvi.

iii. **Generally opposite branches and branchlets;** fig. *bb*.

Undivided main axes, 3-8 in. long, may be 12 in., hollow. Branches and branchlets are narrowed at each end and decrease in length successively away from bottom. Final subdivisions are sharply pointed. Whole plant tends to lie flat in one plane. Very pink. Limp and rather gelatinous feel. Middle and lower shore. Summer only. On rocks and seaweeds. In pools. Widely distributed. Common.

Lomentaria clavellosa pl. xl.

Plant 3-6 in., undivided main axis. Stiff opposite branches and branchlets successively shorter towards top and spread open and wide. Pinkish-purple to, in sunshine, yellowish-red. Low on middle shore and on lower shore. Summer only. Widely distributed. Common. *Laurencia obtusa*

Stiff, gritty feeling, articulated. See p. 250.
Corallina officinalis pl, 35 and xxvii.

iv. **Alternate branches,** 6-12 in long; fig. *cc.*

Plant 2-6 in.; strong, central axis has alternate branches that decrease in length towards top (shape of miniature Christmas tree). Branches with alternate branchlets, which are similarly subdivided. Dark purple. Low on middle shore. On bottom in shallow pools; on limpets and rocks. Widely distributed. Common.
cc   *Laurencia hybrida* (=*L. caespitosa*) pl. xxxvii.

Beware of variations of *Laurencia pinnatifida* (p. 242 and pl. xxxvii) that tend to mask the essentially flat nature of its frond by rolling up; or, when about 1 ft. long, not having really developed the flatness of maturity.

Plant 6-8 in., up to 12 in. Deep crimson. Has strong, hairy main axis, from which come irregularly alternate branches in two lines in one plane, *lower portions showing bare* but at least the outer three-quarters with branchlets and subdivisions giving feather-fine, rather spear-shaped sections. Lower shore. Full development only below low water, but large pieces are commonly cast ashore. Widely distributed. Common. *Heterosiphonia plumosa* pl. 35.

Plant 6-12 in. long. Crimson. Soft. Main stem carries alternate branches with alternate branchlets *clothed right to their point of origin with fine subdivisions.* Much less airy, open texture than *Heterosiphonia plumosa* (above and pl. 35). Lower shore. Summer only. Widely distributed. Probably common, except in Scotland.
Brongniartella byssoides pl. xxxviii.

v. **Rather stiff plants, with dichotomous branches,** attaining uniform height for each plant and so giving somewhat level look to top line of plant. Small plants, about 6 in. long; fig. *ff.*

From interweaving *branched "rootlets"*—claw holdfast—arises a stiff shiny plant, 4-8 in. tall, subdivided 3-4 times at acute angles, to long, cylindrical pod-points in summer, obviously thicker than the branchlets which support them. Dark red-brown. Low on middle shore. Widely distributed. Not uncommon.

Furcellaria fastigiata pl. xxxvi.

As *Furcellaria*, but from strong *disc holdfast*; branched 45°. Fruiting bodies long-oval lumps in branches, not at tips. Middle shore. On rocks; in sandy pools. Widely distributed. Not common.

Polyides caprinus (=*P. rotundus*) pl. xxxvi.

These last two species to be certainly distinguished only by the structure of the holdfasts.

From small disc holdfast arises clean stalk, 1-3 in. tall. Springy, smooth frond, many times dichotomous to level curve of small delicate divisions. Until floated out may appear as tuft. Very dark red, nearly black. Lower shore. On rocks. Widely distributed. Rare, but more often seen on S. coasts. *Gymnogongrus griffithsiae* pl. xxxix.

From small disc holdfast arises tuft 2-10 in. tall, one plant or several close together, ending in blunt short tips. Gelatinous and slimy. Clean pink or brownish-red. Lower shore. Summer only. S.W. coasts occasional; occurrence elsewhere doubtful.

Scinaia furcellata pl. xxxvi.

Although usually a flat plant, *Chondrus crispus* (p. 247 and pl. 38 and xxxviii) has varieties some of which might be described as round in cross section rather than flat.

Stiff, gritty-feeling, articulated, see p. 250. *Jania rubens*

Rather tufted plant, many ends of which are divided into two inward-hooking points (forcipate). See p. 251.

Ceramium rubrum pl. 38.

vi. Stem and branches covered with whorls of little hooks. Irregularly branched. About 6 in. long; fig. *u*.

Plant 3-8 in. long, erect and somewhat rigid, very dark red. Covered with whorls of short spikes, that curve upward and inward, *so close that they overlap*—bottle-brush effect. Middle and lower shore. On exposed shores. In pools higher up; on rocks lower down. Widespread; not common. Disappears in winter.

Halurus equisetifolius pl. 38.

Plant 4-8 in. long, rose-red, rather stiff (but becomes limp after picking), covered with whorls of little hooks far enough apart for *stalk to show through between successive whorls.* Lower shore. On steep-sided pools. Not in N., rare in W. and E., not uncommon in S.   *Sphondylothamnion multifidum*

G. STEM AND BRANCHES A FLAT MEMBRANE. Dichotomous.
About 6 in. long; fig. *v.*

As *Gymnogongrus griffithsiae* (p. 246 and pl. xxxix), but plant narrow, flat membrane branched from near holdfast.   *Gymnogongrus norvegicus*

Disc holdfast. Short stalk, 3-6 in. tall. The most variable of all red seaweeds. Under sheltered conditions it grows almost without a stalk. Wide flat frond which may divide into small rounded dichotomies. Or it may divide sharply. In exposure it may grow narrow, scarcely branched at all and almost rounded in section. But never so finely divided to be confused with *Gymnogongrus.* In pools it may be thin and with small end divisions that glow a watery violet iridescence (pl. 38) which disappears the moment the plant leaves the water. Little pustular fruiting bodies as swellings in the frond in winter. Frond is never inrolled, which is a certain distinction from *Gigartina stellata* (see below and pl. xxxix). Typical colour is dark red. May be pinkish-red. In heat waves the plant may go green, except towards the base, and even white-yellow. Middle shore. On all kinds of shore except mud. Widely distributed. Abundant.   *Chondrus crispus* pl. 38 and xxxviii.

In spite of all this variation *C. crispus* has a pattern and a texture which is characteristic. After a small amount of careful attention, it will come to be recognised in all its forms except the strangest aberrations.

Disc holdfast. Plant 4-8 in. tall, growing rather in·tufts, several times dichotomous. Very dark brownish-red. *Plant is inrolled throughout to form a channel,* much as in *Pelvetia* (p. 226 and pl. xxxiii). Frond may be dotted with characteristic pustular fruiting bodies which emerge almost as minute leaves from surface of the frond. Middle and lower shore. On stones. At that level may be the commonest seaweed. Frequently overgrown with grey, spiny masses of the polyzoan *Flustrella hispida* (p. 172 and pl. iii). Often mixed with other small reds, including *Chondrus*. Widely distributed. Abundant.

Gigartina stellata pl. xxxix.

Both *Gigartina* and *Chondrus* are collected and eaten in Ireland, where they are known as carragheen moss. They are a source of agar.

From *large, thick disc holdfast* may grow several *round stalks gradually flattening* and widening into dichotomous stiff and rose-red, wedge-shaped branches, 2-4 in. tall, with final sections often appearing from extreme tip of next lower down. Lower shore. On rocks. Not in N. and E. Rare in W. Locally not uncommon in S.

Phyllophora palmettoides

As *P. palmettoides*, but tiny disc holdfast. Round stalk leading to dichotomies, one side of which opens into flat fan while other side continues the stalk. On the fan side the change from the round stalk to fan is abrupt. 3-10 in. tall. Edge of membrane may carry proliferations. Brownish-purple or purplish-red. Lower shore. In pools. Widely distributed. Common.   *Phyllophora membranifolia* pl. xxxix.

Tiny disc holdfast, *very short stalk, gradually flattening* into long, thin, red, round-ended sections, lowest of which have slight midrib; dichotomous from tips only. *Proliferations from surface of frond.* Middle and lower shore. In steep-sided pools; on rocks; mixed with other seaweeds. Widely distributed. Locally common.

Phyllophora rubens (=*P. epiphylla*)

With midrib. Irregularly dichotomous. See p. 237.

Membranoptera alata pl. 36.

Tough, opaque texture, 2-4 in. tall, with stalk; dichotomously branching, rounded tips. See p. 238.   *Rhodymenia pseudopalmata*
Broad rounded thin sections. See p. 239.   *Nitophyllum* etc. pl. 37.

H. SMALL PLANTS CONSTRICTED INTO SMALL SECTIONS
articulated together, giving effect of closely strung long-oval or disc beads; fig. *w*.

i. **About 6 in. long.** Constrictions quite obvious.

Plant 3-8 in. long, *articulated throughout*. Irregularly branched and subdivided, *all divisions being at constrictions*. Rather pinkish-red to crimson; shiny. Lower shore. On rocks and other seaweeds; in pools. One of the commonest reds. Widely distributed. Abundant.

Lomentaria articulata pl. 39.

Small disc holdfast. Main stems 6-12 in. long. *Whorls of branches* and branchlets at constrictions. Pinkish, but goes yellow on rocks exposed to sun. Middle and lower shore. Summer only. In pools; on rocks. Widely distributed. Not uncommon.

Chylocladia verticillata (=*C. kaliformis*) pl. 39.

Plant 3-4 in. tall, irregularly branched and falls into lump, but teasing out shows whole plant to be a very long tube of fairy winegums. Dull pink or red. Middle and lower shore. Summer only. Fringing edge of pools; on other seaweeds. W. and S. coasts only. Rare. *Champia parvula* pl. xxxiv.

Stiff, pink strings of beads, with hard calcareous skeleton, see p. 250. *Corallina* spp. pl. 35 and xxvii.

ii. About ½ in. long. Constrictions masked at first sight by general moss-like appearance of whole plant.

From holdfast of interlacing threads plant about ½ in. high, series of irregularly articulated branches. So low that it looks like moss; dark purple that it looks almost black. High on middle shore. *In sheltered cracks* and on sheltered steep faces. Covers considerable areas at same level as and in amongst holdfast of *Pelvetia* (p. 226 and pl. xxxiii) and *Fucus spiralis* (p. 226 and pl. xxxii). No other seaweed has such tiny articulated filaments. Widely distributed. Abundant. *Catenella repens* (=*C. opuntia*) pl. xl.

I. PLANT PINKISH-PURPLE, WITH A HARD SKELETON (coat) of a rough, abrasive texture, of calcium. After death skeleton turns white.

i. Thin and closely encrusting, feeling like surface of rock.

Very thin, pinkish-purple encrustations on rocks from the middle of the shore downwards, becoming richer coloured lower down and in pools. Patches may cover large areas through which other seaweeds grow. Towards edges of patch and at surface of water in pools, the colour tends to be somewhat washed-out, white or dirty pale grey. These same faded colours show on stones cast high up on beach or in patches low down where the plant has died. Only pattern may be that of more or less concentric rings. Surface texture rough. Widely distributed. Very abundant. May cover more rock than any other genus. Tends to be less common in very quiet water.

Lithophyllum spp. pl. 35.

Only microscopically distinguishable from *Lithophyllum* unless the encrustation is gathered into liver wort-like lobes or coalescing protuberances and knobs. May grow on other seaweeds but usually on rocks in pools.   *Lithothamnion* spp. pl. xxxvi.

Closely encrusting, but not gritty. Smooth. Crimson. See below.
Hildenbrandia spp. pl. 35.

ii. Stiff, upright, branched, articulated plants.

Small disc holdfast, tufts 2-5 in. tall. *Branches, branchlets and their further subdivisions exactly opposite.* Close inspection shows at least main stem and main branches to be a long series of minute articulated sections. Plum-colour becoming paler to yellow and eventually to white higher up beach or in greater exposure to sunshine. Middle shore. Fringing pools about 3 in. below their surface. In shady places may almost form carpet pile over rocks. Widely distributed. Abundant.   *Corallina officinalis* pl. 35 and xxvii.

Plant 1-2 in. high, several times *dichotomously branched* with swellings at the divisions in spring. Middle shore. On other seaweeds. Widely distributed. Not uncommon.   *Jania rubens* (=*Corallina rubens*)

J. SMOOTH, STRUCTURELESS CRIMSON PATCHES

i. Shiny, sharply outlined, hard

Patches that lose lustre when dry. Can be picked off with thumbnail. Could be mistaken for paint. Middle shore. On damp, shaded rocks or in moist runnels. Widely distributed. Common.
Hildenbrandia sp. pl. 35.

Much as *Hildenbrandia*, but green-black, see lichen *Verrucaria mucosa*, p. 253.

ii. Velvet-dull carpet pile. Mixed with sand.

Covering quite large areas of rock, with other seaweeds growing through; also on seaweeds. When picked off with thumb-nail, it is seen to consist of crimson hair-threads massed in accumulated sand. Fluffy; ½ in. or less long. Middle shore. Widely distributed. Common. Locally abundant.   *Rhodochorton* spp. pl. 38.

K. RATHER SMALL PLANTS, about 6-12 in. long, *of branched threads.*

i. Dichotomous threads with simple ends; fig. *x.*

Delicate plant, 3-8 in. long, pink-crimson that is at once lost on

contact with fresh water. Under water an *eréct* tuft, a closely growing bunch of many times dichotomous threads. *Reproductive parts appear as stalked dots* scattered on the threads. Lower shore. Rock pools, particularly on more exposed coasts. Widely distributed. Common.

Griffithsia flosculosa pl. 35.

As *G. flosculosa* but plant covered in slimy skin. Strong smelling. Only in spring and summer. Widely distributed. Not common. *Griffithsia corallinoides*

ii. Dichotomous threads with tips divided into two inward hooking points (forcipate). Threads may be banded across with alternate dark and light sections; fig. *y*. *Ceramium* spp. pl. 38.

The genus *Ceramium* may be identified from either or both these characters. *Ceramium rubrum* (pl. 38) is a very common species on rocks and in pools on the middle shore. Has banded threads and forcipate tips. Colour varies from deep red to brownish-red or, in sunshine, even greenish-yellow. 1-12 in. long; in tufts.

Ceramium acanthonotum grows about 2-4 in. tall on middle and lower shore on rocks exposed to wave action. Each thread is clearly banded in alternate pink and silver.

There are at least twenty other species of *Ceramium* and several look very like these two.

iii. Threads irregularly branched and entangled; fig. *z*.

Plant of *stiff, wiry* texture, like a lump of two-amp fuse-wire, about 4 in. across (or, as some say, reminiscent of a piece of a landlady's wig). *Nearly black*. Middle shore. In pools, particularly on exposed beaches. Widely distributed. Common. *Ahnfeltia plicata* pl. xxxix.

Plant 2-4 in. long, no holdfast; growing *among stalks* of *Halimione portulacoides*, sea purslane, and other plants in mid-level of *some saltmarshes*. Widely distributed. Locally abundant.

Bostrychia scorpioides pl. xxxvii.

iv. Others

Small, fine plants, variously branched and ramified, in varying tones of red, are common on the shore. Their identification is beyond the limits of this list. Yet attention should again be drawn to the number of species that are in this group. For instance there are more than twenty species of *Polysiphonia* (pl. xxxviii), five species of *Pterosiphonia*, about fifteen species of *Callithamnion* and so on. To distinguish these needs a microscope, botanical knowledge and patience, and above all a much more detailed key than can be provided here.

LICHENS

ON THE splash zone, i.e. the region between the lowest flowering plant, often a sea-pink or a sea-campion, and the seaweeds, lichens are the dominant form of plant life, most of them closely encrusting and feeling dry and brittle.

The identification of lichens is a technical process. Only a few can be recognised at sight.

Green-grey, stiff, almost brittle, only slightly branched, tufts; may be 2 in. tall, but on higher steeper faces becomes about ½ in. and grows closer together to be almost a sward. Widely distributed. Abundant.

Ramalina spp. pl. 40.

Orange, coarse, rough, small-leafy, orbicular or irregularly shaped encrusted patches, typically 2-4 in. across. Gives dominant colour to zone above high water mark but below *Ramalina*. Widely distributed. Abundant. *Xanthoria parietina* pl. 40.

Dark orange encrustations, closely adherent to the rock, somewhat as *Xanthoria* but not leafy. May be peppered with fine orange granules. Widely distributed. Abundant. *Caloplaca* (=*Placodium*) spp. pl. 40.

Grey encrustations, roughly granular, irregular shaped patches, in which little black cups with white rims (when these are cut into they are dark purple inside). Among orange lichens and upwards. Widely distributed. Abundant. *Lecanora atra* pl. 40.

As *L. atra*, but inside of cups black all through. *Lecanora gangaleoides*

Greenish-brown, khaki, more or less orbicular patches, 1-2 in. across, growing closely on the rock, of narrow, more or less radiating irregular

LICHENS

branches that sometimes straggle. When wet has somewhat spongy texture but dries stiff and almost brittle. At same level as *Ramalina* and *Xanthoria*. Widely distributed. Common. *Pseudophyscia fusca* pl. 40.

Black patches, resembling a minute seaweed, almost furry at sight, but feels stiff. Very small *rounded branchlets*. May well go up exposed cliffs where even spray seldom falls. Widely distributed. Abundant.

Lichina confinis

Black patches similar to *L. confinis*, up to 1 in. high but with *short flattened lobes*, densely tufted; tufts may meet together to cover large area. On middle shore where it overlaps *Pelvetia canaliculata*, channel wrack (p. 226 and pl. xxxiii), down to as far as the *Fucus serratus*, saw wrack (p. 227 and pl. xxxii). Particularly on steeply sloping rocks where no large seaweeds survive. Widely distributed. Abundant.

Lichina pygmaea pl. 40.

Black, encrusted film, *rather like tar*, on upper shore. Covers so much rock that at low tide a black zone is visible along the top of the beach, beneath the much thinner orange (*Xanthoria*) zone and above the grey barnacle zone. May be thinly peppered with fine black granules. Comes off black under thumb-nail (so does tar!). Widely distributed. Very abundant.

Verrucaria maura pl. 40.

Green-black, smooth, sharply defined, closely encrusting, irregular patches, not more than a foot across. Somewhat gelatinous when wet. Green tint obvious if sample picked off under thumb-nail. Middle shore. On beaches where fucoids (wracks) abundant. Widely distributed. Common.

Verrucaria mucosa

Acorn barnacles (p. 90 and pl. vi) and some shells, notably limpets (p. 132 and pl. 17), are often peppered with black pits, minute but easily seen through a hand-lens. This peppering is the growth of the lichens.

Arthopyrenia faveolata or *A. litoralis*

FLOWERING PLANTS

ALTHOUGH the flowering plants are really outside the scope of this book and have been repeatedly described elsewhere we have nevertheless included below *Zostera* and *Ruppia* because they might be mistaken for green seaweeds and four other genera which flourish in the lower levels of salt-marshes where other organisms described in this book may be found.

Dark green, grass-like plants varying in length from 6 in. to 3 ft. arising from a creeping root-system. Leaves are flat and linear, ¼ in. wide or less, alternate, with distinct veins. Grass-like inconspicuous flowers without petals occur in spikes at base of some leaves. On protected shores, up estuaries and creeks. Middle shore and lower. On mud, gravel and muddy sand. Widely but irregularly distributed. Locally common.   *Zostera* spp. EEL-GRASS, SEA-GRASS pl. 40.

Leaves up to ¼ in. wide and 3 ft. long, with at least three veins. Flowering stems branched. Ribbed seeds.   *Zostera marina*

Narrow leaves, 6-12 in. long, with 1-3 veins. Flowering stems branched. Ribbed seeds.   *Zostera hornemanniana*

Very narrow, almost thread-like, leaves, about 6 in. long, with only one vein. Unbranched flowering stems. Smooth seeds.   *Zostera nana*

Stem much branched and, with leaves, thread-thin and dark green. Leaves sheathed at their base, from where the long flower stalks arise. In brackish ditches and salt-marsh pools. Widely distributed. Not uncommon.   *Ruppia* spp. (two species occur) TASSEL PONDWEED

Stiff annual, from up to 2 in. in May to 6 in. or more in August, by when stem has become rather woody. Shiny, succulent, rather fat-jointed, cylindrical sections of stem and the opposite branches all with blunt tips. Fresh green turning reddish in late summer. Very inconspicuous flowers at joints. Abundant at all levels of salt-marshes and may be dominant in lower levels, where dead brown stiff erect stems may persist through the winter; also occasionally on gravelly foreshores. Widespread.
        Salicornia spp. (nine species occur) GLASSWORT, MARSH SAMPHIRE

Rather stiff annual, succulent, cylindrical, hairless, frequently and alternately branched, about 2 in. long by May, and may remain very small, or grow to 9 in. or more by August. Grey or blue-green. The much branched brown remnants persist in winter. Very inconspicuous flowers.

On middle levels of salt-marshes, particularly just above the level at which *Salicornia* is dominant. Widespread. Common.

Suaeda maritima COMMON SEABLITE

Very stiff, hairless, erect grass-stems, either in colonising small groups or in circular patches which progressively coalesce. 2-3 ft. tall. Leaves tough, yellow-green, grooved, tapering to long point. Yellowish flowers in spikes in late summer. On estuarine mud and low down on salt-marshes. *Spartina* spp. (three species occur) CORD GRASS

Pliant stems, low growing, and usually interlocking to cover large areas. Many blue-green, elliptical, succulent, untoothed leaves. Inconspicuous yellow flowers from July to September. On salt-marshes, particularly along edge of scoured runnels. Widespread. Abundant.

Halimione (Obione) portulacoides SEA PURSLANE pl. xxxvii.

Bostrychia scorpioides (see p. 251) is particularly associated with *Halimione*.

Combat between an Annelid and *Corophium longicorne*
reproduced in *A History of the British Stalk-Eyed Crustacea*

FOR FURTHER INFORMATION

THOSE WHO use this guide may well wish to know more about conditions of life on the sea shore, or about the geography of the British coastline or wish to extend the inevitably only preliminary information here provided about the animals and the plants of the shore. The following list represents an attempt to meet these needs. Place of publication is London, except where otherwise stated.

LIFE ON THE SEA SHORE

THE SEA SHORE by C. M. Yonge (*New Naturalist*, Collins, 1949). Essentially a companion volume to this one while the many coloured and black and white photographs, largely by Dr. D. P. Wilson, both add to the illustrations in this book and show many of the animals here described in their natural surroundings. (Far and away the best account of the natural history of the shore. Recommended strongly. J.H.B.)

LIFE OF THE SHORE AND SHALLOW SEA by D. P. Wilson (Nicholson and Watson, 2nd edition, 1951). An admirably illustrated account of shore life including a valuable account of development.

LIFE IN THE SEA by L. Nilsson and G. Jagersten (G. T. Foulis, 1961). Probably the finest collection of photographs of living marine animals from northern European seas and with most informative text. A beautifully produced book.

THE BIOLOGY OF THE SEA-SHORE by F. W. Flattely and C. L. Walton (Sidgwick and Jackson, 1922). A good, although now much out of date, account of the habits, etc. of shore dwelling animals.

BETWEEN THE TIDES by Philip Street (University of London Press, 1952).

THE BRITISH SEASHORE by H. G. Vevers (Routledge & Kegan Paul, 1954). Two clearly written, well-illustrated elementary accounts of shore life.

THE WAYS OF THE SEA by Roger Pilkington (Routledge & Kegan Paul, 1957). First rate account of waves and tides based on the most recent work; a most informative book.

LIFE IN THE SEA

THE OPEN SEA: I THE WORLD OF PLANKTON; II FISH AND FISHERIES by Sir Alister Hardy (*New Naturalist*, Collins, 1956; 1959). These delightful books deal with life off-shore and so complement THE SEA SHORE (above). The first volume includes accounts of the early (planktonic) stages of all groups of animals which live as adults on the shore. The second volume summarises much modern work on fish. Both are liberally and very beautifully illustrated.

NATURE ADRIFT: THE STORY OF MARINE PLANKTON by James Fraser (G. T. Foulis, 1962). A well-illustrated account of the plankton and its importance in the life of the seas.

THE BRITISH COASTLINE

THE COASTLINE OF ENGLAND AND WALES by J. A. Steers (Cambridge University Press, 1946).

THE SEA COAST by J. A. Steers (*New Naturalist*, Collins, 1953). The standard books on the British coastline.

THE SHORE FAUNA

THE LITTORAL FAUNA OF GREAT BRITAIN by N. B. Eales (Cambridge University Press, 3rd Edition, 1961). An indispensable handbook for those who would take this subject further. It is intended for the student, not the general reader, but contains many helpful keys and clear diagrammatic figures. It also lists

FOR FURTHER INFORMATION

the major authorities for each group many of which will not be accessible except in scientific libraries. Reasonably available works on some of the major groups of shore animals are listed below.

ANIMALS WITHOUT BACKBONES by Ralph Buchsbaum (Penguin Books, 2 vols., 1953) and LIVING INVERTEBRATES OF THE WORLD by Ralph Buchsbaum and Lorus J. Milne (Hamish Hamilton, 1960). These contain much zoological information on all the large invertebrate groups, well illustrated with photographs and drawings. Admirable books for amateurs, strongly recommended.

COELENTERATES

A HISTORY OF BRITISH HYDROID ZOOPHYTES 2 vols. by T. Hincks (Van Voorst, 1868). Despite its age, still the standard work although much of the nomenclature is out of date. Easily obtained second-hand.

A HISTORY OF BRITISH SEA ANEMONES AND CORALS by P. H. Gosse (Van Voorst, 1860). Although now superseded by Stephenson (see below) remains a classic work on sea anemones. Has excellent colour illustrations and is easily obtained second-hand.

BRITISH SEA ANEMONES 2 vols. by T. A. Stephenson (Ray Society, vol. 1, 1928; vol. 2, 1934). The standard work on British sea anemones, magnificently illustrated largely by coloured reproductions of paintings by the author.

NEMERTINES AND POLYCHAETES

Difficult groups for the amateur (also for the professional) zoologist; the standard British work is:

A MONOGRAPH OF THE BRITISH ANNELIDS 4 vols. by W. C. McIntosh (Ray Society, 1873-1923). This includes, at the beginning, the Nemertines. The book, though with good coloured plates, is very difficult to use and is now getting out of date. Those who become interested in these animals are best advised to turn to:

FAUNE DE FRANCE Vol. V *Polychètes Errantes;* Vol. XVI. *Polychètes Sédentaires* by P. Fauvel, 1923; 1927.

CRUSTACEANS

The group most likely to interest the amateur is the Decapoda including the shrimps, prawns, lobsters and crabs; these are "stalk-eyed" in contrast to the "sessile-eyed" isopods, amphipods, etc. Excellent general accounts of these groups, although the nomenclature is often out of date are found in:

A HISTORY OF THE BRITISH STALK-EYED CRUSTACEA by T. Bell (Van Voorst, 1853).

A HISTORY OF THE BRITISH SESSILE-EYED CRUSTACEA 2 vols. by C. Spence Bate & J. O. Westwood (Van Voorst, vol. 1, 1863; vol. 2, 1868).

MOLLUSCS

A HISTORY OF THE BRITISH MOLLUSCA AND THEIR SHELLS 4 vols. by E. Forbes & S. Hanley (Van Voorst, 1852).

BRITISH CONCHOLOGY 5 vols. by J. G. Jeffreys (Van Voorst, 1862-1869).

A MONOGRAPH OF THE BRITISH NUDIBRANCHIATE MOLLUSCA by J. Alder & A. Hancock (Ray Society, 1845-1855).

BRITISH NUDIBRANCHIATE MOLLUSCA (SUPPLEMENT) by C. Eliot (Ray Society, 1910).

The above represent the classic works on British molluscs, the first two covering land and freshwater as well as marine species, the last two being con-

FOR FURTHER INFORMATION

fined to the exclusively marine sea slugs. Although again the nomenclature is largely out of date, these are most valuable books and are still to be obtained.

SHELL LIFE by E. Step (*The Wayside and Woodland Series*, Warne, 1945). The only recent general account of molluscs that is at all complete. Has many plates and text-figures but is not systematic and in various respects not up to date; but the best available.

BRITISH PROSOBRANCH MOLLUSCS by V. Fretter & M. Graham (Ray Society, 1962). Although beyond the scope of a beginner, this is a superb book, exhaustive in text and magnificently illustrated. Essential to all who become really interested in marine "snails"; it does not deal with sea slugs and other Opisthobranchs.

OYSTERS by C. M. Yonge (*New Naturalist*, Collins, 1960).

BRITISH BIVALVE SEASHELLS by Norman Tebble (British Museum [Natural History], 1966). Splendidly illustrated and completely authoritative account of the British marine bivalves. A book we have long been waiting for. Can be carried in the pocket.

BRYOZOANS

A HISTORY OF THE BRITISH MARINE POLYZOA 2 vols. by T. Hincks (Van Voorst, 1880). The descriptions in vol. 1 and the figures in vol. 2 remain essential for identification of these rather fascinating animals. Despite its age still often available second-hand.

BIOLOGY AND IDENTIFICATION OF INTERTIDAL POLYZOA by J. S. Ryland (off-printed from *Field Studies*, Vol. 1, No. 4, 1962). A good, new illustrated key.*

ECHINODERMS

A HISTORY OF BRITISH STARFISHES by E. Forbes (Van Voorst, 1841). Undoubtedly the most charmingly illustrated and altogether the most delightful book ever written on any section of the British marine fauna, at the same time a work of high scientific standing. Still freely available second-hand.

HANDBOOK OF THE ECHINODERMS OF THE BRITISH ISLES by T. Mortensen (Oxford University Press, 1927). The standard modern work by the outstanding authority on these animals.

TUNICATES

THE TUNICATA WITH AN ACCOUNT OF BRITISH SPECIES by N. J. Berril (Ray Society, 1950). Supersedes the earlier Ray Society monograph on these animals; by no means a popular work but indispensable to those wanting further information about British species.

FISHES

THE FISHES OF THE BRITISH ISLES by J. Travis Jenkins (*The Wayside and Woodland Series*, Warne, 2nd edition, 1936). A most useful volume which summarises the older, more detailed but large and cumbersome, books by Couch and Day.

THE SHORE FLORA

FLOWERS OF THE COAST by I. Hepburn (*The New Naturalist*, Collins, 1952). Deals with the flowering plants that live along the margin of the sea and so cannot fail to be encountered by those who study the sea shore.

A HANDBOOK OF THE BRITISH SEAWEEDS by Lily Newton British Museum (Natural History), 1931).

FOR FURTHER INFORMATION

MANX ALGAE by Margery Knight and Mary W. Parke (Liverpool Marine Biological Committee—Memoir XXX, The University Press of Liverpool, 1931). Two rather technical books, now somewhat out of date, but still valuable to those closely studying British seaweeds.

BRITISH SEAWEEDS by Carola I. Dickinson (Eyre & Spottiswoode, 1963). Conveniently sized and excellently illustrated. Strongly recommended.

A KEY TO THE GENERA OF THE BRITISH SEAWEEDS by W. Eifion Jones (off-printed from *Field Studies*, Vol. 1, No. 4, 1962). Certainly now the best available key. The glossary and illustrations enable relative beginners to use it successfully.*

†Obtainable from Dale Fort Field Centre, Haverfordwest, Pembrokeshire.

SOURCES OF ILLUSTRATIONS

Most of the animals and plants shown in the text figures and plates were drawn from life, but there remain many that had to be copied, some being more or less adapted to our purpose. We wish to acknowledge indebtedness to the authorities listed below.

ALDER, J. and HANCOCK, A., 1845-55. A Monograph of the British Nudibranchiate Mollusca. Ray Society, pls. 19, 20 & 21 (part).

ALDER, J. and HANCOCK, A., 1905-12. The British Tunicata. Ray Society, figs. 135, 136, 141.

BATE, C. SPENCE and WESTWOOD, J. O., 1863-68. A History of the British Sessile-eyed Crustacea, figs. 57, 59.

BERRILL, N. J., 1950. The Tunicata, with an account of the British species. Ray Society, figs. 131-134, 138, 139, 144-149.

BRAMBELL, F. W. ROGERS and COLE, H. A., 1939. *Proc. Zool. Soc., Lond.*, 109, pl. 28 (*Saccoglossus*).

BÜRGER, O., 1895. Nemertinen. Flora u. Fauna des Golfes von Neapel, 22, pl. 8 (part).

COOPER, J. OMER and RAWSON, J., 1934. Notes on British Sphaeromatidae. Dove Marine Laboratory, pl. viii (part).

DAY, F., 1880-84. The Fishes of Great Britain and Ireland, pls. xxii-xxiv, figs., 151, 164, 169, 170, 175, 176.

EALES, N. B., 1950. The Littoral Fauna of Great Britain, figs, 18, 19, 25, 80, 119, 153, 155, 156, 160, 162, 166, 168, 173, 177.

ELIOT, C., 1910. A Monograph of the British Nudibranchiate Mollusca (Supplement). Ray Society, pl. 21 (part).

FAUVEL, P., 1923. Faune de France 5. Polychètes errantes, figs, 17, 20-24, 26-28.

FAUVEL, P., 1927. Faune de France 16. Polychètes sédentaires, figs. 29-35, 38

FORBES, E., 1841. A History of British Starfishes, figs. 120-124 and vignette on title page.

FORBES, E. and HANLEY, S., 1848-53. A History of British Mollusca and their Shells, pls. xiv (part), xv (part), xvi, xxi, 18 (part), 19 (part), 20 (part), 21 (part).

HARRISON, R. J., 1944. The Linnean Society of London. Synopses of the British Fauna No. 2. Caprellidea (Amphipoda, Crustacea), figs. 68, 75-77.

HARDY, A., 1956. The Open Sea. Its Natural History: the World of Plankton. *The New Naturalist* No. 34, pl. 4 (*Rhizostoma*).

SOURCES OF ILLUSTRATIONS

HINCKS, T., 1868. British Hydroid Zoophytes, figs. 2-15, pl. i (part).

HINKS, T., 1880. A History of the British Marine Polyzoa, figs. 103-108, pl. iii (part).

JENKINS, J. T., 1925. The Fishes of the British Isles, both freshwater and salt, figs. 157, 161, 171, 174.

KENNEDY, M., 1954. The Sea Angler's Fishes, figs. 150, 158, 163.

LANG, A., 1884. Die Polycladen (Seeplanarien) des Golfes von Neapel (etc.). Fauna u. Flora des Golfes von Neapel, II. pl. ii (Turbellaria).

MACAN, T. T., 1949. A Key to the British Fresh- and Brackish-water Gastropods. Freshwater Biological Association Sci. Publ., 13, pl. xv (part).

MCINTOSH, W. C., 1900-23. A Monograph of the British Annelids. Ray Society, figs. 36, 37, pls. iv (part), 8 & 13 (part of each), 9-12.

MEYER, H. A. and MÔBIUS, K., 1865. Fauna der Kieler Bucht. Bd. I, pls. 18, 21 (part of each).

MORTENSEN, Th., 1927. Handbook of the Echinoderms of the British Isles, fig. 122.

MORTON, J. E., 1954. The Crevice Faunas of the Upper Intertidal Zone at Wembury. J. Mar. Biol. Assoc., 33, fig. 87.

NAYLOR, E., 1955. The comparative external morphology and revised taxonomy of the British species of *Idotea*. J. Mar. Biol. Assoc., 34, figs. 54-55, 61, 62.

NORMAN, J. R., 1937. Illustrated Guide to the Fish Gallery, figs. 159, 172.

NORMAN, J. R., 1947. A History of Fishes, figs. 152, 154, 165, 167.

PARRY, D. A., 1944. Structure and function of the gut in *Spadella cephaloptera* and *Sagitta setosa*. J. Mar. Biol. Assoc., 16, fig. 109.

REID, D. M., 1944. The Linnean Society of London. Synopses of the British Fauna No. 3 Gammaridae (Amphipoda), figs. 64, 70, 71.

SARS, G. O., 1892-5. An Account of the Crustacea of Norway: vols. 1 & 2, figs. 63, 65, 66, 69, 72, 73, pls. vii, ix, x and part of viii and xiii.

STEPHENSON, T. A.. 1928, 1935. British Sea Anemones. Ray Society, pls. 5-7 (part of each).

STEPHENSON, T. A., 1944. Seashore Life and Pattern. King Penguin Books, pl. 13 (*Myxicola*).

TATTERSALL, W. M. and TATTERSALL, O. S., 1951. The British Mysidacea. Ray Society, figs. 47-49.

INDEX

The page references in bold type are to the main systematic descriptions of the plant or animal.

INDEX

Chitons, note on, 36; 125-6; pl. xiv
CHITONIDA, 125
Chlamys distorta, opercularis, tigerina, 153, pl. 22; *varia,* 153-4, pl. 22
Chondria dasyphylla, 243, pl. xxxviii; *tenuissima,* 243
Chondrus crispus, 247, pl. 38 & xxxviii
Chorda filum, 228, pl. xxxi; other seaweeds on, 231, 234
Chordaria divaricata, 232; *flagelliformis,* 232
Chrysaora isosceles, 55, pl. 4
Chthamalus stellatus, 91-2, pl. vi, fig. 44
Chylocladia ovatus, 243-4, pl. xl; *verticillata (kaliformis),* 249, pl. 39
Cingula cingillus, 135, fig. 87
Ciona intestinalis, 187, pl. 29, fig. 135
Cirolana cranchi, 99, fig. 59
Cirratulidae, 38-4, pl. 11, figs. 34-5
Cirratulus cirratus, 84, fig. 35; *tentaculatus,* 83, pl. 11, fig. 34
CIRRIPEDIA, 90-93, pl. vi
Cladophora flexuosa, 222; glaucescens, 222, pl. 33; *rupestris,* 222, pl. xxvi, sea-slug on, 146
Cladostephus spongiosus, 233; *verticillatus,* 233, pl. xxx
Clam, 153, pl. 22; burrowing, 25; Soft Shelled, 164, pl. 23
Class, subdivision of Phylum, 38
Clathrus clathrus, 135, pl. xiv
Clave multicornis, 48, pl. 2, fig. 10; *squamata,* 48, pl. 2
Clavelina lepadiformis, 190, pl. 29, fig. 142
Clay, animals of, 25; character of, 20
Cliona celata, 42
Clunio maximus, 121
Clymenella torquata, 85, fig. 37
Coat-of-Mail-Shells, 36; 125-6; pl. xiv
Cockles, 155-7, pl. xvii-xviii
Codium tomentosum, 223, pl. 33; sea-slug on, 145
COELENTERATA, notes on, 45
Comb-Jellies, note on, 37-8; pl. 2
Commensalism, defined 167; 25, 60, 168
Conger conger, 198, 202, pl. xxii
COPEPODA, notes on, 34, 89
Corallina officinalis, 250, pl. 35 & xxvii; *rubens,* 250; spp., 26; bivalve in, 168; confused with hydroids, 45; ribbon worm with, 65; seamat on, 173
Corals, note on, 28; Devonshire Cup, 60, pl. 7; Scarlet and Goldstar, 60-1; Soft, 61, pl. 5
Corbula gibba, 164, pl. 23
Cord-grass, 255
Corella parallelogramma, 187-8, fig. 136

Corkwing, 200, 208, pl. 30
Corophiidae, 109
Corophium volutator, 109, pl. x
Corynactis viridis, 61
Coryne muscoides, 46, pl. i, figs. 7, 8
Corystes cassivelaunus, 24, 119, pl. xii
Cottidae, 209, pl. 32
Cotton Spinner, 183, pl. 28
Cottus bubalis, 200, 209, pl. 32; *scorpius,* 200, 209
Cowries, 136-7; European, 137, pl. xv
Crabs, 21, 22, 34-5; pl. 14-16, xii. Edible, 118, pl. xii; Fiddler, 118, pl. 15; Hairy, 118, pl. xii; Hermit, 23, 35, 116-7, pl. 15; anemones on, 60, pl. 6; commensalism, 25; parasite under tail, 90, 93, pl. vi; white spiral tubes on, 77; Masked, 24, 119, pl. xii; Pea, 25, 119, pl. 16; Porcelain, Broad-clawed, 117, pl. 14; Porcelain, Long-clawed, 117, pl. 14; Shore, 24, 117, pl. 15; parasite of, 25, 90, 93, pl. vi; Spider, Spiny, 119, pl. 16, Velvet, 118, pl. 15
Crangon vulgaris, 112, 114, pl. xi; burrowing, 24
Crassostrea angulata, 155, pl. xvii
Crawfish, 115, pl. 14
Crenella, Green, Marbled, 152, pl. 22
Crenilabrus melops, 200, 208, pl. 30
Crepidula fornicata, 136, pl. 17
Crevices, fauna of, 22
CRINOIDEA, notes on, 37, 177, pl. 26
Crisia spp., 173, fig. 106
CRUSTACEA, notes on, 33-4, 89
Cryptochitonidae, 126
Cryptopleura ramosa, 239-40, pl. 37
Ctenolabrus rupestris, 200, 208, pl. 30
CTENOPHORA, notes on, 37-8, 61, pl. 2
Cucumaria lactea, 183-4, pl. 28; *normani,* 183, pl. 28; *saxicola,* 183, pl. xxviii
Cultellus pellucidus, 163, pl. 23
CUMACEA, notes on, 95-6, pl. xiii, fig. 50
Cushion Star, 179, pl. 25
Cutleria multifida, 229, pl. xxix
Cuttle, Little, 170, pl. xxi
Cuttlefish, notes on, 36, 38; Common, 170, pl. xxi; shell of, 35, 216, pl. xxv
Cyanea capillata, 55, pl. 3; *lamarcki,* 55
Cyclopteridae, 205, pl. 30, fig. 167
Cyclopterus lumpus, 199, 205, pl. 30
Cystoceira tamariscifolia (ericoides), 229 pl. xxxiii; brown seaweed on, 234
Cystoclonium purpureum, 243, pl. xl

Dab, 200, 210, pl. xxiv
Dasychone bombyx, 79, pl. 13

INDEX

267